MW00577179

Dreams

Dreams

The Many Lives of
Fleetwood Mac

MARK BLAKE

PEGASUS BOOKS

NEW YORK LONDON

DREAMS

Pegasus Books, Ltd.
148 West 37th Street, 13th Floor
New York, NY 10018

Copyright © 2024 by Mark Blake

First Pegasus Books cloth edition October 2024

ISBN: 978-1-63936-732-0

10 9 8 7 6 5 4 3 2 1

Printed in the United States of America
Distributed by Simon & Schuster
www.pegasusbooks.com

Contents

Part Five: 'I knew I was going to die and I didn't want to die'

Mark Blake is an acclaimed music journalist and author. Former assistant editor of *Q* magazine and long-time contributor to *Mojo* and *Classic Rock*, Blake has written for many high-profile publications including *Rolling Stone* and *Billboard*.

Among his previous books are *Us And Them: The Authorised Story of Hipgnosis* (Nine Eight Books) *Magnifico!: The A to Z of Queen* (Nine Eight Books), the bestselling *Pigs Might Fly: The Inside Story of Pink Floyd* and *Bring It On Home: Peter Grant, Led Zeppelin and Beyond*, which was listed as a 'Music Book of the Year' by *The Times*, *The Sunday Times*, the *Daily Mail* and the *Daily Telegraph*.

Blake has edited and contributed to titles about Freddie Mercury, Keith Richards, Bob Dylan and punk. He has also worked on official projects for Queen, Pink Floyd, the Who and the Jimi Hendrix estate. He lives just outside London with his wife and son.

Foreword

Stevie Nicks' stretch limousine is so long you can sit with your legs out and not touch the feet of the passenger opposite. On this occasion, it's Stevie Nicks wearing a pair of her signature platform boots.

The morning sun glints off the vehicle's tinted windows, but the singer is cocooned in an ankle-length jet-black overcoat and two matching shawls. She's dressed for a funeral in the Arctic Circle, rather than an airstrip half an hour's drive from Detroit. Fleetwood Mac are on the reunion trail and selling out arenas across the US. Stevie is scheduled to board a private plane flying the group to their next destination: Buffalo, New York.

In the meantime, she's giving an interview. As it's the twentieth century, Stevie is answering questions into a miniature cassette recorder. She talks constantly, but during the occasional pause, takes a mouthful of water, lemon and honey from a glass tumbler on the seat beside her.

'Oh, I could easily have fallen for John,' she says suddenly, between sips. Stevie is talking about Fleetwood Mac's bassist John McVie. 'It's those eyes,' she adds.

Had this happened, it would have brought more turmoil to a group that had already survived three broken relationships between its members. Yet based on past form, Fleetwood Mac would have weathered the storm and spun it into another hit record.

It's tempting to wonder if the band's mainstays, John McVie and drummer Mick Fleetwood, sold their souls to the devil, sometime in the '60s. Fleetwood Mac would go on to sell millions, but to the detriment of their personal lives and mental well-being. A later interview with their troubled ex-guitarist Peter Green brought this truth home to me, and then some. Unlike his former bandmates and successors, Green wasn't seeing out his days in a beachside residence in Maui or a mansion in Bel Air. He was living modestly in Canvey Island in Essex.

In autumn 2023, Stevie Nicks announced that Fleetwood Mac were no more, after the death of their bandmate Christine McVie, 'the one who wrote the really big hits,' she explained. However, Fleetwood Mac had returned from the brink many times before. Since 1967, there had been at least four Fleetwood Macs. There was the original blues band of 'Albatross' hit-single fame; the version that made those curious folky, progressive records in the early '70s; the one behind the multi-platinum-selling '*White Album*' and *Rumours*, and the later fluid incarnation, missing either a Stevie, a Christine, guitarist Lindsey Buckingham, or sometimes all three. There was even a bogus version without any of its existing members.

Dreams draws from many original interviews and eyewitness encounters to join the dots between each version of Fleetwood Mac. It charts their unique journey from post-war London to '70s California; how the '60s British blues boom fuelled the money-spinning West Coast rock of the next decade, and how two gifted female songwriters overcame widespread prejudice to turn a previously all-male ensemble into one of the biggest groups in the world.

Fleetwood Mac may be over, but the music isn't. Instead, it's leapfrogged generations, genres and formats and been used to soundtrack Hollywood blockbusters, television adverts and social media videos.

Then again, emotional anguish and sexual tension never go out of fashion. 'If I wasn't in Fleetwood Mac,' said Stevie Nicks that day in Detroit, 'I would *so* want to be in Fleetwood Mac.'

A Cast of Characters

Who's Who in Fleetwood Mac

Bekka Bramlett, lead vocalist and Stevie Nicks' replacement in 'The Mini Mac', 1993–5. Fired by fax.

Bob Brunning, original bass guitarist in 1967, kept the seat warm before John McVie joined. Died 2011.

Lindsey Buckingham, vocalist, songwriter, guitarist, co-producer, self-confessed 'troublemaker'. Joined in 1975, with long spells away for solo projects and misbehaviour. Rejoined in the '90s, left/pushed in 2018. Sang the hits 'Go Your Own Way', 'Tusk' and 'Big Love'.

Billy Burnette, vocalist and guitarist in 'The Mini Mac', 1987–95.

Mike Campbell, ex-Tom Petty and the Heartbreakers guitarist. Drafted in for the 2018–19 world tour.

Neil Finn, ex-Crowded House frontman and vocalist, guitarist, drafted in for the 2018–19 tour to replace Lindsey Buckingham.

Mick Fleetwood, drummer, co-founder, leader, spokesperson. Helped found the band in 1967 and never left. Most famous moment: the back-to-front drumming on 'Go Your Own Way'.

Peter Green, co-founder, vocalist and guitarist, left in 1970 and never found his way back. Sang the hits: 'Man of the World', 'Oh Well', 'The Green Manalishi (With the Two Prong Crown)'. Died 2020.

Danny Kirwan, Peter Green's prodigy, vocalist and guitarist, 1968–71. Died 2018.

Dave Mason, ex-Traffic vocalist and guitarist in 'The Mini Mac', 1993–5.

Christine McVie, vocalist, songwriter and keyboard player. Joined in 1970, left in 1994, re-joined, left, re-joined . . . Wrote and sang the hits, 'Don't Stop', 'You Make Loving Fun', 'Little Lies', 'Everywhere'. Died 2022.

John McVie, bass guitarist and the 'Mac' in Fleetwood Mac. Joined in 1967, never left. Most famous moment: 'Dum . . . dur-dur-dur-dur-dur-dur-dur-dur . . . Dum' on 'The Chain'.

Stevie Nicks, vocalist, songwriter, figurehead, solo star. Joined in 1975, left in 1991, re-joined in the mid-'90s and stayed till the end. Sang the hits 'Dreams' and 'Gypsy'.

Jeremy Spencer, guitarist and vocalist, 1967–71, left to join the Children of God religious cult.

Rick Vito, lead guitarist in 'The Mini Mac', 1987–91.

Dave Walker, vocalist. Joined in 1973 and fired six months later. Heard (briefly) on the album *Penguin*.

Bob Welch, guitarist, vocalist and songwriter, 1971–4. Sang the non-hits 'Future Games' and 'Hypnotized'. Died 2012.

Bob Weston, guitarist, vocalist, 1972–3. Fired for adultery. Died 2012.

Part One

'I Wanted to be Free'

Peter Green discovers the blues, saves Mick Fleetwood from life as a window cleaner, and becomes a number-one pop star only to abandon his own group.

Peter Green

'I always thought I was a metal worker who should have been doing woodwork.'

'My biggest regret is that I never got to share the stage with him.'
Stevie Nicks

'I'd give anything for a millionth of his talent.'
John McVie

'I wanted to wave a magic wand and have him be the person I wanted him to be.'
Mick Fleetwood

'Everybody was awestruck by Peter.'
Christine McVie

'I love that Peter Green stuff, but it's not me.'
Lindsey Buckingham

Peter Green's greatest Fleetwood Mac moments

'Black Magic Woman'
'Need Your Love So Bad'

'Albatross'
'Man of the World'
'Rollin' Man'
'If I Loved Another Woman'
'Love That Burns'
'Long Grey Mare'
'Stop Messin' Round'
'Oh Well (Parts I & II)'
'The Green Manalishi (With the Two Prong Crown)'

Around the time *Rumours* reached the top of the US charts in spring 1977, Peter Green was being treated for schizophrenia at the Priory clinic in south-west London. Fleetwood Mac's ex-guitarist had been admitted shortly after his arrest for supposedly threatening his accountant with a shotgun. It never happened, but Green's mental health had long been a cause for concern.

It wouldn't be the last time he spent in a clinic or hospital. In April 2012, Green talked about his visits to other residential facilities.

What does he do when he's there?

'I practise my drawing with coloured felt tips and pencils, and I listen to the radio?' he replied.

What does he think of *Rumours*?

'Yeah, I like *Rumours*. Just as well. It sold about 22 million . . . And that was just last week.'

What does he think when he hears Lindsey Buckingham playing his old hit, 'Oh Well'?

'Could be worse.'

Green started chuckling, which he did often during the conversation. It was the last magazine interview he ever gave, and there were many moments of gallows humour, and many more when he headed off on indecipherable tangents.

'I always thought I was a metal worker who should have been doing woodwork,' he once joked. 'I go in the Ladies when it should be the Gents.' He wasn't wrong. Green could be perfectly lucid one minute and confused and confusing the next. It was like being in a room with several 'Peter Greens'.

Peter was sixty-five at the time, bald and with tufts of white hair exploding above his ears. He wore a yellow polo shirt tucked into baggy jeans, and the nails of his long feminine fingers were discoloured and overgrown. The mischievous grin and dark olive eyes hadn't changed, though. When he smiled, he still looked like the Peter Green who played 'Albatross' on *Top of the Pops*.

Green was arguably the greatest guitarist of his generation, and then he wasn't. But he didn't die young or fade into commercial obsolescence; he became ill, rejected the music business for a long time, and never quite found his way back.

Peter Allen Greenbaum was the youngest of four children, born in Bethnal Green, East London, on 29 October 1946, to mother, Anne, and father, Joe, a tailor-turned postal worker. The family background was a melting pot of Polish, Jewish and Ukrainian. When Peter was two years old, Joe Greenbaum changed the family name by deed poll to 'Green' and moved them out to Putney in west London.

By then, Green's siblings had experienced Oswald Mosley's black-shirted fascists marching through the East End, throwing missiles and shouting abuse at the Jewish residents. Green later talked about a childhood marred by anti-Semitism and explored those feelings in Fleetwood Mac's 'Trying So Hard to Forget'. 'I can't stop my mind wondering back to when I was a downtrodden kid,' he sang. 'I would spend most of my days, running and hiding from the world outside.'

'A couple of times local kids would throw stones at the window and shout "Yid!"' recalled Green's older brother, Michael. 'Perhaps it did leave an impression on Peter', whom he described as a 'sensitive child who questioned everything'.

Hearing the theme tune to Disney's *Bambi* once moved young Peter to tears. Years later, he was similarly shaken by a TV news report on starving Biafrans and donated some of his royalties to charity. But an atypically assured and confident Peter Green emerged when he started playing guitar.

Ten-year-old Peter learned his instrument by listening to Gene Vincent's guitarist Cliff Gallup and the Shadows' Hank Marvin, and discovered the blues via a friend's 78-rpm record of Muddy Waters' 'Honey Bee'. His eldest brother Len played guitar, but Peter quickly surpassed him.

After leaving school he found work as a butcher's boy and an apprentice French polisher, while playing bass, first in a west London dance band called the Ken Cats, and, later, with Eel Pie Island regulars the Muskrats.

When he wasn't playing, Green frequented the Crawdaddy in Richmond and the dilapidated hotel on Eel Pie watching the Yardbirds and assessing his competition. His fellow Muskrats realised how far ahead Green was when he mastered Eric Clapton's tricky guitar break from the Yardbirds' 'I Ain't Got You', on the bass.

'I went pro on my own,' Green explained, making it all sound so easy. 'One day I had a stinking row with the foreman at work and just walked out. I decided I may as well make a clean start, so I started to learn lead guitar. I just stayed at home and practised. Then I read that John Mayall wanted a new guitarist and I got in touch with him.'

John Mayall's Bluesbreakers were a boot camp/finishing school for some of the UK's finest apprentice musicians, but their latest prodigy, Eric Clapton, had taken a temporary leave of absence. Mayall appointed a replacement, Jeff Kribbett, but Green was unimpressed when he saw him understudying at London Marquee.

'Peter kept coming down to all the gigs and saying, "I'm much better than him,"' recalled John Mayall, who eventually let 'the pushy cockney kid' take over.

'John paid me a great compliment. He said I was the best guitarist he'd heard since Eric Clapton,' said Green. 'So I tried to float on that compliment. I did my best. But I used to drink before I went on. It seemed to be the thing where everyone went to the pub. I couldn't play properly at all. Most of them gigs I flunked.'

This was the other Peter Green talking: the self-critical one who was still telling interviewers that 'Oh Well (Part II)' should have been the A-side of Fleetwood Mac's single, more than forty years after it was a hit.

Green's tenure as a Bluesbreaker lasted around a week in August 1965, until Clapton came home early and asked for his job back. In February of the following year, Green auditioned for a new R&B group, Peter B's Looners. 'Peter B' was keyboard player Peter Bardens, and the band's gangling 6-foot, 6-inch drummer was Mick Fleetwood.

Green landed the job, but with his jeans and T-shirt and, what he called, 'riverboat captain's sideburns', he'd yet to embrace the boutique fashions of the era: 'Peter Bardens would say to me – "You look like a dustman."'

For Green, the music always came first. He made his recording debut with Peter B on a Booker T. & the MGs-inspired single, 'If You Want to be Happy'. But the group morphed into Shotgun Express, with lead singer Rod Stewart, before breaking up soon after.

Then, when Clapton quit the Bluesbreakers to form Cream in July 1966, Green took his place again. The group's second album, *Blues Breakers With Eric Clapton*, had only just been released. Future guitar heroes, including Queen's Brian May, and Eddie Van Halen, would attach near-biblical status to this LP. But in October 1966, Mayall and the group were back at West Hampstead's Decca Studio, minus its superstar guitarist.

Producer Mike Vernon scoffed when John Mayall told him that 'the new guy' would soon be better than Clapton. But the next album, *A Hard Road*, featured two Peter Green compositions, including 'The Supernatural', on which he sketched out the sinuous improvised style explored later on 'Oh Well' and 'Black Magic Woman'.

Out on the road, though, Green faced sceptical audiences. 'I don't know anyone who wouldn't be worried about having to follow Eric,' he admitted. There were hecklers. But Green won them over, just as he did Mike Vernon.

Green was an instinctive musician who eschewed the flash and braggadocio of some of his contemporaries. Clapton, Jeff Beck,

Jimmy Page and Ten Years After's Alvin Lee ushered in the era of the lightning-fingered guitar god, but Green condemned the craze for what he called, '7,541 notes a minute'.

'Eric Clapton had energy, but Peter had a deftness, a more melodic style . . . deeper blues,' explained Vernon.

Before long, Green had become restless in his day job. 'I didn't agree with the kind of material which was being played in Bluesbreakers,' he said. 'It was becoming less and less of the blues. And we'd do the same thing, night after night. John would say something to the audience and count us in, and I'd groan inwardly.'

Green formed Fleetwood Mac in July 1967, but as their label boss and producer Mike Vernon discovered, Green was neither a born leader nor a self-publicist. The obvious marketing strategy would be to call the new group 'Peter Green's Fleetwood Mac'. Green refused and graciously told Fleetwood and McVie that leaving his name out of it would enable them to carry on in his absence.

Green also insisted on sharing the spotlight with not one but two other guitarists, Jeremy Spencer and then Danny Kirwan. It was as if he knew he wouldn't be staying around.

Musically, too, he had a conflicted relationship with the blues. Fleetwood Mac's 1969 jam session at Chess Studio, alongside giants of the genre Willie Dixon and Buddy Guy, dented Green's confidence. He thought he played too loudly and aggressively to make up for his lack of life experience. 'There are levels in the blues,' he said later, 'that most people, including me, never get anywhere close to.'

This self-questioning proved a blessing and a curse. It drove his songwriting but also drove him apart from the band. 'I use guitar sounds as colours and shades, that you might use to paint a picture,' Green explained.

Those colours on 'Albatross', 'Man of the World' and 'Need Your Love So Bad' set Fleetwood Mac apart from their twelve-bar peers and suggested that Green was creating a new blues, out of his personal life experiences. He'd stopped interpreting and had started creating.

Green wasn't just using the guitar either. His voice was Fleetwood Mac's most undervalued instrument, and expressed a range of emotions, from lascivious to heartbroken, without lapsing into the 'Richmond Delta' drawl beloved of many white British bluesmen.

A prime example was 'Man of the World'. Green was barely twenty-three, but sounded like the oldest, saddest man on the planet. Mick Fleetwood later called the song 'a cry for help'.

None of this was good enough for its composer, though. 'I thought the lyrics were corny,' sniffed Green in 2012. 'But the solo is nice.' He was even more dismissive of his vocals. 'I had to do the singing, and I really shouldn't be doing it.'

When Fleetwood Mac broke away from Vernon and Blue Horizon, Green shouldered even more responsibility. He was utterly focused on where he wanted to take the music on the band's third album, *Then Play On*. 'He was like the simple blues maestro turned Brian Wilson,' said Mick Fleetwood.

But Green had become a one-man band, delivering many of these songs as a *fait accompli*, and telling his bandmates what to play. Jeremy Spencer was barely contributing, and Danny Kirwan had to be pushed into writing songs. They were all more reliant on Green than ever.

His mindset was elsewhere, though. In 1968, Mick Fleetwood's future wife, Jenny Boyd, accompanied the Beatles on their pilgrimage to Rishikesh to see Maharishi Mahesh Yogi. Jenny later shared a taxi ride with Green during which he asked about her subsequent spiritual journey. 'I had from Notting Hill Gate to Marble Arch, in which to describe the most important aspect in my life,' she recalled. 'Yet he spent most of the time telling me he could feel himself changing, that he'd become more aware of a spiritual side.'

Green's quest wasn't unusual. The Who's Pete Townshend, Pink Floyd's Syd Barrett and the Beach Boys' Mike Love shared the Beatles' interest in Eastern philosophy. Green and his girlfriend, Sandra Elsdon, were regulars at the esoteric bookshop Watkins Books in Covent Garden and had attended a Tibetan Buddhist retreat. But Green's spiritual journey was partly engendered by

LSD. He'd taken it for the first time with Fleetwood Mac in the US. It opened his mind to a universe of possibilities but rendered him unable to play on stage in New Orleans.

The debate still rages as to whether drugs caused Green's mental decline or exacerbated an existing problem, and how much pop stardom and the music business played a part. There was a lot of inner conflict. One moment Green was searching for spiritual salvation, the next he was flattered by the teenage girls congregating outside his house, desperate to meet a pop star. 'I'm in a terrible state of "don't knows" right now,' he said at the time.

In the spring of 1969, he performed 'Man of the World' on the BBC, dressed like an Old Testament prophet in sandals, a white robe and with a crucifix around his neck. Sandra made the robe and thought it signified the moment that Peter's God complex began to take hold. 'He was acutely aware he had a gift which then became a power,' Elsdon told Green's biographer, Martin Celmins. 'As I see it, he wasn't strong enough to contain that power.'

'Oh Well's lyric, 'Now when I talk to God, I know he understands', was a giveaway. 'There was a time,' confirmed Green, 'when I did start reading about Jesus and thinking along the lines of, "He has returned and I am Him".'

Green renounced his Judaism and embraced Christianity. 'But it only lasted two or three weeks,' he told *New Musical Express*. 'Although my faith was strong, it was jarred by people who didn't want to know and I made the mistake of trying to explain it to them.'

Green was now required to approach strangers on the street and spread the word. In 2012, he recalled the experience with bemused good humour. 'I think it was a soldier first of all, in Denmark,' he grinned. 'I said something to him about Jesus, but you're bumbling and stumbling. Then a city gent type went by in a suit, and he slaughtered me.' Green started laughing. 'He knocked it right out of me, and I didn't bother again.'

Most of Fleetwood Mac believe that Green's LSD trip at a Munich commune in March 1970 was the moment they truly lost him. Apparently, his wine was spiked with acid and he spent the night jamming in the commune's basement, before being rescued by Mick Fleetwood and the road crew. Green finished their German tour, but with his mind tuned to another wavelength. He could still play, beautifully at times, but was mentally out of kilter with the others.

Fleetwood and John McVie have always blamed 'the rich German brats', whom they believed destroyed their guitarist. Jeremy Spencer isn't so sure. 'LSD might have been Peter's tipping point,' he said. 'But I think there has been a bit too much blame on it for his demise. Unfortunate mental afflictions have been around for centuries before the existence of drugs.'

However, the post-Munich 'Peter Green' immediately donated thousands of pounds to Save the Children after seeing TV footage of starving Biafrans. Green believed that giving away his money would purge him of his power and return him to a purer state of mind. He urged his bandmates to donate some of their royalties too, but they refused.

Green wrote the cautionary 'The Green Manalishi (With the Two Prong Crown)' and made even more money when the single became a hit. But when news of Green's charity donations became public knowledge, he was inundated with begging letters.

Green said he wanted to leave Fleetwood Mac long before he did. But their manager, Clifford Davis, persuaded him not to: 'He said, "Stay on for the boys, 'cos they've got families and you're doing so well, writing the hits".' 'He didn't leave us in the shit,' insisted Fleetwood, after Green's final show at London's Lyceum in May 1970. 'He gave us plenty of notice. He was completely and utterly responsible. But behind all that was this seething emotional disturbance.'

The rest of 1970 was a confusing time for Green. He was now living with his parents in 'Albatross', a house he'd paid for in New Malden, Surrey. A visiting journalist listed some of the items in the property: a Buddha statuette, a Superman poster, a leather whip, a stuffed crocodile, a tiger's head, a double-handed sword, a parrot named 'Parrot'.

11

Green's first solo album, *The End of the Game*, was the musical equivalent: a headrush of free jazz improvisation and disembodied solos. Green called it his 'LSD album', and an attempt to reach a place he'd only managed before with hallucinogenics. *Melody Maker* described it as 'the most disturbing album release this year'. This was Green shedding his so-called God-like power and creating pure music without any commercial expectation. As creatively satisfying as this was, *The End of the Game* was a commercial dud.

Green started drifting and didn't stop for the rest of the '70s. In the summer of 1970, he spent time travelling the US and stayed at the Godard Free College in Vermont, where he was remembered floating around in a kaftan, talking about God, and taking synthetic mescaline. 'I still haven't returned from that,' he said. 'You're not allowed to return. It's like someone's playing with you.'

Green claimed to have taken LSD once more, with friends at a house in Surbiton. 'And I listened to Donny Hathaway. It was a really beautiful night,' he recalled. But the experience, he said, left him 'halfway between this' – he held his hands apart in the air as if gesturing towards something unseen – 'and that – and *that*'s no good.'

In his 2012 interview, this was the moment that Green's cheery demeanour faded into one of befuddlement and frustration. 'You feel dozy and stupid,' he added quietly.

One of Green's hosts in Surbiton helped him find a job at nearby Mortlake Cemetery. He enjoyed the lack of responsibility and nobody knowing or caring that he'd once been *that* Peter Green. Then he was lured back to Fleetwood Mac when Jeremy Spencer left in the middle of a US tour. He played the shows as a favour to Clifford Davis but asked to be billed as 'Peter Blue'.

The shows were warmly received, despite the band playing without a setlist. At a club in Long Island, Green led the others on a deathless version of 'Black Magic Woman' that lasted until 4 a.m., despite the promoter threatening to pull the plug at midnight.

Green wasn't interested in re-joining the band, though. *Kiln House*, the album they'd just made without him, held little appeal.

'I couldn't identify with it,' he said. 'It wasn't blues, it wasn't anything.'

In the meantime, Green kept his family afloat with bumper royalty cheques and looked for charities to donate the rest to. Parents, siblings and girlfriends learned to accommodate his eccentricities. After re-embracing his Judaism, Green spent weeks on a kibbutz in Israel but returned home claiming that he felt more sympathy with the Arabs. At one Christmas dinner, Green declared himself a vegetarian and flung the freshly roasted turkey into the garden.

Davis tried to get him to make music again. But a stint with blues-rockers Stone the Crows never made it out of the rehearsal room. Green told the rest of the band that he was worried they were going to be too successful and didn't want to go through what he had with Fleetwood Mac.

Unfortunately, his mood swings and erratic behaviour grew worse, and Green was soon admitted to a mental hospital in Epsom. He was later taken to St Thomas's Hospital in south London and received controversial electro-convulsive therapy, where his brain was shocked with electricity to alleviate the symptoms of mental illness. This treatment and high doses of medication rendered Green docile and impaired his judgement. By 1977, he could be found either at his parents' new house in Essex or sleeping on friends' floors and sofas, until he wore out his welcome and moved on to the next.

In January 1977, Green returned to London from visiting a girlfriend in Canada. In his account of events, he telephoned Clifford Davis from a payphone at Our Price Records, asking for some money. Davis told him their accountant had some cash for him. At which point Green threatened to shoot him. He later said that it was meant in jest. But Davis wasn't taking any chances and called the police.

The trouble was, Peter had just bought a .22 fairground rifle in Canada but had not declared it at customs. The weapon was miles away at his parents' house, but Green was subsequently arrested and charged with possession of an unlicensed firearm.

'The Shotgun Incident' quickly took on a life of its own. On 27 January 1977, the *Daily Express* erroneously reported how Green had arrived at Davis's office brandishing a 'pump-action shotgun' and demanding *not* to be given a £30,000 royalty cheque. Davis was quoted in the article, complaining about how much money Green was donating to charity. The uncomfortable truth was that Green's largesse was impacting on his manager and his loved ones, many of whom relied on him for financial support. The magistrate in the subsequent court case sectioned Green for further treatment, resulting in his stay at the Priory.

Green was now corresponding with a Californian violinist and born-again Christian named Jane Samuels. Green underwent another religious conversion and married Jane in January 1978. The couple later had a daughter, Rosebud, but the marriage didn't survive.

Green's time in California with his new wife coincided with Fleetwood Mac making *Tusk*. He dropped by Village Recorder studio to play on the song 'Brown Eyes', and Mick Fleetwood persuaded Warners' boss Mo Ostin to offer his old friend a record deal. Then with the contract in front of him to sign, Green changed his mind, claiming that it was the devil's work.

After this, his family launched a concerted attempt to get Green working again. Michael Green was employed as a radio plugger for PVK Records, an independent label established by an entrepreneurial businessman named Peter Vernon-Kell. Green signed to PVK Records. 'They gave me an E-type Jag as my advance, but I pranged it on a bollard in the rain,' he recalled. The label put him in the studio with musicians he knew, including former bandmate Peter Bardens and Snowy White. Green's contribution to his second solo LP, *In the Skies* (released in 1979), was minimal and many of the songs were co-written by his bandmates and his brother.

Green had formed a publishing company with Michael, which put him under pressure to deliver songs. The subsequent albums, including *Little Dreamer*, *Whatcha Gonna Do?* and *White Sky*, sold modestly but prompted Green back onto the gig circuit. His performances were variable and Green sometimes seemed barely *compos mentis* on stage. Yet there were still flashes of clarity and of the gallows humour that never deserted him. When he was on, he was *on*. 'You're taking me to Brighton,' he yelled at one session musician in the studio, 'when I want to go to Shepherd's Bush.' Better still, the musician understood what he meant.

Green's final studio solo album, 1983's *Kolors*, gave him the name for a new band, comprised of younger musicians. For most Kolors gigs, Green sang and played rhythm guitar, letting his Ghanaian bandmate Alfred Bannerman take the solos. Green was sufficiently together to play Kolors gigs overseas, including Israel, and a charity fundraiser in a Camden club on the day of Live Aid. However, mismanagement and Green's reluctance to handle the business side of the group eventually derailed the project. By the late 1980s, Green's property in Richmond had become a drop-in centre/doss house for itinerant musicians and hangers-on, not all of whom had his best interests at heart.

In his absence, an Essex farmer and amateur guitarist convinced several musicians and journalists that he was Peter Green, and cadged guitars and blagged a record deal, until Green's family intervened. While this was happening, the real Peter Green received a police caution for hitting his neighbour over the head with a loaf of bread. 'It made me very sad,' said John McVie of this time. 'It was such a waste of talent.'

Green eventually moved into a property near Great Yarmouth with his brother Len's family and their mother. Peter had gone from being the 'Green god' of the '60s blues boom to a poster boy for acid casualties, even if the truth of the matter was more complex than that. In a rare interview from 1994, he was asked what he did all day. 'Oh, I just zombie around,' he replied. 'I'm taking tablets of some kind. I don't know what they're supposed to do for me. I fall asleep in the daytime. I never used to do that.'

Two years later, though, Green appeared at a memorial concert for Alexis Korner. With his family's support, he'd changed his medication and was no longer 'zombieing around'. Nevertheless, his role in what became the Peter Green Splinter Group was secondary to the one he'd had in Fleetwood Mac. To begin with, the band's co-founder, Nigel Watson, took the lead role, and Green, in his trademark pillbox hat, seemed more like a figurehead. 'Peter's not coming back the same as he was in 1969,' cautioned Watson. 'Nobody does that – not even Muhammad Ali.'

Over time, Green's confidence grew, in tandem with his willingness to revisit what he called 'that old stuff'. 'I relate to people through my playing,' he explained. 'I relate better with the guitar than with words.'

Splinter Group musicians came and went, including superstar drummer Cozy Powell, who died in a car accident in 1998. Shortly before Powell's death, Mick Fleetwood told *Q* magazine that he thought the drummer was pushing Green too hard and he needed a gentler approach. 'I'd love to help Peter,' Fleetwood insisted. 'I'd love to get a little blues band together and get him back on track.'

Of course, it never happened. The Fleetwood Mac juggernaut was too big to stop. Instead, Green broke up the Splinter Group and began recording blues covers albums and touring as Peter Green and Friends, before retiring from the road in 2010.

Green's 2012 interview was set up as part of a tentative plan to get him making music once more. He had spent time in residential institutions again but was now living comfortably in Canvey Island, cared for by a support network of family members and trusted friends. Mick Fleetwood kept a private box free for him at the London Palladium when he was MC at the Tribute to Peter Green concert. The box remained empty all night, and Green was conspicuous by his absence on stage.

In 2012, Green revealed that he often played along to his Peter Green and Friends CDs at home. 'I sit on the couch,' he said, 'speaker here, speaker there and find a middle and play along with it. I try and improve what I'd done on the CD. Nobody's watching me, so I can't go wrong.' It was a blunt reminder that one of the world's greatest guitar players had never been a natural showman.

Why did he leave Fleetwood Mac?

'I don't know,' he replied. 'I probably could remember if I tried . . . Let me see . . . I wanted to be free.'

Green died peacefully in his sleep on 25 July 2020. 'Losing Peter Green is monumental,' wrote Mick Fleetwood at the time. Fleetwood and the others had lost him many years before. But they couldn't quite escape him. Peter Green was there, somewhere, in Fleetwood Mac up until the end.

Bob Brunning

Fleetwood Mac's Bass Guitarist 0.5

Bob Brunning, Fleetwood Mac's original bass player, was once interviewed for a music magazine's regular spot, 'The Pete Best Corner'. Most musicians wouldn't want to be compared to the Beatles drummer fired soon after their first recording session, but Brunning didn't care.

It was the early '90s and he was now the headmaster at Churchill Gardens Primary School in Pimlico, and playing the blues in his spare time. 'All along, I'd known teaching was what I wanted to do,' he told the magazine.

Robert Brunning was born in Bournemouth, two years before the end of the Second World War, and played bass in a local group called the Sabres along with future BBC DJ Tony Blackburn. He moved to London to attend teacher-training college and formed an R&B group, Five's Company, who released several flop singles before breaking up.

Then, in July 1967, Brunning answered a small ad in *Melody Maker*: 'Bass player wanted for a Chicago-type blues band.' He rang the telephone number, only to discover that it had been printed incorrectly in the advert: 'But a hunch told me to pursue it and I called the paper to get the correct number.' Brunning was summoned to a flat in Putney and introduced to Peter Green. 'I said, "Do you know about the other Peter Green? The one in

John Mayall's Bluesbreakers?" Peter said, "That's me, you fucking idiot!" And after that we got on really well.'

Brunning 'fumbled and bluffed' his audition and was surprised to get the job. He was even more surprised to discover Fleetwood Mac would be making their live debut in a month at the Windsor National Jazz and Blues Festival. At his audition, Green told Brunning his place in the band was temporary. 'Peter had put the embryonic Fleetwood Mac together,' he explained. 'But at the last minute, John McVie had got cold feet, and that's why they put the ad in *Melody Maker*.'

Fleetwood Mac made their debut on Sunday 13 August 1967, under the watchful gaze of Eric Clapton and Jeff Beck. Brunning joined them on the road for the next two months, playing in pub backrooms, clubs and colleges. Then, in early December, John McVie arrived and Brunning stepped aside. 'I always knew I was temporary,' he said, 'plus I went on to join Savoy Brown, who at the time were actually better known.'

Fleetwood Mac's self-titled debut album (aka '*Dog and Dustbin*') was released in February 1968, with Brunning playing on one song 'Long Grey Mare'. However, he also recalled visiting the studio one night, when John McVie fell asleep, and playing on what became the band's first single, 'I Believe My Time Ain't Long', and its B-side 'Rambling Pony', both included on the 1969 compilation, *The Pious Bird of Good Omen*.

Brunning eventually left Savoy Brown to pursue a full-time job as a schoolteacher in Croydon. He'd also married and was about to become a father. Nevertheless, music still played a huge part in his life, and before the '60s were over, he'd recorded and toured with the Brunning Sunflower Blues Band and re-assembled Five's Company to make a lo-fi concept album, *The Ballad of Fred the Pixie*, which he later disowned.

Throughout the 1970s and '80s, Brunning worked with ex-Fleetwood Mac guitarist Danny Kirwan, wrote books about Fleetwood Mac and the blues, contributed to numerous albums and played hundreds of gigs, 'While making sure I never missed a day of school.' He took early retirement in 1999 to focus on running a blues club in south London. And he was still playing when he suffered a fatal heart attack on 18 October 2011. 'People have said to me, "You must have felt sick, living on a teacher's wage when they were making millions,"' he admitted in 1992. 'And you can bet there were times when it got me down when I was supporting my wife and kids on forty quid a week. But even if John McVie hadn't joined, the day Peter Green walked out of the band I'd have walked out with him. That, to me, *was* Fleetwood Mac.'

Mick Fleetwood

'I'm the Devil! I'm the Beast!'

'We have no democracy in Fleetwood Mac. Mick is the king.'
Stevie Nicks

'Mick will go on until they put him against the wall and shoot him.'

John McVie

'Mick was a raving lunatic.'

Christine McVie

'Mick, in the best possible sense, doesn't have a clue about what he's doing.'

Lindsey Buckingham

'It's not just the beat, it's what he does with it.'
Guitar hero, B.B. King

Mick Fleetwood's Greatest Fleetwood Mac Performances

'Rattlesnake Shake'
'Oh Well (Part I)'

'Love That Burns'
'Hypnotized'
'Dreams' (even though it's an eight-second drum loop)
'The Chain'
'Go Your Own Way'
'Gold Dust Woman'
'Walk a Thin Line'
'Tusk'

Mick Fleetwood's last proper job was at Liberty's department store in London's Regent Street. He was a sixteen-year-old, polo-shirted mod with long hair. Fleetwood was given a pile of paperwork and told to vet potential customers for credit; a big problem, as he had undiagnosed dyslexia. Soon, the jumble of words and the shop's strict dress code became too much, and he was fired. 'That was the end,' he wrote, years later. 'I've never had another job since.'

From a young age, Michael John Kells Fleetwood was an inveterate daydreamer who created a bubble around himself; the vital life skills for surviving Fleetwood Mac. Born on 24 June 1947 in Redruth, Cornwall, to Mike and Bridget 'Biddy' Fleetwood, he spent his early childhood overseas. Mike Fleetwood was an RAF pilot who later worked for NATO. So, Mick, his mother and two sisters, Sally and Susan, followed him to postings in Egypt and Norway. Back in England, though, Fleetwood acquired the habit of running away from boarding school. He was always caught, with one headmaster even chasing a bus to bring him back. It was a challenging time, as dyslexia wasn't a recognised condition in '50s Britain, and Fleetwood struggled academically.

Still, he excelled at fencing and acting in school drama productions. His 6-foot-plus height, long reach and willowy build lent themselves to both wielding a fencing foil and playing Ophelia in Shakespeare's *Hamlet*. 'I looked like a girl,' he said. 'I was quite an effeminate creature.'

Then Mike Fleetwood bought his thirteen-year-old son his first drum kit. Mick taught himself by listening to the Shadows' Tony

Meehan and Buddy Holly's Jerry Allison. Like John and Christine McVie doing the same in west London and the Midlands, respectively, he was smitten with that first generation of rock 'n' rollers.

One afternoon, after another academic disgrace at his latest *alma mater*, King's School, Sherborne, Fleetwood climbed a tree, where he spent a few hours, daydreaming. 'I was very unhappy,' he recalled, 'so I imagined the place I wanted to be – which was London. I was going to London to be a drummer.'

Fleetwood fulfilled this daydream. After convincing his parents he'd never make it to university, he moved to London and into his sister Sally's house in Notting Hill. Their father later composed a poem about fifteen-year-old Mick's departure. 'Gloucester Station, wet and dreamy,' he wrote. 'A mum, a dad and a teenage boy stand together, dreading the last goodbye . . . The whistle blows, it's all too much. Dad blows his nose, Mum sheds a tear. The embryo rock star hides his fear . . .'

Mick slept in Sally's attic and kept his drum kit in the garage, which is where his neighbour, organist Peter Bardens, first heard him play. Fleetwood never forgot the lesson learned at his first booking in a Notting Hill pub. 'I walked in with my drum kit, and said, "Where do I set up?" In my mind I'm going, "There's a stage! This is a thing!" The landlord didn't even look up, "Oh over there." "Well, where's the stage?" "Over there, on the *carpet*." "Oh."'

By the summer of 1963, Fleetwood and Bardens were playing together in the Cheynes (named after the hip Chelsea thoroughfare, Cheyne Walk). The group opened for the Yardbirds and backed Ronnie Spector on a UK tour but never had a hit. A similar fate befell Fleetwood's next group, the Bo Street Runners before he reunited with Bardens in Peter B's Looners. Their guitarist, Peter Green, didn't stay long and left to join the Bluesbreakers.

Fleetwood had now spent three years in the capital, playing in Soho dives and aristocratic country houses, and mixing with swinging London's beautiful people. But all his groups struggled to have hits. Fleetwood was now out of work. It was a rude awakening. In desperation, he borrowed money to buy a set of window cleaners' ladders but failed to land a single job. Then Peter Green rang and asked if he wanted to join the Bluesbreakers. Fleetwood accepted the offer but was woefully out of his depth. His predecessor, Aynsley Dunbar, was an adept soloist who'd later play with Frank Zappa. Audiences loved Dunbar and Fleetwood arrived on stage to cries of 'Where's Aynsley?', which stopped only after bass guitarist John McVie told the audience to 'Fuck off and listen!'

Fleetwood and McVie became inseparable, finding a musical groove, encouraged by an increasingly boozy friendship. It couldn't last, though, and Mayall fired Fleetwood after a gig in Ireland when he was too pissed to keep up. Though Mayall later claimed it wasn't Fleetwood's drinking so much as the limitations in his playing.

Fleetwood's tenure as a Bluesbreaker had lasted six weeks, but long enough for him, McVie and Green to cut a demo. Among the tracks was the instrumental that Green christened 'Fleetwood Mac'. Fleetwood often talks about serendipity and coincidence, and two months later, Green rang him with another job offer. And so began Fleetwood Mac.

At the time, Fleetwood was a failed window cleaner with a Jimi Hendrix-style perm and had just had one of his periodic break-ups with model girlfriend Jenny Boyd. 'So I thought I'd cheer him up,' joked Green. On Green's watch, Fleetwood flourished as a drummer and a performer. But Green could be Mick's fiercest critic. He'd sometimes sit behind the kit to demonstrate the beat himself. At one gig, Fleetwood lost his way so Green took his hands and put him back in time. Green told him to listen to Jimmy Reed's drummer, Earl Palmer, on the *Rockin' with Reed* album. Fleetwood listened and realised how close he was to replicating Palmer's lazy shuffle. He just lacked confidence.

Green also encouraged Fleetwood's showmanship. Mick acquired a West African talking drum, from Georgie Fame's Ghanaian percussionist 'Speedy'. The drum contained leather cords that could be manipulated to mimic speech-like sounds. One night, Fleetwood liberated a lavatory chain with wooden balls from a club toilet and started wearing it as a belt. Now, during gaps between songs or when his bandmates were changing strings, he'd play his 'wooden bollocks' like a percussion instrument, or lope around the stage, hollering at the audience and making his drum talk. Fleetwood was still performing a hi-tech version of this act in the '80s, via a waist-coat containing digital drum pads, which saw him flailing to the beat like Rasputin performing a ceremonial haka.

Fleetwood's height and appearance made him the band's totemic figurehead. He was practically naked on the cover of 1968's *Mr. Wonderful*, and, in drag for the US compilation, *English Rose*. Fleet-wood reappeared, again naked, save for the art director's wife's knickers, on 1974's *Heroes are Hard to Find*. But he was fully clothed for the '*White Album*', playing a champagne-sipping suited gentle-man, while a kneeling John McVie juggled a crystal ball. *Rumours* reinforced Fleetwood's *numero uno* position, with Mick holding the crystal ball towards a balletic Stevie Nicks.

'I got into the habit with *English Rose*, and all these weird pics of me half naked and making faces,' explained Fleetwood. 'I didn't think about it then, but now, I wonder if people might think, "This chap has a terrible ego." But I was a weird-looking guy anyhow.'

Fleetwood had also found a costume that would sustain him for the rest of his performing career. 'I still had my school gym kit and fencing gear,' he explained. 'I wore the knickerbockers, tore the sleeves off the jacket to make a waistcoat and put my gym shoes on. That was the start of my stage costume, captured on the *Rumours* cover, and I've worn some version of that ever since.'

In 1970, Peter Green's decision to quit the band shook his drum-mer's confidence. But Fleetwood never forgot Green's willingness to take a chance on him: 'Having been told I was no good at school, and knowing I wasn't a natural blues drummer, what Peter did was just incredible.' Now Fleetwood fell into the role of acciden-tal bandleader. He willed Fleetwood Mac to carry on, despite one setback after another. Christine McVie later revealed the band's standing joke: that Mick was to blame 'for driving us all mad'. Hence the departures of Green, Spencer and the rest.

'Being in this band is like going to that Gordonstoun school in Scotland that fucked Prince Charles up,' said Fleetwood. 'This band is peppered with people who have had some very sad things happen. This band is a cauldron of shit.'

Fleetwood married Jenny Boyd for the first time in 1970. The couple went on to have two daughters, Amelia and Lucy, but the family came second to Fleetwood Mac. When Fleetwood Mac all lived together, Mick's role included father figure, landlord, appeaser, protector and ringmaster. But the core trio of Fleetwood and the McVies insulated themselves, while others fell by the wayside. This was a valuable coping mechanism, but affected Jenny hugely, and triggered her affair with guitarist, Bob Weston.

It didn't last: Weston was sacked and Jenny and Mick had reconciled before the year was out. But the fact that Fleetwood tried to carry on working with the cuckolder said much about his priorities.

Fleetwood was always superstitious and loved the serendipity of meeting Lindsey Buckingham and Stevie Nicks. Over the years, Fleetwood has embroidered the myth: how he glimpsed 'this beautiful girl' through the studio glass and how Lindsey Buckingham's guitar playing reminded him of Peter Green's.

With Stevie and Lindsey falling apart as a couple, the chemistry in the band became even more precarious. Fleetwood the appeaser took over: sweet-talking his new guitarist and lead singer, and trying to stop them from killing each other or, worse, leaving the group. 'I was also the only one spared being in a band with my partner,' he said. 'Though I was still with these other four people in emotional hell.'

Naturally, Fleetwood's personal life was as tortuous as everyone else's. Despite reconciling with Jenny, he began a relationship with Stevie on the final leg of the *Rumours* tour (he and Jenny divorced in 1976, only to remarry the following year and divorce again twelve months later). Mick and Stevie seemed to have survived the tryst without the lingering aggravation that she experienced with Buckingham.

A greater challenge came when Fleetwood began a relationship with Stevie's friend, Sara Recor. It started at a Halloween party in

1978 and the couple were living together a month later. Sara's husband, Jim, was a friend of Mick's, and the couple found themselves *persona non grata* among their acquaintances. No wonder the mood was tense when the group began making *Tusk* – Stevie was barely talking to Mick.

Fleetwood fell back on his superstitions and rituals: dispensing cocaine like a doting uncle handing out sweets to his favourite nieces and nephews, or dipping into his mojo bag of magic charms and I Ching coins, hoping to fend off evil spirits, even the ones he was conjuring. With so much cocaine in the mix, though, Fleetwood's superstitious nature became more pronounced. During one lost weekend, Sara Recor and co-producer Richard Dashut drew '666' on a comatose Mick's chest in semi-permanent lipstick. When he woke up and saw it, Fleetwood freaked out. 'He ran out of the shower after trying to wash it off,' recalled Dashut. '"Look! I'm the devil! I'm the beast! I told you I was possessed!"' Even after they'd explained the prank, Fleetwood wasn't convinced.

The group were in their reckless pomp and Fleetwood was the worst behaved despite also being their manager. There were times when he ingested so much cocaine he'd lose the power of speech. Instead, he'd gurn mutely and point to whatever he needed: a glass of wine, a cigarette, his drumsticks, etc.

'He would make the occasional appearance at home,' recalled Jenny. 'His face haggard, buried under his long scruffy beard, blowing his nose and smelling strongly of patchouli oil.'

He also fell victim to some pre-internet catfishing. One afternoon on tour, the telephone rang in Fleetwood's New Orleans hotel suite and a young female voice told him she was 'Whitney' and could she please have tickets for the show. Fleetwood was flattered and kept her on the line for an hour. Whitney's friends came backstage after the show and told him she'd had to go home early. But he continued chatting to her on the phone every day and told friends he'd fallen in love.

Whitney told him she was a wealthy fashion model, wrote him long letters and sent him photographs of a beautiful young woman, claiming it was her. She never asked for money, but her so-called friends were soon sharing stretch limos paid for by Fleetwood on other dates.

After eight months of Whitney finding excuses not to meet him, Fleetwood hired a private detective. He discovered she wasn't the model in the photographs, but a dowdy postal worker puttering around New Orleans in a dilapidated Volkswagen. The pair never spoke again.

Throughout all the madness, though, Fleetwood maintained a strong work ethic that he nicknamed 'Fred'. 'Fred' was the angel on one shoulder trying to drown out the devil on the other. 'Fred would go, "Mick, you'd better get to sleep now?" And I'd go, "What the fuck do I want to go to sleep for? I'm twenty grams in and I'm up for ten days." Fred would say, "Because you've got eight more shows to do and you're going to make a fool of yourself."'

He also still managed to play the drums despite it all. As insecure as he was, especially in the early days, it's impossible to imagine Fleetwood Mac without Fleetwood. 'I'm not Gene Krupa,' he said. 'I'm just a guy who gets out his own emotions through a pretty simple technique. I pride myself on time.' Fleetwood's technique involves hitting everything hard except the kick drum and placing his tom-toms in a jumbled order. The results were unmistakably Mick: shuffling softly on 'Sara', mimicking a drum machine on 'Hypnotized', dancing like a man with a broken leg on 'Go Your Own Way' or channelling something deeply primal on 'Tusk'.

Tour manager John Courage once said that Fleetwood's drumming suggested he had 'African blood in him somewhere'. Fleetwood made his first trip to the continent in 1974. Six years later, he flew to Ghana on a musical whim. He wanted to tour remote villages with a mobile studio and record the country's great undiscovered musicians. It was a white saviour's pipedream, which ended with Fleetwood's manager being relieved of his briefcase containing passports, cash, credit cards and plane tickets.

Fleetwood refused to give up, though, and returned a year later with a solo deal. Fleetwood recorded *The Visitor* in Ghana and included new versions of 'Rattlesnake Shake' and 'Walk a Thin Line' and a map of Africa on the sleeve. It didn't trouble the charts, but it offered him a respite from the day job.

En route to Ghana, though, Fleetwood discovered he'd maxed out his credit card. He called the bank and deployed the same charm he used to keep Fleetwood Mac afloat and persuaded them to extend his credit. To celebrate, he splashed out on an $8,000 Rolex in the duty-free shop and filed for bankruptcy soon after.

The rest of Fleetwood Mac knew about his financial worries and had fired him as their manager in 1979. Fleetwood now tried to hold himself, his band, his children and his relationship together, while living beyond his means. Playing music allowed him to forget his woes, for a time.

In 1983, Mick Fleetwood's Zoo, a group of musicians and drinking buddies released *I'm Not Me*, a collection of Beach Boys covers and ritzy soft-rock, with help from Buckingham and Christine McVie. The Zoo toured small theatres and played to even smaller audiences. With funds dwindling, Fleetwood called the bank from truck stops and motels around the US. The following year, he filed for bankruptcy for a second time, with newspapers claiming he'd lost $8 million 'and most of it up my nose'.

However, Fleetwood hadn't forgotten the lesson learned in a Notting Hill pub in 1963. 'I got back over there on the carpet,' he said. He also persuaded Fleetwood Mac to reunite for 1987's *Tango in the Night*, a huge hit, but the first album on which Fleetwood seemed partially absent. Fleetwood could still be heard on 'Big Love', 'Little Lies' and the explosive title track, but he was distant in other ways. He was out on the town with a hardcore Hollywood crowd, including comedian Robin Williams, and staying up for days. Buckingham rented a Winnebago that he parked on his driveway where Fleetwood and his familiars could either carry on or sleep it off.

Fleetwood married Sara Recor in 1988 and kept a version of Fleetwood Mac recording and touring for the next few years. He also published *Fleetwood: My Life and Adventures with Fleetwood Mac*, a *New York Times* bestseller, which kept his creditors but not all his former bandmates happy. 'I don't think I could have brought myself to read it, because it was so trashy,' complained Buckingham.

Away from music and publishing, Fleetwood made his Hollywood debut with a bit-part in Arnold Schwarzenegger's *The Running Man*, followed by cameos in other films and television shows. Although his one foray into TV presenting, co-hosting the 1989 BRIT Awards with model Samantha Fox, was a disaster. The pair screwed up several introductions and missed their cues, while Mick, resembling a pony-tailed rabbit in the headlights, blamed his dyslexia and a malfunctioning teleprompter.

Mick and Sara divorced in 1995. By then, Fleetwood was with his third wife-to-be, Lynn Frankel, with whom he'd have twin daughters, Tessa and Ruby, and conquer some of his demons. Early in the relationship, Mick and Lynn took a vacation on Maui, but Fleetwood spent it boozing with friends and hangers-on. Lynn threatened to leave, but Fleetwood begged for one more chance. He went to the bathroom and was shocked by his reflection in the mirror: 'My beard was down here, I was a greasy, sweaty blancmange. I looked at myself and said, "This is it."' So began Fleetwood's long journey back to what he called 'the real world'. His marriage to Lynn wouldn't survive. But he stopped taking cocaine and curbed his drinking. Before long, he had a touring blues band, Blue Whale; had recorded another Zoo album, *Shakin' the Cage*, and reunited with Jeremy Spencer on 2004's Mick Fleetwood Band LP, *Something Big*.

'Mick Fleetwood, the Brand' had also begun, with an early venture into the hospitality industry. Regrettably, Fleetwood's LA Blues in Santa Monica closed after a few months, as one of his business partners was affiliated with the Gambino crime family, and the FBI blocked their liquor licence. He fared better with Fleetwood's On Front Street, an ocean-view restaurant in Maui, noted for its herb-and-panko crusted mahi mahi, and where the boss sometimes sat in with the house band.

In 2007, Fleetwood launched Mick Fleetwood Private Cellar Wine, offering a range of Chardonnay, Pinot Noir and more from his Santa Barbara vineyard. This was followed by Mick Fleetwood Coffee, whose signature Hawaiian blend still promises an 'aromatic blend of fruits, nuts and cocoa'. 'If coffee could go platinum,' enthused Fleetwood, 'this is the stuff.'

In 2021, Mick became the new face of pop star Harry Styles' skin and nail-care brand, and recently launched House of Fleetwood, promising a 'journey of lifestyle and designs', including handcrafted Hawaiian jewellery and scented candles.

Tragically, parts of Maui were devastated by wildfires in August 2023, with a huge loss of life and livelihood. Fleetwood was in Los Angeles when he learned that his restaurant had been destroyed by the fire. He chartered a plane, filled it with emergency supplies, returned to the island, and helped organise a charity concert the following month.

Mick Fleetwood once said that when Fleetwood Mac is finished, 'I'll probably still be standing there, totally deluded and thinking everyone was still around me, waiting to go on stage'. Somehow, somewhere, he's still standing.

The Windsor National Jazz and Blues Festival

Fleetwood Mac Meet the People

'Pete, you'll never be a star if you dress like that,' smirked Eric Clapton. It was backstage on Sunday 13 August 1967 at the Windsor National Jazz and Blues Festival. Peter Green was wearing Levi's and a white T-shirt. Clapton was in what appeared to be a mauve-and-pink bedspread, with his hair frizzed out, à la Jimi Hendrix, and rings glinting on every finger. Green smiled but said nothing before Clapton swanned off.

Fleetwood Mac were like the anti-Cream. While Clapton's super-trio were launched in a blaze of publicity, Green's new group stumbled into the limelight, almost by accident. Yet, instead of playing their first gig somewhere under the radar, Fleetwood Mac debuted at the Windsor National Jazz and Blues Festival before 10,000 paying punters and a coterie of hard-to-impress music journalists.

Like many of their contemporaries, Fleetwood Mac had signed to the Gunnells booking agency, run by entrepreneurial East End siblings Rik and Johnny. Green wanted to do things differently, though. He saw how many other groups were in hock to the Gunnells for their equipment and transport, and immediately bought a second-hand van. Then he and Mick Fleetwood scavenged several old amps and mic stands from roadies attending the International Love-In Festival at Alexandra Palace.

Fleetwood sweet-talked his parents into guaranteeing hire purchase agreements, and Green moved out of the Paddington love nest that he shared with girlfriend Sandra and back in with his parents. Fleetwood's father, Mike, briefly acted as their manager while the band rehearsed at Fulham's Black Bull Tavern and Sandra's parents' country house.

However, Fleetwood Mac had barely been together a month before they played live. The three-day festival at the Royal Windsor Racecourse offered the Small Faces, the Crazy World of Arthur Brown, Cream, Chicken Shack, Jeff Beck, the Move, Ten Years After and more for fourteen shillings and sixpence. The festival's 1,000-watt PA was woefully inadequate but loud enough to attract complaints from local residents and the masters at Eton over a mile-and-a-half away across the Thames.

Fleetwood Mac arrived on stage to face an audience impatient to see Cream. 'I remember stepping up to the microphone to announce the band and the first number,' recalled bassist Bob Brunning. 'I said, "We'd like to play . . ." and completely forgot the song's title.'

It was 'Talk to Me Baby', with Jeremy Spencer's bottleneck slide and lead vocals roaring away over a wavering tempo. 'I'm Coming Home to Stay' sounded like a work-in-progress version of 'I Loved Another Woman' (later included on '*Dog and Dustbin*') and was followed by Elmore James's 'I Need You' and the instrumental 'Fleetwood Mac', demoed during the group's first studio jam.

By the time Spencer returned to the mic for 'Fine Little Mama', the band had found its groove. Brunning's memory deserted him briefly while trying to introduce 'The World Keeps on Turning' before everyone piled into 'Shake Your Moneymaker', which was loud enough to defy the dreadful PA and presumably get wing collars flapping across the river at Eton.

Fleetwood Mac performed again that evening in a marquee on the racecourse, where they played for over an hour and let their metaphorical hair down. Mick Fleetwood saw John McVie watching in the wings: 'He was there with the Bluesbreakers, and a few weeks later, he called Peter to tell him he was ready to join us.'

Dreams

The group pocketed £40 for their first gig and waited for the reviews to arrive. 'Peter Green's Fleetwood Mac made an impressive debut,' wrote *Melody Maker*'s Chris Welch, 'but Eric Clapton is still two-hundred and forty miles ahead of other guitarists in his field.' Not 200 or 250, but *240* miles? It was a good start, but Eric and his mauve-and-pink bedspread were in the lead. For now.

Jeremy Spencer

The Curse of the Fleetwood Mac Guitarist, Part I

After joining Fleetwood Mac in 1967, Jeremy Spencer moved in for a time with Bob Brunning. He was a terrible flatmate, apparently. Every time Spencer forgot his keys, which was often, he'd smash a window and break in.

'Jeremy would be genuinely surprised at my anger,' said Brunning after calling out a glazier for the umpteenth time. 'He's always been an odd character.'

Spencer's dramatic exit from the band to join the Children of God religious movement was even odder. But he'd always been a mass of contradictions. In Fleetwood Mac, he'd play the most sublime blues before telling what working men's club comedians used to call 'blue jokes' in between songs. He'd also fling condoms filled with milk or beer over the audience and received a lifetime ban from London's Marquee for strolling on stage with a dildo jutting from his fly. Then, he'd sit in the van on the way home, reading the Bible. In hindsight, Spencer was never going to stick around, but he played on four Mac albums and helped shape their original sound.

Jeremy Cedric Spencer was born in West Hartlepool, County Durham, on 4 July 1948. His father worked for the RSPCA and encouraged his son to take piano lessons. Jeremy followed his advice but was soon distracted by Elvis, Cliff Richard and the 'lonely guitar' echoing away on the Righteous Brothers' 'Unchained Melody'.

While studying at Stafford Art College, a friend played him Mississippi bluesman Elmore James's 'The Sun Is Shining'. Spencer was smitten by James's slide guitar technique and discovered that a copper tube over his little finger created an authentic bottleneck sound. 'It was like I'd discovered a way to express emotion,' he said later.

In the summer of 1967, Spencer was training to be a bank clerk by day and pretending to be Elmore James by night in a three-piece called the Levi Set. Producer/talent scout Mike Vernon saw the trio play in Birmingham. He didn't rate the rhythm section but was impressed by the diminutive Spencer playing slide on a guitar that looked too big for him. Vernon brought the group to London to make an audition tape. He played it to Peter Green, telling him to ignore the other two and focus on Spencer. Green was impressed. He was still in John Mayall's Bluesbreakers but plotting to form Fleetwood Mac and adamant he wanted a second guitarist.

Vernon arranged for the Levi Set to play during the interval at Mayall's upcoming date at Birmingham's Le Metro club. 'Peter wanted to hear me play because he was forming a new band and intense about doing straight Chicago blues,' recalled Spencer.

The trio rattled through a half-hour set, but Spencer wasn't convinced he'd passed the test: 'John Mayall played their second set, and I'd discounted any idea of Pete wanting me in his new band. Then, to my surprise, he invited me for a drink, and we stood by the bar, where he talked as though I was already in the band.

'He was saying, "Well, you can do a couple of Elmore things, and then I do a couple of B.B. King's . . ." I finally said, "Are you serious? Do you like what I play?" He said I was the first guitarist who made him smile since Jimi Hendrix. Can you believe it?'

Green then took a notebook out of his pocket and showed Spencer something he'd written on the journey up to Birmingham: 'It was like a prayer that said, "I can't go on with this music like it is. Please have Jeremy be good, please have him be good . . ."'

Bob Brunning was replaced by John McVie, and Fleetwood Mac released their self-titled debut, commonly known as *'Dog and*

Dustbin', in February 1968. Spencer was credited with three originals (all of which cheekily borrowed from existing blues numbers) and ripped it up on covers of Elmore James's 'Shake Your Moneymaker' and 'Got to Move'.

Fleetwood claims Spencer was a model of restraint to begin with. He also had commitments. In the summer of 1968, he'd married his sixteen-year-old girlfriend, Fiona, after she'd given birth to their son, Jeremy Jr, known by his middle name Dicon. Bob Brunning recalled congratulating Spencer on the new arrival, only to discover that Jeremy couldn't remember the baby's name.

Before long, another Jeremy Spencer emerged on stage: a sort of Artful Dodger for the British blues boom – all honking slide guitar, leery grins and penis jokes. 'He was a dynamo,' said Fleetwood. 'A whirlwind of raw power.' This version of Jeremy Spencer also had a knock-on effect on the others, and Peter Green encouraged the vulgarity. But there were times when it backfired: like the dildo-down-the-trousers incident at the Marquee or when Green joked on stage about shy John McVie taking 'months to fuck Christine Perfect', leading to John threatening him in the middle of the gig.

However, *this* Jeremy Spencer also engaged his bandmates in deep conversations about God. 'I didn't understand it myself,' Spencer admitted years later. 'Why I was such an irreverent so-and-so on stage and yet off stage, I had these religious inclinations. But I believed in God and read the Bible and other spiritual books, looking for the answers.' Decades later, Spencer was also reluctant to discuss the dildo and the bawdy jokes. 'I prefer that people are more acquainted with me as a musician, past and present,' he said. When he did talk about it, he blamed youthful over-exuberance and a warped sense of humour.

Spencer's savant-like mimicry extended to other musicians besides Elmore James. He impersonated Elvis Presley with such conviction that it became a part of the act. But Spencer sometimes refused when his bandmates asked him to 'do Elvis'. 'It went back to his schooldays, when he didn't like being told what to do,' explained Peter Green, who recalled a gig in Essex, where Spencer started playing the hall

37

piano instead of unloading his gear. 'Bob Brunning said, "Would you get your amplifier in please, Jeremy, before you start doing that?" and Jeremy said, "No, the last time I was told to do something, I was at school."'

He was also reluctant to write new songs or play on other people's. When Green asked Spencer to play back-up on his songs, he'd find an excuse not to because he wasn't confident enough. 'While Jeremy could be good fun, he was limited as a player beyond doing Elmore James,' suggested Mike Vernon.

In contrast, Green's latest new recruit, eighteen-year-old guitar prodigy Danny Kirwan, was a fount of new ideas, making Spencer even more reticent. Instead of playing on the hit 'Albatross', he made a solo album of '50s pop and surf-music parodies. Spencer also oversaw an LP's worth of spoof songs and covers, which he wanted to include on the second half of 1969's *Then Play On*. Some of the material later appeared on *The Vaudeville Years* and *Show-Biz Blues* compilations but was nixed at the time for being too self-indulgent.

Green was also on what he called a 'Jesus kick', and he and Spencer planned a concept album based on Christ's life. 'We believe in God, and this is a serious venture,' said Green at the time. But it never happened.

Then again, old Buddy Holly songs and singing about Jesus were more to Spencer's tastes than the progressive sounds on *Then Play On* or its calling card single, 'Oh Well'. Besides a snippet of his piano playing, Spencer was absent from the album and the single. 'I had no inspiration,' he explained. 'I couldn't think of anything new. There was nothing to really sing about anymore. So if I sang about a girl, what girl? . . . I suppose I could sing about my wife.'

But Green's sudden departure thrust Spencer and Kirwan into the spotlight. Their next LP, *Kiln House*, leaned heavily on Jeremy's cod-rock 'n' roll but also included a song about God called 'One Together'. Spencer claimed his interest in religion accelerated after he tried LSD in 1968. He was looking for something but didn't know what: 'I'd never thought seriously about death or my life or anything . . . and then when I took acid, it just freaked my mind.'

In February 1971, Fleetwood Mac were booked to play four nights at Los Angeles' Whisky a Go Go. They were now being chauffeured around in Rolls-Royces and regularly offered cocaine. But Spencer, already in a fragile state after taking mescaline, felt alienated by the band's music and their lifestyle.

He was still doing his Elvis routine on stage with a gold lamé suit, and his hair teased into a towering pompadour. At San Francisco's Fillmore West, he was so in character that he singled out an audience member trying to slip away to the bathroom. 'Nobody!' he drawled, pointing a quivering finger, 'but *nobody* leaves when Elvis is on stage.' Spencer hid behind this persona. The rest of the time, he seemed withdrawn and distracted. Just before Fleetwood Mac arrived in LA, a major earthquake had torn through the city. 'Jeremy was in the window seat on the plane, and he turned to me and said, "What the hell am I doing here?"' recalled John McVie.

The night before the first Whisky gig, Spencer was listening to a recording of a Peter Green-era show and winced when he heard himself playing 'Stranger Blues': 'I blurted out, "This sounds like shit!" I went to my room and prayed to God to get me out of it.' The following afternoon, Spencer told the others that he was going to a bookshop on Hollywood Boulevard. When he hadn't returned by six o'clock, road manager Dennis Keane led a search party. Nobody in the shop recalled seeing him, but the street was teeming with young people handing out leaflets and talking about Jesus.

Fleetwood Mac cancelled the show, the police were notified, and radio stations broadcast urgent pleas for information. Some claim Spencer was missing for three days; others as many as five. At some point, a fan showed up at the band's hotel to tell them Jeremy was with the Children of God, one of the groups seen preaching on the Boulevard.

Manager Clifford Davis and some of the crew arrived at the Children's mission in downtown LA. At first, the members denied Spencer was there. So Davis falsely claimed Fiona Spencer had been taken ill back in the UK, and they had to speak to her husband. Finally, Jeremy appeared, apparently with his hair cut short, wearing a pair of trousers several sizes too big and insisting that they call him 'Jonathan'. Davis spent several hours trying to persuade him to leave. But Spencer told him that the earthquake was a bad omen, and he'd found a new calling. Fleetwood Mac had lost yet another guitarist. 'We faced ruin,' said Fleetwood. 'We couldn't promote *Kiln House*, and I feared we were done.'

The circumstances surrounding Spencer's departure ran like Chinese whispers and were soon steeped in hearsay. Coming so soon after Green's 'bad acid trip' in the Munich commune, how could they not be? Within days, the music press claimed that Spencer had been abducted by a religious cult and was found 'walking around like a zombie with a shaved head'.

A different version of events emerged later. In a 1974 *NME* interview, Spencer said he'd been approached on Hollywood Boulevard by a young man named 'Apollos' who was strumming a guitar and asked if he wanted to hear a song. Spencer thought a fan was hustling him: 'But he'd never heard of Fleetwood Mac, and he didn't seem like a regular freaked-out doper.' Apollos asked if Jeremy had ever invited 'Jesus into your heart'. Spencer wasn't sure how to answer but joined him in a prayer and followed him to the Children of God's mission. Fleetwood Mac's showtime came and went, but Spencer was too busy talking about the meaning of life with his new friends.

Spencer insisted that he wasn't abducted and hadn't shaved his head. He'd willingly cut his hair short earlier because the band were scheduled to play in Texas, and he thought his flowing locks would upset the locals. Although he did admit to wearing oversized trousers and changing his name to 'Jonathan'. He also remembered Clifford Davis suggesting that he stay with Fleetwood Mac and 'just follow these people in his spare time', but his new friends drowned Davis out with their communal singing. Ultimately, Spencer was disillusioned with music and drugs, and believed he'd found an alternative.

The Children of God (or 'The Family', as it was later known) were an evangelical Christian organisation promoting 'spiritual salvation, revolution and happiness' by radical and uncompromising means. Devotees had to change their names, and children were sometimes separated from their parents and sent to live in other parts of the world. Later, the organisation was fiercely criticised for its authoritarianism and brainwashing; for encouraging under-age sex, and for female members using sex to attract male followers. The Children of God's leader, David Berg (who died in 1994), was accused of multiple sexual offences by past members. Spencer was also accused online and in print by former Family members of sexual misconduct, which he described in 2009 as 'slander and controversy . . . and misinformation'.

After Spencer disappeared, Fleetwood Mac didn't see him again for nine months, until he turned up, unannounced, at a gig in Seattle. Apparently, they forgave him for his sudden exit: 'But the way I left was wrong and a mistake. I should've told them right away. A phone call or something.'

Fiona and Dicon had now joined Jeremy in the organisation, and CBS had released *Jeremy Spencer and the Children*, a poorly recorded LP of devotional songs. 'It was a horrible album,' shuddered Fleetwood.

The Children of God also gave Spencer special dispensation. Perhaps having an ex-rock star in the organisation was good for business? 'Jonathan' was allowed to revert to 'Jeremy' and play the electric guitar but not use a distortion pedal – that was the devil's plaything. In 1974, Jeremy Spencer and the Mountain Children performed at the Poorboy Club, a Family mission in London's Finchley Road, where Spencer revisited some of the bawdy blues he'd played in Fleetwood Mac.

As the Family required its members to spread the message globally, he spent the rest of the decade between the UK, the US, France, Brazil and Italy, recording devotional music and writing and illustrating the group's literature.

Spencer secured another record deal in 1978. *Rumours* was selling millions, and Atlantic Records boss Ahmet Ertegun hoped an ex-Fleetwood Mac member would be bankable. But the Jeremy Spencer Band's *Flee* was *Rumours*-lite, with added disco and a religious subtext. 'The record company started by telling us our ideas were great,' Spencer grumbled. 'Next thing, we're being told to listen to a pile of two-bit funk albums as a reference point.'

Flee was Spencer's last album for over two decades before 2006's *Precious Little*. In the intervening years, he wrote and drew, played festivals and performed charity shows for the blind in India.

It's believed that Spencer had more children with Fiona before meeting his second wife, known as both 'Julie' and 'Dora'. He spent the 1980s with her in the Philippines, Japan, Greece and Sri Lanka and the '90s and '00s in Brazil, Mexico, Switzerland, Germany and Ireland. 'I have to be ready to go or stay, sometimes at a moment's notice,' he explained.

In 2006, the rock group Jynxt – comprising some of Spencer's children, including Dicon (now known as 'Jez') – released the album *Bring Back Tomorrow*. The siblings had rejected the Children of God and blamed their parents' joining the organisation on Jeremy's LSD use and Fiona's immaturity. In interviews, they talked about their unusual childhoods, in which they'd been airlifted out of Sri Lanka during the Tamil uprising and once spent a freezing winter in Omsk. They claimed their father was 'the most impractical man in the world.' He couldn't drive a car, ride a bicycle, swim or cook. Everything Spencer had went into practising his religion and playing the guitar. These were the two constants in Spencer's life. At times, he's complained about being haunted by the past. 'As you probably understand,' he said in 2012, 'it's not inspiring to re-tread old ground.' But he's not always shy about doing so.

In 2020, Spencer held the audience spellbound with his version of Elmore James's 'The Sky is Crying' at the Peter Green tribute concert. The two musicians hadn't shared a stage in half a century. After it was done, Mick hugged him, and Jeremy looked awkward.

He'd spent three-and-half years in Fleetwood Mac and has been in the Family for over fifty years. Perhaps he'd found what he was looking for after all. 'I believe God wants me to impart my passion for the blues,' he once said, 'and I am grateful for the opportunities "He" has given me.'

X-Rated

*The Inside Story of Harold the Dildo and
Mick Fleetwood's $128,000 Balls*

Mick Fleetwood: We'd been to the red-light district in Holland
or Germany [in 1968], and found this huge dildo which we nicknamed 'Harold' and decided to make a part of the show.

Huw Pryce (road manager): Some nights I used to come on stage
carrying a tray of drinks for the band. They'd introduce me, lark
about, and point out Harold lying on the tray.

John McVie: We did this a lot at the Marquee. Harold appeared
quite regularly. He was a stand-up guy.

Ian Anderson (vocalist, Jethro Tull): I remember supporting
Fleetwood Mac at the Marquee, who produced a very large dildo
on stage. It brought about a huge amount of mirth, but I found it
rather vulgar. There was no guarantee it hadn't been *used*.

Mick Fleetwood: We did it to get a reaction from the audience.
We'd take Harold off the tray and put him on my bass drum, where
he'd undulate as we played. Then Jeremy Spencer began to get
very vulgar. He'd fill condoms with milk or beer and hang them
from the pegs of his guitar, and swing them out over this audience
of appalled blues purists.

43

Christine McVie: I used to go and see them before I joined. Fleetwood Mac were gregarious, charming and cheeky. Very cheeky. But Jeremy Spencer was really dirty. At the Marquee one night he put the dildo in his trousers, came out and impersonated Cliff Richard. Half the women left, escorted out by their boyfriends.

Mick Fleetwood: We got banned from the Marquee after that until 1971.

John Gee (The Marquee manager, overheard running on stage): Bloody well pack it in!

Mick Fleetwood: Harold's showbiz life came to a crashing end at an American Southern Baptist college, where we were nearly arrested. Much to my wife's chagrin, he ended his days sitting on our pine corner cabinet.

Jeremy Spencer: I'm not proud of a lot of those antics. But we were a bunch of silly kids, really – boys in the band, acting up.

Mick Fleetwood: The whole ethic of the blues is suggestive. I got into the spirit of things by nicking a pair of wooden balls from a pub lavatory chain and hanging them from my belt whenever we played. I walked out on stage with these wooden balls hanging down. The original balls disappeared, but were replaced, and I've never played a Fleetwood Mac show without them – and I wore them on the cover of *Rumours*.

Julien's Auction Catalogue (Los Angeles, December 2022): For sale, the two wooden balls worn by Mick Fleetwood as part of his attire for the album cover of *Rumours*. The balls feature a dark finish that has been worn away in a band around the circumference of each ball . . . Attached to leather cords and housed in a soft maroon cloth drawstring case with the words 'Open Sesame' embroidered in gold-tone thread. Lot Closed – sale price $128,000.

John McVie

'Like a loaf of crusty bread . . .'

'I could have easily fallen for John, but he drinks too much.'

Stevie Nicks

'John is like the greatest dance partner. He's the type who knows what you're going to do before you do it because they've been leading you all along.'

Mick Fleetwood

'I never hung out with John ever.'

Lindsey Buckingham

'John really made his basslines count, They're almost like little songs within the song.'

Bob Welch

'Oh, Johnny!'

Christine McVie

John McVie's Greatest Fleetwood Mac Moments

'Rattlesnake Shake'
'Oh Well'
'The Green Manalishi (With the Two Prong Crown)'

'Bare Trees'
'World Turning'
'The Chain'
'You Make Loving Fun'
'Say You Love Me'
'Beautiful Child'
'Tusk'

John McVie remembers the moment he realised he could never be a tax inspector. He was an eighteen-year-old trainee working behind the counter at the inland revenue's office in Brentford, west London. 'I was a no-nothing kid and I was also useless at maths,' said McVie. 'There were a couple of breweries in the area and some of the customers used to come in pretty wasted.' Excessive alcohol and an excessive tax bill proved an explosive combination. One day a customer jumped over the counter and tried to attack him.

McVie started at the tax office the same day that he joined John Mayall's Bluesbreakers, in February 1963. McVie only landed the gig because his neighbour turned it down and passed on John's phone number. 'Luck has been a big part of my life,' he admitted.

The 'Mac' in Fleetwood Mac was born John Graham McVie on 26 November 1945, in Ealing, west London, to parents Reg and Dorothy. McVie learned to play the trumpet before discovering the guitar at fourteen years old, and was smitten when his cousin played him Buddy Holly and the Crickets' 'Rave On': 'He kept on playing it over and over, and from that moment on I was hooked.'

McVie joined his first group, the Krewsaders, in 1962. The Ealing blues scene was incestuous, and McVie was friends with their drummer, John 'Speedy' Keen, who'd later work with the Who. The Krewsaders needed a bass player and McVie told Keen that his father would buy him one if they offered him the job. The trade-off worked, and the group landed a coveted spot at the Ealing Jazz Club.

By now John had met an older musician, Cliff Barton, who lived opposite and played bass in the Cyril Davies R&B All-Stars: 'Cliff turned me on to Chuck Berry, Jerry Lee Lewis and Little Richard.' But Cliff also turned down John Mayall and suggested McVie for the job.

Davies' group (which at various times hosted a young Jimmy Page, Jeff Beck, Eric Clapton, Bill Wyman and Charlie Watts) was considered a safe bet. John Mayall was an unknown quantity: a thirty-year-old commercial artist and part-time musician who'd moved to London from his native Manchester and started sourcing musicians for a new group. Mayall auditioned McVie at the White Hart pub in Acton. He passed. 'John took a chance and gave me a bunch of blues albums to listen to and learn from,' recalled McVie, who turned professional after nine months. 'My parents, bless their hearts, were very supportive. But it was a sort of bemused tolerance.'

Mayall adopted a similar attitude towards his latest Bluesbreaker. Mayall didn't drink alcohol but the band, especially McVie, made up for it. 'I never drank for pleasure, it was more of an environment thing in the Bluesbreakers,' McVie admitted. 'I met a lot of people in those days who drank, and it snowballed until I'd be drinking half a bottle of spirits every gig.'

One night, Mayall dumped McVie at a bus stop on London's Old Kent Road to prevent him throwing up in the band's van. He also sacked him several times – once for some boozy on-stage acrobatics involving a speaker cabinet, which is difficult to imagine, as McVie barely moved on stage with Fleetwood Mac – but he was too good to lose for good. Benign tolerance became the key to the two Johns' working relationship. Mayall's Bluesbreakers were now the go-to backing band for visiting American bluesmen such as John Lee Hooker and Sonny Boy Williamson.

McVie made his recording debut on 1965's *John Mayall Plays John Mayall*, followed a year later by *Blues Breakers With Eric Clapton*, aka '*The Beano Album*', as its cover photo showed Clapton downplaying his guitar-hero status by posing with a copy of the famous comic. McVie sat next to him, glowering from under a hard fringe and unruly eyebrows.

Mick Fleetwood's earliest memory of seeing McVie was in Soho's Flamingo club. 'I noticed John because he was always turned out in classic blues band style,' recalled Fleetwood. 'He'd have on perfectly faded jeans, a pair of gym shoes, a white T-shirt and his "Fu Manchu" moustache. He had a very cool, "Don't fuck with me" air to him.'

McVie played on Fleetwood Mac's original demo, and Fleetwood and Peter Green wanted him to join their new group. But McVie turned them down. 'It was a good gig with John Mayall, a regular wage,' he reasoned.

In August 1967, McVie watched Fleetwood Mac make their debut without him at the Windsor National Jazz and Blues Festival. Mayall's Bluesbreakers and Chicken Shack (with pianist Christine Perfect) were also on the bill. 'Chris was in the next tent,' recalled McVie, 'I went over and heard this young lady playing and we kept bumping into each other around the circuit.' McVie had just seen his future band and his future wife. 'I finally got up enough courage to ask Christine out when we were playing at the Thames Hotel in Windsor. It was a pretty quick courtship – six or seven weeks, I believe.'

McVie also phoned Fleetwood and told him he was leaving the Bluesbreakers. 'John Mayall started bringing horns in,' he grumbled. 'I thought it was getting too jazz, which it wasn't, but I wanted it to be Chicago blues. I was very blinkered.'

During a Bluesbreakers gig in Norwich, McVie overheard one of the horn players asking Mayall what sort of solo he wanted on an upcoming song. 'Just play freeform,' Mayall replied. This was a step too far for McVie, who slipped out during the interval. 'I phoned up Peter and said, "Hey, you need a bass player? I'm in."'

McVie's blues purism was indulged on Fleetwood Mac's first two albums. But Danny Kirwan's arrival dovetailed with Green pushing the band out of its comfort zone. McVie was baffled when he first heard their future number-one hit 'Albatross'; but he did as he was asked. 'Danny and Peter would bring these tapes in and there wasn't much interaction. "This is how it goes." "Okay, I'll play this."'

McVie's influences encompassed pop, jazz and blues, from Paul McCartney to Charles Mingus to Willie Dixon. But neither he nor Fleetwood were songwriters, so they focused on becoming a telepathic rhythm section, on which different guitarists, vocalists and songwriters could rely. 'I always try to get in with the kick drum,' McVie explained. 'Mick knows where I'm going, and I know where he's going, so the song locks.'

In later years, McVie played down the impact of Peter Green's departure in 1970. Privately, he was furious and frustrated. He'd given up a gig with John Mayall to join a group whose principal member had walked out as soon as they started selling records.

McVie found it similarly traumatic when Jeremy Spencer disappeared in the middle of a US tour the following year. Joining the Children of God religious movement, his departure was so sudden, that his bandmates wondered if he was dead: 'Just the fact that he disappeared like that, *anything* could have happened.'

McVie also threatened to leave the group. While making their first post-Green LP, 1970's *Kiln House*, he told Fleetwood he was fed up with the music business and wanted to be a roadie instead. Three years later, he stormed off to France for a time. His uneasiness and frustration were usually down to alcohol, marital problems or the band's general instability; or a combination of all three.

In keeping with his later love of all things nautical, McVie's role became that of the chief mate who never plotted the ship's course but helped keep it afloat. 'We got used to the traumas,' he said. 'Oh shit, here we go again.' Unfortunately, though, he couldn't stop his marriage from capsizing.

John and Christine had wed in 1968, after which she abandoned Chicken Shack and a blossoming solo career to stay home and become, in the parlance of the times, 'John's old lady'. It didn't last, and she soon became a member of Fleetwood Mac. But living and working together tested their resilience. None of the band were abstemious, but McVie *really* drank, and by 1973, his relationship was in jeopardy. 'I was over the top, way over the top, and she couldn't handle it anymore,' he admitted. 'We were doing something down in Florida when I got the message, she'd rather be with our lighting director than me.'

Christine tried to keep her new relationship with lighting director Curry Grant secret; but failed. While making 1977's *Rumours*, the studio became like the stage in a Whitehall farce, with band members ensuring that Grant left by one door whenever McVie entered via another. Then John introduced a new girlfriend, Peter Green's ex, Sandra Elsdon (the real-life 'Black Magic Woman'), into the mix.

From the start, Christine was keen to move on. John found it harder. At the time, he strove to maintain a stiff upper lip and focused on the music. McVie's contribution to 'The Chain' was inestimable. Imagine it without that bass run? But he also added those wonderfully elastic lines to 'You Make Loving Fun' (a song about Grant) and 'Don't Stop' (a song about him). For decades, John claimed not to know who his estranged wife was singing about. Perhaps it was easier for him that way.

The cliché of the 'quiet one' followed him around like a shadow. *Rumours*' co-producer, Ken Caillat, claimed that it was a literal description: 'John had the strange talent of being able to enter a room without a sound.' 'I have no problem with "quiet",' said McVie. 'I have an ego and it's nice to have people applaud. I just have a hard time dealing with compliments.'

McVie was no shrinking violet, though: whether having a penguin tattooed on his arm after an afternoon's heavy drinking or going nose-to-nose with Lindsey Buckingham in the studio. 'Lindsey was and is a pretty intense guy,' he said. 'It took quite a while to get used to him, and vice versa. But I wasn't about to be a session player and just go along with Lindsey's commands.'

In 1977, *Rolling Stone*'s Cameron Crowe interviewed McVie, who was now living on a ketch moored in the Marina del Rey. He bristled at the suggestion that Buckingham and Nicks had saved the group. 'Fleetwood Mac was doing fine before,' he insisted. 'People are always asking me, "How does it feel to have made it?" If that's the case then what do I do now?' The dichotomy between

Fleetwood Mac's success and his marriage's failure wasn't lost on him. 'It still affects me. I'm still adjusting to the fact that it's not John and Chris anymore. It goes up and down.'

Success didn't spoil his fashion sense either. McVie spent the late '70s looking like he'd just come from his sailboat, by sporting a succession of baseball shirts, longshoreman caps and frayed denim shorts. Ken Caillat found the shorts especially disconcerting because when John was playing his big-bodied Alembic bass it looked like he was naked from the waist down.

Soon after his divorce in May 1978, John married his secretary Julie Rubens at a ceremony in same Hollywood Hills house that he'd once shared with Christine. There was no time for the McVies to take a honeymoon as there was another tour booked and another album to make. McVie was off sailing to Tahiti once he'd recorded his bass parts for 1979's *Tusk*. But his 28-tonne boat was rammed by a whale, hard enough to put a dent in the hull and remind him of the power of Mother Nature.

McVie sometimes found animals easier to deal with than humans. His fascination dates back to childhood and the '60s when he and Christine lived near Regent's Park and were frequent visitors to London Zoo. Decades later, McVie sold his Cabo 35 Express fishing vessel because he didn't like watching the marlin die on the deck after being caught.

Fleetwood Mac spent most of the '80s off the road. The McVies landed themselves in trouble in 1981 when the Honolulu police department found seven guns and a package containing four-and-a-half grammes of cocaine in their house. McVie didn't know he'd broken Hawaiian gun law, as he presumed the rules about ownership were the same as mainland US. He also passed a lie-detector test during which he denied knowing about the package of cocaine. The old McVie luck kicked in and the couple escaped with a $1,000 fine and a hefty donation to a drugs charity.

The following year, McVie joined a reunited Bluesbreakers for dates in the US, Australia and Asia. But he suffered performance anxiety when Fleetwood Mac began work on 1987's *Tango in the Night*.

51

An alcoholic seizure that year saw him hospitalised and under doctors' orders to give up drinking. It would be some time before McVie made that change, though. Two years later, aged forty-four, he finally received his US citizenship, and he and Julie became parents to a daughter, Molly Elizabeth.

McVie has fewer than a dozen writing credits to his name with Fleetwood Mac, but he helped sell a lot of records and invested in property: a house in Maui (which he later sold to Mick Fleetwood), another in Honolulu, and 1950s crime novelist Raymond Chandler's old place in Brentwood, Los Angeles.

But when he wasn't with Fleetwood Mac, he didn't work. *John McVie's Gotta Band*, a 1992 collaboration with the American blues vocalist Lola Thomas, came and went without many noticing.

Fleetwood Mac's 1997 tour was their first in over a decade with all five members of the *Rumours* line-up. It stirred up old emotions. After the shows, McVie told journalists that his ex-wife was 'a lovely, lovely lady . . . even though she told me to fuck off.'

It was no secret McVie was sometimes 'in his cups' on stage. Not that it seemed to affect his performance. Wearing a billowy white shirt and a bandanna that made him look like a tipsy pirate, he locked into Fleetwood's kick drum and swung effortlessly through 'The Chain', 'Dreams', 'Gold Dust Woman', 'Go Your Own Way' and the rest. One night after a date in Detroit, McVie accidentally knocked over a table full of drinks in the bar of an upscale hotel. He calmly waved for a waitress to clean up the mess and carried on signing autographs.

McVie's reluctance to grant interviews reinforced the 'quiet one' image, and he rarely figures highly in those 'Greatest Bass Players of All Time' magazine polls. 'Yet is one of the most instinctive and tasteful players I've ever met,' according to Ken Caillat. McVie, lost for words in a rare interview, described his style of playing like so: 'Deep, but still tight. Like a loaf of crusty bread. It just has a nice edge, and there's a kind of doughy thing.'

Other musicians understand. R.E.M.'s bass guitarist Mike Mills was once interviewed about his band's 1991 hit, 'Losing My

Religion'. 'The song was complete and I was coming up with all these different basslines but I couldn't find something that fitted,' said Mills. 'Then it popped into my head – "What would John McVie do?"' The answer was, 'Something simple, but with just enough of a weird note to make it strange, slightly unsettling.'

Not that McVie sought anyone's approval other than his own. The making of Fleetwood Mac's 2003 comeback album, *Say You Will*, was documented in the fly-on-a-wall film, *Destiny Rules*. McVie spent most of it sat on a couch in Buckingham's home studio, observing the others. He looked impassive and a little sad sometimes too. Partway through the film, McVie described his role in the band more eloquently than ever: 'I'm not privy to where the writers want the songs to go,' he said, sitting next to Fleetwood and opposite Stevie and Lindsey. 'I do my bass parts, and after that, it's back in the writer's court, and after that, it's repeat, repeat, *repeat* and that's where I get completely bored.' The others could be heard laughing, but McVie sounded frustrated. 'So I'd rather be anywhere else but sitting in the same room – bless their hearts, it's not personal it's business – listening to the same bloody thing going over and over two hundred thousand times a day . . .'

'Johnny, you're being brutal on yourself,' chipped in Fleetwood.

'No, it drives me to distraction unless I play it,' replied McVie, 'and it's always been that way. I wish I could have more of an input into the product, but I can't see into people's heads.'

'I want to say something,' announced Fleetwood, while McVie sighed deeply. 'You've been more present on this project than any other.'

'I was just gonna say that,' replied McVie. 'That was my wind-up bit . . . Christ almighty! . . . Anyway, that was the end of it, thanks.'

McVie cast a doleful eye at the camera and presumably went outside to smoke the cigarette he'd been waving around for the last few minutes.

In October 2013, McVie was diagnosed with colon cancer. It was his spur to stop drinking. He responded well to treatment, and in 2018, joined the rest of Fleetwood Mac for what seems likely to be their final tour. Even before Christine's death, though, McVie felt that his time as a touring musician was ending. 'It's not the music, it's the peripherals, the travelling,' he told *Mojo* magazine. 'What must I fucking look like – this old fart up there.'

Once again, luck played its part in McVie being there in the first place. 'Luck has been such a big part of my life. One phone call from Cliff Barton to John Mayall . . . Lucky that I caught the cancer so quickly. I'm a lucky guy.'

John McVie was once asked where his role began and ended in Fleetwood Mac. 'Playing bass,' he replied. 'I'm not a dedicated musician particularly, but it's the one thing I enjoy doing.' He smiled and then looked like he'd rather be doing something, anything, rather than being interviewed.

'Dog and Dustbin' and Mr. Wonderful

Two Albums, Two Canines, One Naked Man

For those who saw Fleetwood Mac at Tolworth's Toby Jug or any British blues club in the '60s, 1977's *Rumours* must have sounded like the work of imposters. But every successive line-up has struggled to escape the one before. 'When we joined, there was all this history, all this *past*,' said Stevie Nicks. 'And we'd hear all these stories about Peter Green.'

Fleetwood Mac's self-titled debut (nicknamed *'Dog and Dustbin'*) and its follow-up, *Mr. Wonderful*, arrived within seven months of each other in 1968. Where every note on *Rumours* sounded polished, everything on these two sounded like it was recorded on the hoof – which it was.

By the summer of 1967, John Mayall, the Bluesbreakers bandleader, knew he couldn't hold on to Peter Green for ever. Fleetwood Mac was born when Green, Mick Fleetwood and John McVie accepted Mayall's gift of free studio time and recorded a handful of tracks for fun, including a Chicago-style blues instrumental they called 'Fleetwood Mac'.

When Mayall proposed introducing a horn section into the Bluesbreakers, Green bailed out. Fellow Bluesbreaker John McVie had similar misgivings but didn't want to lose his £40-a-week wage.

Bassist Bob Brunning took his place temporarily, alongside new recruit, slide guitarist Jeremy Spencer.

A buzz developed following the band's debut at the Windsor Festival in August. After signing to producer Mike Vernon's Blue Horizon Records, Fleetwood Mac released a single, 'I Believe My Time Ain't Long' before rushing off to finish their debut album.

There was precious little time, budget or thought involved. John McVie had finally joined the band and the recording sessions were squeezed in between pre-Christmas dates at the Marquee and other venues. Vernon produced the LP at CBS Studios but also sneaked the band into Decca (where he'd recently been house producer) after hours when nobody was looking. The idea was to make the album sound as much like their live show as possible. One night, the band returned from a gig at the Nottingham Boat Club to start recording at three o'clock in the morning. In fact, there's a whiff of cigarette breath and armpits around the whole album.

While the band was Peter Green's baby, Jeremy Spencer's honking slide and Elmore James impressions dominated half the record. His opening song, 'My Heart Beat Like a Hammer', showcased a blood-pumping riff and a lascivious-sounding vocal. As with many British blues records, the credits deployed great poetic licence. The song was credited to Spencer but bore a striking resemblance to Buster Brown's 'Don't Dog Your Woman' and James's 'Dust My Broom', among several others.

Spencer was similarly noisy on 'Shake Your Moneymaker' and 'My Baby's Good to Me', which re-imagined the blues through the eyes of a pint-sized white boy from Hartlepool. But Spencer swapped the slide guitar for piano on a reworked 'Hellhound on My Trail', a Robert Johnson number with Peter Green's name in the credit, despite Green being absent from the song.

The album's scattershot nature was also apparent on Green's mellow 'Merry Go Round' and his harmonica-driven rumba, 'Looking for Somebody'. Despite his love of Chicago blues, Green was pushing the genre's limits. There were too many competing influences for him to be restrained by just one.

'Long Grey Mare' was inspired by Green's girlfriend Sandra Elsdon, but the music was sparkier than its suggestive lyric; Green played the unfaithful narrator pleading for forgiveness on 'I Loved Another Woman', while his acoustic playing took centre-stage on 'The World Keeps on Turning' (the blueprint for the *White Album*'s 'World's Turning' seven years later).

Fleetwood Mac was released in February 1968, and, despite Green insisting otherwise, was pressed in some territories as '*Peter Green's Fleetwood Mac*'. The band were relegated to the back, while the front cover showed the group's name rendered in a graffiti-style typeface and Sandra Elsdon's pet mutt nosing around a Soho alleyway.

Green apparently grumbled about having dustbins on the cover. The image was trying to recreate the scuzziness of a downtown Chicago street but didn't need to. Despite its musical origins, there was something terribly English about Fleetwood Mac's blues, while the sleeve could have graced a punk LP a decade later.

'*Dog and Dustbin*' died in the US, but went top five at home, where *Melody Maker* declared it 'the best English blues LP ever released'. With barely a pause for breath, *Fleetwood Mac* was followed by two non-album hit singles, 'Black Magic Woman' and 'Need Your Love So Bad'. Both demonstrated how Green was outgrowing the blues, but the next album showed that not all his bandmates were keeping up.

In April, Vernon took Fleetwood Mac back to CBS Studios to record *Mr. Wonderful*. Even by the standards of the '60s, this was a swift turnaround. The lack of new material was obvious, but so too were Jeremy Spencer's limitations. Man management and pastoral care were in short supply, and Fleetwood Mac operated in a state of permanent dysfunction. 'Jeremy wouldn't play on my tunes,' said Green, 'but I don't know why.' 'In hindsight, I should have been more accommodating,' said Spencer.

Besides covering 'Dust My Broom' itself, Spencer used the same riff on 'Need Your Love Tonight', a cover of James's 'Coming Home' and Buster and J.T. Brown's 'Doctor Brown'. 'The first album was a good spontaneous release,' he said. 'The second was too much of me flogging the "Dust My Broom" riff to death.'

Despite Green's earlier resistance to working with a horn section, brass was added to several songs. 'We wanted a dirtier, gutsier sound,' said Vernon, who strove to recreate the ambience of Chicago's Chess Studio and recorded the horn players through an ancient Vox amp. Among the hired hands was alto sax player Steve Gregory, who later performed on the Rolling Stones' 'Honky Tonk Women' and Wham!'s '80s ballad, 'Careless Whisper'.

Gregory and his colleagues added a peppy swagger to Green's 'Stop Messin' Round' and 'Rollin' Man', and a mournful echo to 'Love That Burns'. Green shared his writer's credit on all three songs with the band's new manager Clifford Davis (real name Clifford Adams). Elsewhere, his protégé, country bluesman Duster Bennett, blew harmonica and Christine Perfect, John McVie's fiancée, played the piano.

If the canine on *'Dog and Dustbin'* foreshadowed the beagle mix on the cover of *Tusk*, then *Mr. Wonderful* established Mick Fleetwood as the group's go-to cover model. For reasons never disclosed, Fleetwood appeared naked on the front of *Mr. Wonderful*, with his modesty preserved by some strategically arranged foliage and what appeared to be a stuffed dog.

The BBC's underground DJ John Peel's rambling sleeve notes added to the air of eccentricity. 'Mick Fleetwood is a classified giant, whatever that means,' wrote Peel. 'I expect it's good. He fires .22 pistols at 3 o'clock in the morning. He wants an old house and thousands of children without having to get married. Help him . . .'

Mr. Wonderful was released in August and became a UK top-ten hit but didn't attract the praise heaped on its predecessor. Even some of the band weren't enamoured. 'It was recorded in four days and it sounds like it,' complained Fleetwood. The cover image and Peel's ramblings were the only visible nods to the counterculture. Fleetwood Mac's Delta blues and Elmore James rip-offs seemed like the antithesis of *Sgt. Pepper* or *The Piper at the Gates of Dawn*. But Green was already muddling his way towards a more progressive sound.

Before long, Fleetwood Mac had recruited another guitarist, Danny Kirwan, and were at number one with their blissed-out instrumental, 'Albatross'. In the space of three months, they'd forged a new sound and attracted a new audience. Tolworth's Toby Jug, the Nottingham Boat Club and even Jeremy Spencer would soon be consigned to history.

'Black Magic Woman'

Her Name was Sandra

Pablo Picasso supposedly said, 'Good artists borrow, great artists steal.' Like the rest of the '60s Brit blues generation, Fleetwood Mac did a lot of borrowing and stealing.

Exhibit A: their March 1968 hit, 'Black Magic Woman'. The chords were almost a straight lift from Peter Green's earlier Bluesbreakers composition, 'The Supernatural', which, in turn, sounded like Otis Rush's earlier single 'All Your Love', and so on, presumably all the way back to the devil's crossroads.

What was unique, though, was the black magic woman herself: Peter Green's partner, Sandra Elsdon, who drifted in and out of Fleetwood Mac's story for more than two decades. Sandra and Peter met at London's hip Cromwellian Club in 1967. Sandra was a fashion model, had dated Eric Clapton, and her parents' house was a salon for many future pop stars.

Green apparently wrote three songs for the woman he nicknamed 'Magic Mama'. In 'Sandy Mary', he raved about Sandra's 'bony bare looks/Enough to drive a vegetarian insane', and in 'Long Grey Mare' he compared the poor woman to a horse that wouldn't let him ride her.

The same frustration inspired the third, 'Black Magic Woman'. The couple had recently stayed at a Buddhist retreat and been told to abstain from sex to achieve a higher state of consciousness.

'Unfortunately, we weren't on the same page,' recalled Sandra, who spurned Green's advances while she was trying to meditate. Lyrics such as 'Don't turn your back on me, baby/Because you might break off my magic stick' were straight from the bluesman's book of double entendres. But 'Black Magic Woman's minimalist take on the genre was all Fleetwood Mac's. Every guitar note and ruminative sigh was vital to the work.

Released as the group's third single in March 1968, 'Black Magic Woman' nudged into the UK top forty. But it was Latin-rockers Santana's cover that became an American top-five hit two years later. Santana dialled the original up with some testifying lead vocals and plenty of Afro-Cuban swagger. Green liked Santana's version but was confused by the royalties he earned off it. But by then, he was confused by most things.

Sandra and Peter split up soon after. But she moved to LA with the band in 1974 and embarked on a year-long relationship with John McVie before marrying their art director, Larry Vigon. Sandra is now a Jungian psychotherapist living in Santa Barbara, California, and credits the career change to Fleetwood Mac. One night, watching yet another psycho-drama unfold during the making of *Rumours*, she realised that it was worthy of scientific study. 'I have a special interest in dreamwork, active imagination and the creative process,' she explained.

Sandra last saw Peter Green backstage at a Fleetwood Mac show in 2015. 'Peter was a kind and humble man, but he had some pretty deep issues,' she said. That night, the original black magic woman smiled and said hello, while her ex-boyfriend stared straight through her.

'Need Your Love So Bad'

B.B. King's Favourite Fleetwood Mac Song

The late, great B.B. King considered 'Need Your Love So Bad' one of Peter Green's greatest guitar performances. For King, it wasn't what Green played as much as what he didn't. But his voice was as much the lead instrument here as his guitar. 'Peter was a natural singer,' said producer Mike Vernon. 'He made use of his voice beautifully, especially on this song.'

Fleetwood Mac's cover of Michigan R&B singer Little Willie John's 1955 hit was another step away from straight Chicago blues. Green bookended the song with some trademark guitar lines, but his voice emphasised its gospel roots. This was Green, the balladeer, rather than the blues shouter.

But the song was a battle of wills between the guitarist and producer. As their previous single, 'Black Magic Woman', had barely scraped into the UK top forty, Vernon was determined to make this one a hit. 'I wanted a string arrangement on the song,' he explained. 'Because that would increase its chances of getting played on the radio. But Peter didn't.'

Vernon suggested the American jazz musician, Mickey Baker, who was one half of the R&B duo, Mickey & Sylvia, and had played guitar on Little Willie John's original. It took Vernon some time to convince Green, though: 'Peter was 100 per cent against having strings until I explained that I wanted Mickey to write the chart.'

Green could still veto the strings if he didn't like them, but Vernon took a chance anyway, despite the cost. He flew to Paris, where Baker was living, and sold him on the idea. So, in May 1968, Baker rocked up to London's CBS Studios with charts for the horn and string players.

The orchestration was lush but subtle and augmented by Christine Perfect playing some stately sounding organ. Most importantly, it took the song out of the spit-and-sawdust blues clubs and onto BBC daytime radio. 'Need Your Love So Bad' became Fleetwood Mac's highest-charting single yet at number thirty-one. 'I buffed my fingernails on my lapels after that,' admitted Vernon.

A string-free version of the song was later included on the compilation, *The Pious Bird of Good Omen*. Green reprised the song in 2020 when his original home demo vocal was merged with Pink Floyd guitarist David Gilmour's guitar and arrangement, and released as a limited-edition track with the official Green photo book, *The Albatross Man*. Green loved this new version and signed off on it shortly before his death.

'Need Your Love So Bad' did its job in autumn 1968. But years later Mike Vernon confessed that while Green gave in, he was never a fan of those strings: 'At the end of the day, regardless of what I or anybody else thought, I don't think he really liked them at all.'

English Rose

Mick Fleetwood's Drag Act

Terence Ibbott was an unofficial court photographer/artist during the late '60s British blues boom. Sometimes credited as 'Terence', sometimes 'Terry', his images were occasionally rejected for being too outré and tasteless. But the tamer ones graced the covers of albums by many Blue Horizon artists, including Chicken Shack (whom he photographed as Robin Hood and his merry men) and the New Orleans boogie-woogie pianist Champion Jack Dupree, whom he dressed up as a court jester.

When it came to Fleetwood Mac, Ibbott had an unerring knack for getting Mick Fleetwood out of his clothes and either naked or in drag. Ibbott's cover shot for the group's second album, *Mr. Wonderful*, plumped for the former (but with some artfully arranged foliage protecting Fleetwood's modesty). But his image for 1968's US compilation, *English Rose*, saw the drummer exploring his feminine side.

However, Fleetwood, in his platinum wig, blood-red lipstick and matching feather boa, looked less like the shy English rose eulogised by Elizabethan playwrights and more like a blues-rock Widow Twanky, whose wild staring eyes followed record buyers around the room. It was also a bold image for a prurient US market, unused to cross-dressing English music hall artists and pantomime dames. *Mr. Wonderful* had been denied a US release, but after 'Albatross' became a hit, *English Rose* was rushed out in time for Christmas.

It was a hotch-potch of singles ('Albatross', 'Black Magic Woman'), *Mr. Wonderful* album tracks (including 'Stop Messin' Round) and tasters from the band's still-unreleased third album, *Then Play On*.

A year later, Blue Horizon cashed in with a UK compilation that included some of the same tracks. Instead of Fleetwood in drag, though, *The Pious Bird of Good Omen* came with a picture of a nun carrying a stuffed albatross. Audiences would have to wait until 1974's *Heroes are Hard to Find* for Mick to strip off again. 'I don't why. Maybe it's a British thing, but I was quite happy to dress up as a woman,' he said. 'But I also think it's because I'm just a dreadful show-off.'

Status Quo

'Dinka-dinka-dink...'

Psychedelia didn't suit every pop group, but when the Beatles started writing songs about strawberry fields and Lucy in the sky with diamonds, others followed. Status Quo's first single, 'Pictures of Matchstick Men', in January 1968, was a Butlins holiday camp take on psychedelia. Status Quo had never tried LSD, but frontman Francis Rossi still made his guitar sound like an acid trip.

A year later, the band were in a mess. 'We were a rock group with a psychedelic single,' grumbled Rossi. 'It was destined not to work, so we'd gone back to playing rock 'n' roll like we did when we started. The Quo sound is a bit of blues, rock, country, Irish jigs . . .' And a lot of Fleetwood Mac.

Driving home in the van after gigs, Status Quo listened to '*Dog and Dustbin*' and their contemporaries, Chicken Shack's *O.K. Ken?* 'It would be good for the image to say, "Oh, Robert Johnson and Muddy Waters", but I learnt my shit from Stan Webb of Chicken Shack and Fleetwood Mac,' said Rossi. 'And don't forget, the audience was so stoned, everybody would sit cross-legged on the floor and let you play a thirty-five-minute solo.'

Status Quo were reborn as what Rossi called 'a dinka-dinka-dink blues-rock group', à la the early Fleetwood Mac. They swapped the last vestiges of psychedelia for broom-dusting riffs and went on stage wearing the same jeans and T-shirts that they'd had on all day.

Status Quo's 1970 album, *Ma Kelly's Greasy Spoon*, included a cover of Fleetwood Mac's 'Lazy Poker Blues', and the two groups appeared together on the German TV music show *Beat-Club. Here*, the Mac's troubled guitarist, Danny Kirwan, threw up so violently that Rossi intervened: 'Danny was so drunk he fell into the toilet. Nearly killed himself.'

In Spring 1974, Quo opened for Fleetwood Mac in the US. Unbeknown to them, they were supporting the 'fake' Mac, assembled by the management when Mick Fleetwood took the real band off the road. 'It all fell to bits,' said Rossi. They were all splitting up, and I got pleurisy, and we went home after two weeks.'

Status Quo opened for Fleetwood Mac one last time at the Day on the Green concert at the Oakland Coliseum in April 1976. But this was the new Fleetwood Mac, whose latest LP, the '*White Album*', had already sold a few million. This audience wanted Stevie Nicks twirling around the stage, singing 'Rhiannon', not Status Quo. 'We tried in America, but not that hard,' said Rossi. 'I was always worried if we stayed there too long, we'd lose it back home.'

Staying home worked out fine. Status Quo have had almost twenty UK top-ten hits and sold more than 118 million records. Their 1996 hit covers album *Don't Stop* was named after their version of the Fleetwood Mac song, and it suited them because its composer, Christine McVie, always retained the 'dinka-dinka-dink . . .' too.

A year later, Peter Green gave a rare interview and was asked who his favourite guitarists were. 'There are loads of them,' he replied. 'I like Francis Rossi. He plays quite interesting notes.' At the time, Green had just been recording in Rossi's home studio in Surrey. 'I never quite knew what he meant by *interesting*,' said Francis. 'But it's nice to be appreciated, and we really did take a lot from Fleetwood Mac.'

'Albatross'

The Beatles' Favourite Fleetwood Mac Song

One day in September 1969, Fleetwood Mac were listening to Radio Luxembourg on their way to play a gig in Scotland. John Lennon was talking to DJ Tony McArthur about the new Beatles album *Abbey Road*. 'This is where we pretend to be Fleetwood Mac,' said Lennon, before playing 'Sun King'. 'It was wonderful,' recalled John McVie. 'Even Peter Green was slightly impressed.'

Twenty years later, George Harrison confirmed that Fleetwood Mac's 1968 hit had inspired the reverb-heavy guitars in 'Sun King'. But Fleetwood Mac had a conflicted relationship with the song. 'Albatross' was an instrumental unlike anything else in their catalogue. It became a hit twice – and was their only UK number one – but they refused to perform it live after Peter Green left.

Green claimed to have had the idea for 'Albatross' years earlier. Its title came from the seabird in Samuel Taylor Coleridge's poem *The Rime of the Ancient Mariner*, which he'd learned at school. But he was reminded of it when he heard Traffic's 1967 hit, 'Hole in My Shoe', where their label boss Chris Blackwell's stepdaughter, Francine, recited the line, 'I climbed on the back of a giant albatross . . .'

But it was the arrival of Fleetwood Mac's guitar prodigy, Danny Kirwan, which prompted Green to finish the song. 'Once we got Danny in, it was plain sailing,' he said. 'It wouldn't have happened without Danny.'

'Albatross' was recorded at CBS's New Bond Street Studios in October 1968 and released a month later. Green was vague about his musical inspiration. Others have pointed out similarities to the Hawaiian guitars on Santo & Johnny's 1959 hit 'Sleep Walk', and the pastoral work of Green's favourite composer Ralph Vaughan Williams.

The somnolent melody of 'Albatross' and its gentle slide guitar were a sharp contrast to the honking blues on Fleetwood Mac's latest album, *Mr. Wonderful*. John McVie's initial reaction was a stunned, 'What the fuck is this?' Green argued that 'Albatross' wasn't traditional blues, but it was his blues.

Opinion was divided. 'Albatross' introduced Fleetwood Mac to an audience unaware of their previous work or bawdy live show. On stage, the band had a rubber sex toy nicknamed 'Harold the Dildo' stuck to drummer Mick Fleetwood's kit. Now they were on *Top of the Pops*, smiling beatifically but still looking like they'd slept behind the bins in Denmark Street.

'People heard "Albatross" and imagined they would look like the Shadows,' recalled their future keyboard player Christine McVie. 'Then they were astonished to turn on the TV and see these long-haired beatniks.'

Confusion reigned. Classical string players asked the BBC where they could buy the sheet music for this wonderful instrumental, while the Beeb's underground music champion, John Peel, turned up his nose and played the B-side, 'Jigsaw Puzzle Blues', instead. When 'Albatross' reached number one, purists accused them of selling out. 'I didn't care,' said Fleetwood. 'We were on TV, in the charts and playing bigger venues.'

However, Fleetwood Mac's fortunes dipped after Green left in 1970. Three years later, CBS re-released 'Albatross' (alongside Doris Day's 'Move Over Darling') as part of a nostalgic-hits series. *Top of the Pops* re-broadcast an old clip, and host Kenny Everett told viewers Fleetwood Mac had broken up. The band tersely informed the press that they were alive and well and insisted the BBC broadcast a retraction.

Now, though, they were competing with themselves. The single reached number two, Fleetwood Mac's *Greatest Hits* outsold their new LP *Penguin*, and audiences began asking them to play 'Albatross'. 'What's the point of us doing it,' protested their new lead singer, Dave Walker. 'Some fucker would just say, "Where's Peter Green?"'

'"Albatross" will never date,' declared Green in 1969. 'It's one of those great old instrumentals, like [the Shadows'] "Apache". It might even become a standard.'

Green was right. The German auteur Rainer Werner Fassbinder was the first to license the song, in his 1973 sci-fi serial, *World on a Wire*. After this, it became a shoo-in for any TV nature programme featuring birds. It didn't have to be an albatross either; anything with a wingspan was fair game. Since then, 'Albatross' has been sampled by the dance act/art project KLF, covered by the Shadows, and blazed a trail for what record-company marketing departments call 'chillout'. The opening bars alone evoke the soundtrack to a couples massage at a Balian beach resort.

However, peace and well-being have since been replaced by gluttony. In 2005, the retail giant Marks & Spencer used 'Albatross' in their 'This is not just food, this is M&S food . . .' TV ad campaign. While Peter Green twanged, the Irish actor Dervla Kirwan rhapsodised about 'pan-shaken, ready-to-roast, extra-crispy King Edward potatoes.' When the ads became the subject of much piss-taking, M&S changed tack but didn't give up on 'Albatross'. Instead, its 2019 Christmas ad campaign showed a children's choir chanting its wordless melody in a snow-dappled farmer's market, while TV personalities Emma Willis and Paddy McGuinness roamed between stalls buckling under the weight of bronzed meat and calorific puddings. The kids did their best 'Peter Green' as Emma chewed on a de-boned turkey leg and McGuinness drooled over a pyramid of cognac-laced mince pies. Somewhere, one liked to imagine 'Harold the Dildo' wobbling in his rubbery grave.

Danny Kirwan

The Curse of the Fleetwood Mac Guitarist, Part II

Bar Oporto, on the corner of High Holborn and in the heart of London's theatreland, closed its doors for good during the 2020 pandemic. In the '80s and '90s, though, the Oporto's proximity to the *Melody Maker*'s office made it a popular rendezvous for music journalists and their musician friends. Members of the Damned and Sigue Sigue Sputnik would hold forth over expense-account drinks, with their vampiric make-up or brightly hued hairstyles attracting comments from other patrons.

Fleetwood Mac's ex-guitarist Danny Kirwan could sometimes be found nursing a drink in the corner of the same pub. He'd been a member of the biggest band in the world, but few people paid him any attention. In 1989, Kirwan was still recognisable from the back cover of Fleetwood Mac's *Future Games* LP – presuming one knew what to look for. The blond-haired, angel-faced guitar prodigy was now pushing forty, usually unshaven and looking decidedly ragged around the edges.

Little wonder. Kirwan had been diagnosed with paranoid schizophrenia and now lived in a nearby hostel. *Melody Maker* writer and Oporto regular Carol Clerk had taken Kirwan under her wing, and he'd become a fixture in the pub; a one-time poster boy for the Brit blues boom, cast adrift in the era of Bon Jovi and Guns N' Roses. While Kirwan was officially homeless, his former bandmates lived in English country houses and Hawaiian villas with ocean views. How had it come to this?

Born in Brixton, south London, on 13 May 1950, Danny Kirwan learned to play the guitar as a teenager and gravitated towards jazz, big bands and the blues. In 1967, Peter Green chanced upon the seventeen-year-old performing with his first group, Boilerhouse. Kirwan started showing up at gigs and even working as a roadie for Fleetwood Mac. Green tried to find him a new band, before asking him to join his.

'It came as a surprise and no surprise,' said Jeremy Spencer. 'The "surprise" was to suddenly see Danny sitting in the van, ready for the next gig. The "no surprise" was that I was timid about stepping out with new ideas, whereas Danny was brimming with them. It gave Peter a new lease of life.'

Kirwan's haphazard lifestyle sometimes threatened to overshadow his musical achievements. He'd taught himself musical theory and perfected a stinging vibrato technique more seasoned guitarists struggled to achieve. In 1968, he stunned critics, fans and musicians with a playing style way beyond his years. Soon after joining Fleetwood Mac, Kirwan was in the studio with most of them, backing Chicago blues pianist Otis Spann. Green stepped aside and let Kirwan take several solos on Spann's album, *The Biggest Thing Since Colossus*.

'Danny was *the* white English blues guitarist,' explained Christine McVie. 'Nobody else sounded like he did. I was a huge fan of that incarnation of Fleetwood Mac. I was in Chicken Shack at the time but would go and see them whenever I could. Danny and Peter gelled so well. Danny had that very precise, piercing vibrato – a unique sound.'

Christine was so enamoured she recorded Kirwan's song 'When You Say' for her 1970 solo LP, with Danny arranging the strings. Peter Green later said Fleetwood Mac's number-one hit 'Albatross' wouldn't have 'been possible without Danny'. Kirwan debuted his signature vibrato on the Mac's famous instrumental, while his sparky version of the 1933 standard 'Jigsaw Puzzle Blues' made it onto the B-side. Kirwan's nickname in the band was 'Ragtime Cowboy Joe', due to his love of country and western and big-band music.

While Spencer was almost absent from the band's next album, *Then Play On*, Kirwan and Green's sabre-rattling twin lead guitars defined songs such as 'Oh Well' and 'The Green Manalishi (With the Two-Prong Crown)'. But Kirwan was a complex individual and prone to self-sabotage. He sought Green's approval while simultaneously challenging and goading him – and the others. 'Danny brought inventiveness and melody to the band, but he was like a bull in a china shop,' said Spencer. 'It left some less than positive feelings.'

When Green quit Fleetwood Mac in August 1970, Kirwan had his chance to step into the limelight. But it didn't work. The band's next album, *Kiln House*, was titled after their communal retreat in rural Hampshire. Kirwan and his fiancée, Clare Morris, moved in, but Danny clashed with everybody. 'He was a troubled man,' said Christine. 'He was a loner and – I say this with the greatest respect – he didn't know how to treat a woman. I respected him as a musician, but we didn't always see eye to eye.'

Spencer left Fleetwood Mac in 1971, and Kirwan's writing and spectral-sounding guitar dominated *Future Games*, and 1972's *Bare Trees*, which included his musical version of Rupert Brooke's poem 'Dust'.

But a gruelling US tour pushed him to breaking point. Jeremy Spencer had quit suddenly, and Green was drafted in temporarily to finish the tour. Kirwan supposedly felt frustrated and worried he was being upstaged. Backstage before a gig, Kirwan, who'd been drinking heavily, smashed up his favourite Les Paul and started banging his head against a bathroom wall. His blood splattered the tiles as he shouted, 'I'm not going on! I'm not going on!' He didn't, and Kirwan was soon on the next plane home. The band played the show without him.

Kirwan re-appeared in 1974 with a new group, Hungry Fighter, who played one gig before splitting. 'Danny had a touch of genius,' said their former piano player Paul Raymond in 2018. 'As soon as I heard Fleetwood Mac's "Jigsaw Puzzle Blues", I thought this guy has a special talent. But the poor fellow was a bag of nerves. I found it hard to have a conversation with him.'

Raymond stayed on for Kirwan's debut solo album, 1975's *Second Chapter*: 'But it was a bit bizarre. The demos Danny did were so much better.' Two more solo records followed, then Kirwan seemed to vanish after 1979's *Hello There Big Boy!* Instead, his erratic solo career and personal life were blighted by alcoholism and mental-health issues.

While his visits to the Oporto were an open secret among music journalists, nobody told Mick Fleetwood. In 1993, Fleetwood issued a public plea to trace his former bandmate and said that the last time he'd seen Kirwan was backstage at Wembley Arena in 1980. 'Danny looked derelict,' recalled Fleetwood. 'He told us he had worms and had slept on a park bench the night before.' When Fleetwood tried to hug him, Kirwan pulled away. 'No, don't do that,' he said. 'I don't ever want to be touched.'

The *Independent* newspaper quickly discovered that 'a cheerful, dishevelled' Danny Kirwan was staying in St Mungo's hostel in London's West End. 'He has been living on social security and dribs and drabs of royalties from the band's early days,' they revealed. When asked why he'd quit the music business, Kirwan replied: 'I couldn't handle the lifestyle and the women and the travelling.'

Jeremy Spencer last saw Kirwan in 2002, along with Danny's exwife, Clare, and their son, Dominic. 'It was pleasant enough, even though he was a bit in his own world,' Spencer recalled. By then, Kirwan's personal circumstances had improved. He now lived in a residential care home in south London, where family and friends visited him regularly. He remained there until his death, aged sixtyeight, from pneumonia, on 8 June 2018.

Mick Fleetwood released an official statement the day after. 'Danny's true legacy, in my mind, will forever live on in the music he wrote and played so beautifully in Fleetwood Mac,' he wrote.

This tortured, damaged man had alienated many of his bandmates, but none of them disputed his musical legacy. Least of all, Christine McVie. 'Nobody talks about that era anymore,' she said at the time. 'That's because of *Rumours* and what happened after. But listen to Danny's songs 'Woman of a 1000 Years', 'Sands of Time', 'Tell Me All the Things You Do'. . . . Danny was a fantastic musician and a fantastic writer.'

'Man of the World'

Fleetwood Mac's Saddest Song

'Man of the World' is all about Peter Green's voice and words, which is why nobody else can quite do it justice. Touring Fleetwood Mac vocalist/guitarist Neil Finn tried on their 2019 outing and at the Green tribute show the following year. But any song that includes the line 'I just wish I had never been born' challenges its interpreter. Finn didn't sound desolate enough.

Fleetwood Mac started recoding 'Man of the World' in New York in January 1969 and finished it back in London. 'Peter was very focused,' recalled producer Mike Vernon. 'He knew exactly what he was trying to achieve. If they were doing acid at that point, there was no sign of it.'

It was the saddest of songs, but Green parked his mental anguish to coach his bandmates through the music. 'We had a mammoth job recording it,' said Vernon. 'We had to do it bit by bit, as it was so hard for the band to play.'

'Man of the World' was released as the follow-up to the number-one hit 'Albatross' in April. Green and Danny Kirwan threw in some familiar spectral-sounding guitar, but the sentiment carried the song. This bespoke version of the blues was raw, honest and personal; the flipside to the beery Fleetwood Mac, who'd been banned from the Marquee for waving a sex toy around. 'It was how I felt at the time,' said Green. 'It's me at my saddest.'

Green felt conflicted about his love life, pop stardom and the pressure to keep writing hits. Not that the others realised. 'We had no idea he was suffering as much as he was,' admitted Mick Fleetwood. 'But if you listen to the words now, it's crucifyingly obvious.'

Green was under even more pressure to deliver now that the group's manager, Clifford Davis, wanted to take them to a bigger label. After 'Albatross', Davis saw pound notes flashing before his eyes and signed Fleetwood Mac to Immediate Records for a large sum of money, rowing Mike Vernon and Blue Horizon out of the picture. Green didn't want to leave either party, but the decision wasn't his. 'Man of the World' gave Fleetwood Mac a UK number-two hit, but it wasn't enough to prevent Immediate going belly up soon after.

Mike Vernon is adamant Blue Horizon would have renegotiated Fleetwood Mac's existing deal and matched Immediate's offer but wasn't given a chance. 'I love "Man of the World",' said Vernon. 'It's poignant because it's the last record I produced with them. It was us saying goodbye. We both knew we wouldn't see each other again, and that's pretty much what happened.'

Neil Finn isn't the only musician to have braved the song. Moody Blue Justin Hayward performed it with the London Philharmonic Orchestra in 1989, and Ultravox's Midge Ure recorded a gastro-pub electronica version in 2008. However, an anti-drunk driving TV ad campaign in 2000 contained the bleakest version yet. Here, unnamed session musicians delivered a faithful reading, while a Sunday league footballer got drunk and crashed his car on the way home from the clubhouse, killing a child. It made Peter Green's song sound sadder than ever.

The Chess Sessions

Coals to Newcastle

'Peter Green said to me, "We stole the black man's music,"' claimed Danny Kirwan, years after his departure from Fleetwood Mac. 'What we did was wrong.' Kirwan's legacy can be heard on those early hits, but also on the lesser-known *Blues Jam in Chicago* album, where Fleetwood Mac performed with the musicians that Kirwan thought they'd ripped off.

In January 1969, the group opened for one of their idols, Muddy Waters, at Chicago's Regal Theatre. While in town, producer Mike Vernon secured two days at Chess Records' fabled studios. It made sense for the Brits to make a pilgrimage to the home of the blues, even if there was an air of bringing sand to the desert about the venture.

At Chess, Fleetwood Mac were joined by such old hands as Willie Dixon, Buddy Guy, David 'Honeyboy' Edwards and J.T. Brown. For Fleetwood Mac, some of these were names that previously existed only on record sleeves.

Blues Jam in Chicago contained a double album's worth of standards by Howlin' Wolf, Jimmy Rogers and more, and several original numbers, including Kirwan's charming 'Talk With You'. Meanwhile, guitarist Jeremy Spencer was like a kid in a sweet shop, playing Elmore James's 'Madison Blues' with Elmore's real-life horn player J.T. Brown. It made sense as Fleetwood Mac's two LPs so far were filled with his homages to the late bluesman.

However, not everyone remembered the sessions fondly. 'These guys made it quite clear they didn't give a shit about who we were,' grumbled John McVie, who was convinced Willie Dixon disliked him from the moment he walked through the door. 'There was a little bit of "Who are these whiteys coming into our music?"' concurred Spencer, who later wrote a song, the clunkily titled 'You Don't Have to Be Black to Be Blue', about the sessions. 'It smoothed over after a while, but in a way, I don't blame them. We all felt a bit like, "What are we doing, coming in here?"'

'As soon as Peter Green's respect for the music became apparent, they stopped treating us like tourists,' insisted Fleetwood. 'The music was fine too, as long as the Scotch whisky kept flowing.'

However, Green complained that his lead vocals on the album sounded like he 'was singing down the toilet' and he felt inferior to his black American counterparts. Others have suggested that any antipathy towards Fleetwood Mac was due to there being too many session musicians and not enough sessions. Professional jealousy and suspicion were rife at Chess.

Some also realised that there was money to be made from associating with a white British blues band. The session's piano player, Otis Spann (whose lead vocal on 'Hungry Country Girl' was one of the album's highlights) invited Green, Kirwan and McVie to play on his next LP.

Spann's *The Biggest Thing Since Colossus* and *Blues Jam at Chess* (also issued as *Blues Jam in Chicago, Volumes 1 and 2*) were released later that year on Vernon's Blue Horizon label. Both collections showcased Green and Kirwan at the height of their powers and free of Fleetwood Mac's internal politics. The pair spent too much time worrying that they were musical imposters. Sadly, their personal and professional tailspins after Fleetwood Mac suggested both had the blues more than they realised.

'Somebody's Gonna Get their Head Kicked in Tonite'

Fleetwood Mac Help Invent Punk

Fleetwood Mac's 1969 hit 'Man of the World', was inspired by Peter Green's heartache and despair. What a surprise then to hear the B-side: a rockabilly head charge in which the group ripped up chairs, tore down walls and left 'a pool of blood on the dancefloor'.

'Somebody's Gonna Get their Head Kicked in Tonite' was an Elvis pastiche sung by Jeremy Spencer and credited to the fictitious Earl Vince and the Valiants. Spencer didn't play on 'Man of the World' or Fleetwood Mac's next album, *Then Play On*. Instead, he poured his energy into parodies such as this, inspired by the night his bandmates were attacked in a northern club.

'I wrote it as a stab at the type of characters who spoil the fun for everyone,' explained Spencer. 'The sad thing is, some people didn't get the point, and it became a jukebox play for the very crowd it was spoofing.'

The trouble is, Earl Vince and the Valiants sounded like they were having more fun than Fleetwood Mac on the A-side. Peter Green was disintegrating, and their manager was working them like dogs. No wonder they pretended to be a different group.

Come 1978, Fleetwood Mac had gone Hollywood with the arrival of Lindsey Buckingham and Stevie Nicks and the multi-platinum *Rumours*. In Britain, though, the Clash, the Damned

80

and the Sex Pistols had stripped rock 'n' roll back to basics and denounced Fleetwood Mac and their ilk as passé.

Among the new guard following punk's lead were a Scottish group called the Rezillos. A cover of 'Somebody's Gonna Get their Head Kicked in Tonite' appeared on the band's debut album, *Can't Stand the Rezillos*. Only those scrutinising the credits would have known where the song originated. Against the odds, Fleetwood Mac's pseudonymous ode to mindless violence had become a punk anthem.

Camden Borough Fringe Festival

When Fleetwood Mac Gigs Go Wrong

By 1969, the more successful Fleetwood Mac became, the more it seemed to make Peter Green uneasy. One of his solutions was offering their services for free, and Fleetwood Mac headlined the gratis Camden Borough Fringe Festival that summer.

Blackhill Enterprises, the company behind recent free shows in Hyde Park, organised the event in north London's Parliament Hill Fields. On the evening of 30 May, Irish power trio Taste (starring guitar hero Rory Gallagher), young bluesman Duster Bennett and proto-punk rockers the Edgar Broughton Band all took turns on a cramped bandstand before Fleetwood Mac. As the night wore on and the local pubs called time, an initial crowd of hundreds swelled to thousands, and the hill became a sea of denim and Afghan coats. Then came the trouble. According to eyewitnesses, the 'marauding skinheads' only numbered twenty or so, but they gathered in front of the stage and began throwing punches and empty cider flagons during the Edgar Broughton Band's set. The violence escalated when Fleetwood Mac appeared shortly after midnight. As the sound of 'Albatross' drifted across the borough of Camden, the skinheads began pelting the bandstand with coins and bottles and taunting the police with chants of 'Harry Roberts is our friend! He kills coppers!' (Roberts had been jailed for murdering two police officers in 1966). Fleetwood Mac eventually fled amid a hail of missiles.

The band never discussed the incident. That fell to Peter Green's father, Joe, who wrote a letter to *Melody Maker*, published under the headline, 'Sterner Measures For These Hoodlums'. 'My son travels all over the country playing to different audiences practically every night, and last Friday was one of his nights off,' wrote J. Green of London W14: 'But instead of taking advantage and resting, he offered his services to play for free at an open-air concert along with other artists. Everything would have gone off fine when along came a small group of hoodlums – not, I may add, long-haired freaks, as is their usual description – but a gang of crew-cut young thugs who seemed to delight in spoiling a night out for the vast majority of people who were there to enjoy themselves. After many nasty incidents, the concert had to be abandoned, much to the disgust of the organisers, who went to a great deal of trouble to arrange it. It is time sterner measures were taken by the law and stiffer sentences imposed on these so-called citizens of the future.'

'Rattlesnake Shake'

Fleetwood Mac's Bad Sex Guide, Part I

Mick Fleetwood is one of rock's great over-sharers. His lack of filter is a gift to interviewers and readers of his two autobiographies. As a teenager, Fleetwood fell hard for his first girlfriend, model Jenny Boyd, so much so that he married (and divorced) her twice. However, Fleetwood occasionally gave in to temptation on tour. Or he tried to. 'But every time, I got caught. Some rock star! Every fucking time!'

On one occasion, Jenny rang his hotel, and Mick's companion at the time answered the phone. Fleetwood hopped across the room with his pants around his ankles, grabbed the receiver and insisted several people were hanging out in the room, and there was noth-ing to worry about, *honest, my darling*: 'But inside, I was dying.'

Fleetwood's reluctance to act 'like a pig on the road' inspired Peter Green to write 'Rattlesnake Shake' in his honour. 'I know this guy, his name is Mick, now he don't care when he ain't got no chick,' crooned Green. Fleetwood admitted the song was about his preference for masturbation rather than anonymous sex. 'I'm the guy who does the rattlesnake shake to jerk away my sadness,' he explained.

'Rattlesnake Shake' failed to rise to the occasion when released as a single but was a highlight of 1969's *Then Play On*. Green's filthy riff, paired with Fleetwood's syncopated handclaps and shuffle, sounds like a 'How To' manual for Free, Bad Company and future dynasties of hard rock bands. Aerosmith later cut a version of 'Rattlesnake Shake' and lead singer Steven Tyler performed it at the 2020 Peter Green tribute concert. Rightly so, as it sounds like Aerosmith before Aerosmith.

Fleetwood also overcame any embarrassment he might have felt and embraced 'the wanking song'. He likes it so much he's covered it twice: on his first solo LP, *The Visitor*, and *Blue Again!*, a live album recorded with the Mick Fleetwood Blues Band. For *The Visitor*'s version, he even lured Peter Green back to sing and play guitar and piled on choral vocals and tribal percussion from a choir and musicians he'd met in Ghana. But the original is still the best, with its final off-piste jam. 'You hear me being incredibly free to break into the shuffle,' said Fleetwood. 'Which was not supposed to happen, but it did. It incorporated the freedom to go off on a tangent, to jam. On stage, it could last half an hour.'

Peter Green's jokey tale of solo sex was Fleetwood Mac finding their freedom. It sounds like the '70s arrived a year early.

'Oh Well (Parts 1 & 2)'

Fleetwood Mac's Mini Sgt. Pepper

In 1970, guitarist Jimmy Page was seeking somewhere quiet for Led Zeppelin to make their fourth album. Page wanted a residential facility without noise restrictions or noisy neighbours. Mick Fleetwood recommended Headley Grange, a former poorhouse in Hampshire, where Fleetwood Mac had recently rehearsed.

Page took his advice, and Led Zeppelin later emerged with several new songs. One of them, 'Black Dog', featured the guitar and lead vocal playing tag. 'Ah, ah child, way you shake that thing,' shrieked vocalist Robert Plant over the echo of Page's clanging guitar riff.

This was the same call-and-response trick Fleetwood Mac used on their 1969 hit, 'Oh Well (Part I)'. 'But I don't want people thinking it's a rip-off,' said Page when asked about the comparison. 'But Fleetwood Mac had been at Headley Grange, so perhaps their energy came to me.' Mick Fleetwood thought so. Ask him what Fleetwood Mac would have become if Peter Green had stayed, and he usually suggests some variation on Led Zeppelin. No song illustrates this as clearly as 'Oh Well', the follow-up to 'Man of the World'.

'Oh Well' was an unruly beast, which encompassed classical, flamenco, blues and what critics soon called 'heavy metal'. 'It represents my two extremes,' explained Green. In 'Part I',

86

Green's lyric – 'Can't help about the shape I'm in, I can't sing, I ain't pretty . . . and my legs are thin' – was prefaced by a brawny acoustic riff before Danny Kirwan's electric guitar blasted out of the mix. Fleetwood Mac didn't just play the song's riff; they played around with it. 'Peter bent the chord so that certain notes sounded like other notes,' explained Fleetwood, who found the recording challenging. Fleetwood's cowbell interlude was a mistake that Green insisted on keeping. 'So I had to re-learn my mistake, which was not easy.'

'Part I' was a tutorial in dynamics and tension. Green let the song build up a head of steam before taking it back down again. Two minutes before the end, a gentle acoustic reverie cued up the instrumental B-side. 'Part II' belonged to some flurrying Spanish guitar and Green's girlfriend Sandra Elsdon's recorder. It sounded like the soundtrack to a scene in a spaghetti western where a poncho-clad Clint Eastwood faces down bandits in the town square. Finally, Green indulged his current passion for playing the cello as Mick Fleetwood beat out a funeral march, and Jeremy Spencer played what he described as 'some Exodus-style piano.'

There were several clues to Green's mindset in the song. The 'Part I' lyric, 'Now when I talked to God, I knew he'd understand', was inspired by his recent conversion. He'd abandoned Judaism for Christianity and would later perform 'Oh Well' on *Top of the Pops*, wearing a monk's robe and a crucifix. Implausible as it sounds, Green also wanted 'Part II' to be the A-side and denounced 'Part I's famous guitar riff as 'naff and throwaway'. He was over-ruled, but the others still bet him £5 that the song wouldn't be a hit. They were all proved wrong when it reached number two and was hastily added to later US pressings of their new album, *Then Play On*.

'Oh Well' was Fleetwood Mac's *Sgt. Pepper*, crammed into eight minutes and sixty-one seconds. The days of flogging a twelve-bar riff into the ground were over; this was – whisper it – 'progressive' rock, in the true sense of the word. Years later, you could still hear its jarring tension in some of Lindsey Buckingham's songs. No 'Oh Well', arguably no 'Tusk'.

'It's in the top three Peter Green songs,' insisted Mick Fleetwood, this century. 'It influenced a lot of people in bands.' He paused. 'Certainly, a *lot* of things Led Zeppelin did.' Blame it on the energy at Headley Grange.

Then Play On

Like Tusk for the 1960s

Sometime in 1969, an unannounced Peter Green burst into the offices of *Melody Maker* and began rifling through the filing cabinets. Within minutes, there were pictures scattered across the floor. Green loudly declared that he hated all photographs of himself and didn't want them published. To begin with, everybody just stared at him. Finally, a staff member intervened and gently persuaded him to go home.

Peter Green had become Britain's most reluctant pop star. He was disillusioned with fame and had begun experimenting with LSD. His raid on the *Melody Maker* office was another example of his increasingly unpredictable behaviour.

Before Green disappeared, though, he recorded Fleetwood Mac's third album, *Then Play On*. After two top-five hits, 'Albatross' and 'Man of the World', Clifford Davis had lured them away from Blue Horizon and onto a major label, Warner-Reprise. Without Blue Horizon's Mike Vernon, they decided to produce themselves.

Then Play On was created at London's De Lane Lea and CBS Studios, with four of the five members and engineer Martin Birch behind the desk. Jeremy Spencer didn't play a note: 'Peter asked if I had any new stuff, and I said no, only 1950s rock 'n' roll stuff, which wouldn't have fitted the direction he and Danny [Kirwan] were going.' Instead, Spencer's doo-wop, acid rock and country

music parodies were hived off onto an EP, some of which resurfaced on 1998's *The Vaudeville Years* compilation. 'The record company thought the whole thing was a wank,' admitted Mick. 'But we
took it seriously.'

Green's approach to making *Then Play On* veered from wanting
to micro-manage everybody to not wanting to lead. One moment,
he was the 'Green God', playing the drums because he thought he
could do better than Fleetwood; the next, he was frustrated by his
docile bandmates waiting to be told what to do.

Green tasked Danny Kirwan with composing some of the
album's fourteen songs. Kirwan took the commission seriously, but
his inexperience showed. He seemed to run out of lyrics on 'When
You Say' and fell back on bog-standard blues for 'One Sunny Day'.
In contrast, 'Coming Your Way' stripped the meat off the blues and
threw rattling Afro-Cuban percussion, voodoo rhythms and incantatory lyrics into the mix.

The word 'progressive' was bandied around a lot then, but it
fitted the bill here. The best of *Then Play On* reimagined the blues
through the prism of post-war London, folk, African, classical and
English music hall influences. Green's 'Rattlesnake Shake' was an
ode to masturbation full of teeth-gnashing guitars. Like the group's
two non-album singles, 'Oh Well' and 'The Green Manalishi (With
the Two Prong Crown)', it was another blueprint for heavy rock in
the '70s.

The flipside to all this was Green's reflective 'Closing My Eyes'
and 'Before the Beginning'. 'Songs full of sorrow and self-pity,'
recalled Fleetwood. Even 'Showbiz Blues' upended its jaunty handclaps and twelve-bar rhythm with a self-questioning lyric.

The non-writers, Fleetwood and McVie, were credited with a
song apiece. 'Fighting for Madge' and 'Searching for Madge' were
instrumental dust-ups filleted from the same marathon jam. Close
your eyes, and you can imagine Fleetwood gurning like a lanky
scarecrow while the others huddle together, fingers-a-blur, trading
stoned grins. Future dynasties of guitar heroes took their cues from
this. The titular 'Madge' was an uber fan from Darlington who

followed Fleetwood Mac around the country. 'To this day, I've never seen anyone so faithful to a band,' said Fleetwood.

Then Play On was released in September, but legal issues following the change of labels delayed its arrival in the US. After 'Oh Well' became a hit, the LP was reissued in the States with the single replacing Kirwan's 'My Dream' and 'When You Say'.

The album reached the UK top ten but baffled some of the fanbase. *Then Play On* sounded like a group trying to escape themselves. 'Coming Your Way' and 'Rattlesnake Shake's instrumental codas alone signposted a new direction, even if they were still determining what it was.

Decades later, Fleetwood compared Danny Kirwan's approach to songwriting with Lindsey Buckingham's and *Then Play On* to 1979's *Tusk*. But unlike *Tusk*, nobody was steering the ship. 'The trouble is, Peter was a reluctant band boss, and so was Danny,' explained Mike Vernon.

Mick Fleetwood never fell out of love with *Then Play On* or what might have come next. 'Had Peter stayed, we would have been experimenting with sounds, styles and orchestras,' he said in 2018. 'We would have had a place like Led Zeppelin in America.' Instead, Peter Green slipped away from the rest of Fleetwood Mac and everybody else.

Mike Vernon

The Mentor's Tale

The last time Mike Vernon saw Peter Green was when he turned up unexpectedly on his doorstep in 1998. There wasn't much in the way of 'Hello' or 'How are you?'. Instead, Green asked if Vernon had an album by the country-blues guitarist Black Ace and, if so, could he could borrow it?

'I told him I'd had it but had just sold part of my record collection,' recalled Vernon. 'Peter said, "Oh, that's a shame, nice seeing you, goodbye." And off he went. That was it.'

Vernon wasn't surprised or offended. He'd produced Fleetwood Mac's early hits, including 'Albatross' and 'Man of the World', and had heard about Green's subsequent decline. But Vernon also understood the nature of the music business: 'I knew once we finished working together that Peter and I wouldn't see each other again.'

Mike Vernon began in the business as a gofer at Decca Records in 1962. 'Make the tea, go for this, go for that,' he recalled. But he was at blues clubs every night and hustled his bosses into acknowledging the scene, particularly John Mayall's Bluesbreakers. Within a few years, Vernon's production CV included David Bowie's novelty hit 'The Laughing Gnome' and the Bluesbreakers' *'Beano'* album, featuring Eric Clapton. Vernon was expecting Clapton when Mayall's band showed up to make their next single, 'Looking Back', in the winter of 1966. Instead, he spotted an unfamiliar-looking amplifier and a curly-haired guitarist wearing a lumberjack jacket. 'I said to John Mayall, "Where's Eric?". Mayall answered, "He's not with us anymore. He left us a few weeks ago." I was in a state of shock, but Mayall said, "Don't worry, we've got someone better." I said, "Hang on, wait a second, this is ridiculous. You've got someone better than Eric Clapton?" John said, "He might not be better now, but you wait, in a couple of years. . ."'

Vernon would spend the next two years working with Green, producing him on the Bluesbreakers' *A Hard Road* album and Fleetwood Mac's first two LPs and six singles. In the meantime, he'd also set up three independent labels, including Blue Horizon, launched with a limited-edition single by Howlin' Wolf's guitarist Hubert Sumlin and recorded in Vernon's parents' house. Blue Horizon swiftly became *the* blues aficionados' label and struck a distribution and licensing deal with CBS. Vernon resigned from Decca and signed the newly formed Fleetwood Mac to his boutique label.

By then, Vernon shared John Mayall's enthusiasm for Green. 'It struck me then that Peter was a very languid player,' he said. 'In some ways, the opposite of Clapton. Peter had that deft touch, very sweet. He could show a bit of anger and toughness when required, but that was more live than in the studio.'

While Vernon oversaw Fleetwood Mac's seat-of-the-pants '*Dog and Dustbin*' debut and its follow-up *Mr. Wonderful*, he thinks Green did some of his best work under the radar: with John Mayall's Bluesbreakers on unearthed live recordings from 1967; with Rod Stewart late one night at Decca, and on the Otis Spann album, *The Biggest Thing Since Colossus*. 'These recordings showed where Peter was going with his style and how unique it was. There was no discussion about who it was. You listened, and you *knew* it was Peter Green.'

As Fleetwood Mac's label boss and producer, it was also Vernon's job to sell records. He fought big battles with Green over naming the band ('I wanted Peter Green's Fleetwood Mac – and Peter didn't') and overruled him by adding radio-friendly strings to their single, 'Need Your Love So Bad'.

Blue Horizon's signings now included Champion Jack Dupree and Elmore James and their acolytes Chicken Shack with singing keyboard player Christine Perfect (soon to become McVie). The ultimate accolade came in 1969 when the satirical music and poetry ensemble the Liverpool Scene recorded 'I've Got the Fleetwood Mac Chicken Shack John Mayall Can't Fail Blues' and named Vernon and Blue Horizon in the lyrics.

However, they needed help to hold on to their first signing. Blue Horizon's contract with Fleetwood Mac only ran for a year, with an option to renew if the label wished. The band's wily new manager, Clifford Davis, kept quiet about the renewal date, and the label didn't notice when it passed. Davis had gone shopping and told Vernon that Fleetwood Mac had received an offer from Immediate Records and were moving on. 'CBS would have matched or bettered that offer,' said Vernon. 'Okay, we made an error, we admitted it. But we weren't given the chance to ask CBS.'

To make the loss worse, Fleetwood Mac's current single, 'Albatross' had just reached number one. Although Davis promised that the follow-up, 'Man of the World', would be released on Blue Horizon as a goodwill gesture, it came out on Immediate, whose subsequent financial woes meant the £250,000 contract was worthless.

Davis then signed Fleetwood Mac to Warner Bros for less than CBS would have paid given the opportunity. Mike Vernon stepped down as producer during the making of 'Man of the World', and the band's engineer, Martin Birch, finished the mix. '"Man of the World" is a terribly sad song,' said Vernon. 'It's a great song, but still quite painful for me to listen to.'

The blues boom wouldn't last forever, and Blue Horizon ceased production in 1972. Vernon and his brother Richard continued to run their facility, Chipping Norton Studios in Oxfordshire, where Mike produced records for Eric Clapton and John Mayall and new artists, including Level 42, in the '80s.

'I only saw Peter a handful of times after Fleetwood Mac,' he recalled. 'I heard about the acid trips and the visit to Germany, though I saw no evidence of any problem when I worked with him. Later, I saw Peter's first concert in the eighties in Guildford with the Splinter Group, which I thought was embarrassing. I felt bad for him.'

After losing the band, Vernon saw Green struggling to lead Fleetwood Mac and produce their next album, *Then Play On*. 'John Mayall was a bandleader, Peter wasn't,' he said. 'That wasn't Peter's strength.'

Years later, Green was asked for his thoughts on this time. 'We weren't completely aware of the producer's job,' he admitted. 'We should have kept Mike Vernon. I didn't want to leave Blue Horizon, but Clifford Davis was going for bigger money.' But, like Mike Vernon, Green wasn't destined to stay with Fleetwood Mac either.

'The Munich Jet Set'

The Night German Art Revolutionaries
Kidnapped Peter Green

Keith Richards once described his old friend, former fashion model Uschi Obermaier, as 'the Bavarian barbarian'. During a night of passion in the 1970s, Uschi accidentally tore out the Rolling Stone guitarist's earring, leaving him with a blood-soaked pillow and what he described as a 'permanent malformation of the right earlobe.'

So wild was Uschi's life, her memoir, *Das Wilde Leben* ('*The Wild Life*'), was turned into a movie, but her brief encounter with Peter Green was barely mentioned. Even today, though, Mick Fleetwood and John McVie blame Uschi's former associates for dosing their guitarist with LSD and encouraging his departure from Fleetwood Mac.

Peter Green's acid trip at a Munich commune is a less fanciful rock legend than the one about Keith Richards' Swiss blood change because it actually happened. It's just that nobody involved can agree on *what* happened. Was Green really kidnapped by beautiful revolutionaries, and did he really spend three days in their druggy clutches?

Fleetwood Mac first tried LSD together in the winter of 1968 at New York's Gorham Hotel. They were opening for the Grateful Dead, and the drug came courtesy of the Dead's friend and chemist, Augustus Owsley Stanley III. Mick Fleetwood found the trip disturbing. 'I looked at Peter Green,' he recalled, 'and saw him

96

dead, a skeleton without flesh, but moving. It was a horrible, help-less feeling. We hadn't the foggiest notion what to do, and we began to weep and blubber for help.'

Owsley phoned their suite at the Gorham Hotel to check on the group's progress, heard their distress, and gently talked the band members down. 'It worked and we weren't scared anymore,' said Fleetwood. 'Taking LSD was a bonding experience that we did together on other occasions. But it never became a regular thing for us in the way that hash and pot did.'

Peter Green, however, had a more intense relationship with LSD. In March 1970, Fleetwood Mac played a show in Munich. Afterwards, road manager Dennis Keane recalled a group of fans crowding around Green backstage. The ringleader was 'a gorgeous girl' who invited them to a party. The others weren't interested, but Green and Keane agreed to go. However, Mick Fleetwood is certain the same delegation had met them at Munich airport, hours before the show. 'They were a bunch of rich German hippie brats,' he recalled. 'We called them, "The Munich jet set".'

'They met us at the airport and they had fur coats on,' Green recalled. 'One of the girls was a famous model.' This was Uschi Obermaier, and her entourage were members of the High-Fisch Kommune, an art collective that had grown out of two previous organisations, Berlin's Kommune 1 and Munich's Amon Düül.

In 1968, Uschi was working as a model and actor and playing maracas in Amon Düül's house band, when she met Kommune 1's charismatic activist Rainer Langhans and joined him in the newly formed High-Fisch Kommune. Uschi and Rainer became a counterculture power couple, a sort of German John and Yoko. He had the fur coat and a head of long corkscrew curls, and Uschi had just bagged 20,000 Deutschmarks for a nude photo shoot. Keith Richards insists she was a dilettante, though. 'She had never taken the ideology seriously,' he said. 'She was openly drinking banned Pepsi-Cola and upsetting other commune dictates.'

On the night in question, Dennis Keane recalled being driven several miles out of Munich to the commune's remote rented castle,

believed to be Schloss Kronwinkl, near Landshut. Kronwinkl was
flanked by parkland and forest and had twenty-six bedrooms and
a basement studio, used by the commune's new avant-garde music
group, Amon Düül II. The sleeve to the group's second album, *Yeti*,
showed their sound engineer who'd recently died of hypothermia
during an acid trip. It was a bad omen. Not that Green or Keane
knew this when accepting glasses of wine dosed with LSD.

'All hell broke loose,' said Keane. 'I felt dreadful and realised our
drinks had been spiked.' Keane remembers the commune members
taking them out into the garden and 'marching round in a proces-
sion'. Next, he heard 'a freaky electronic droning noise' coming
from the basement, where Green was playing the guitar with members of Amon Düül II.

'I made some music in the basement while I was there,' said
Green in 2012. 'They gave me a tape of it and when I got married
many years after, I left it in a duffel bag in my wife's broom cupboard. I left it there. And she won't talk to me now . . .'

Green's abiding memory of the night was his brain 'thinking so
fast it ran out of thoughts' and being put to bed by one of the commune members, 'lying there on my own on a mattress and thinking
I was made of crystals.'

When the trip subsided, Keane called their hotel and asked
Clifford Davis for help. This is where the story becomes blurred.
Davis has suggested that guitarist Danny Kirwan was also at the
castle, and took some 'bad, impure LSD . . . and was never the
same again.' Mick Fleetwood has never mentioned Kirwan being
present, but believes Dennis Keane was one of the rescue party who
joined him on the journey to Kronwinkl.

Fleetwood recalled 'a weird place with weird stuff happening in
every room'. When they found Green, he was lucid but insisted he
wanted to stay at the commune. They eventually persuaded him
to return with them and finish the tour. Claims that Green was
abducted by the commune members and spent several days at
the castle aren't true. Green went willingly. 'I was only there for a
couple of nights, maybe only one,' he insisted.

Fleetwood Mac also performed in Nuremberg two days later. Though Green was still feeling the aftershocks of the LSD: 'That night I did this thing with my guitar where I made it sound like an air radio siren. I said to Mick, "What did you think of my playing?" Mick said, "You were mad tonight, mad!"'

Nevertheless, Fleetwood believes Green was never quite the same after Munich. He also claims that the commune members followed him back to England, where they took more LSD, and drove a wedge between him and the rest of the band.

Shortly after his return, Green urged the rest of Fleetwood Mac to donate some of their royalties to charity and credited High-Fisch with freeing him up as a musician. 'When I played at the commune in Germany, I found how much I've changed, through playing personally for them,' he explained. 'When the pressure is off, it all comes out naturally.'

Green left Fleetwood Mac soon after and the Munich jet set's beautiful couple also split up. Rainer Langhans became a writer, filmmaker and TV pundit, and in 2011, was among the jungle campmates on *Ich Bin Ein Star, Holt Mich Hier Raus!*, Germany's version of *I'm A Celebrity . . . Get Me Out Of Here!*

Meanwhile, Uschi Obermaier married a Hamburg nightclub owner and spent several years travelling the world before her husband's death in a motorcycle accident in 1983. Uschi later became a jewellery maker and was last heard of living in the Portuguese Algarve.

Uschi has never spoken about Peter Green. But in 2021, Langhans gave an interview to the German edition of *Guitar* magazine. He confirmed that he and Uschi met Fleetwood Mac at Munich airport, but that they did this with many bands, including the Grateful Dead. 'We invited them to jam and celebrate with us,' he said. However, Langhans jokily reminded the interviewer that if you could remember the '60s, 'you weren't really there'. He sidestepped a question about whether Green was spiked with LSD, but was adamant Peter was happy and peaceful at the castle and spent the night 'making beautiful music'.

Langhans also confirmed that he and Uschi spent time with Green in London, but were shocked when he met them at Heathrow Airport, dressed like a rock star and driving an E-type Jag. At Langhans' request, Green brokered an introduction to the Rolling Stones, whom High-Fisch wanted to play a free festival in Munich. Uschi duly befriended Mick Jagger and Keith Richards and later had an affair with Jimi Hendrix.

Langhans didn't know Fleetwood Mac blamed the commune for Green's decline until he read an interview with them in *Rolling Stone* during the early '90s. Langhans explained that several German communes were set up by the offspring of those who'd served in the military under Hitler, and promoted peace partly as an atonement for the sins of their fathers. He blamed Fleetwood Mac's accusations on lingering prejudice from the Second World War, and said the Brits had been duped into believing High-Fisch were 'evil super Nazis'. 'They made a horror story out of it because it was so inexplicable to them that Peter Green left this successful band,' he argued, before revealing that despite Green's interest in Uschi, she found him 'too hairy' and much preferred the Rolling Stones.

At the time of writing, the wounds still hadn't healed, though. 'Peter Green had so much talent that was lost because of these people – and I despise them for that,' said John McVie. 'If they see me, don't ever cross my path.'

Part Two

'Doesn't that guy know he's lost his leg?'

Fleetwood Mac stumble blindly into the '70s, lose more guitarists, and fall victim to a religious cult and a mischievous managerial coup.

Kiln House

When 'Elvis' Left the Building

It happened often. Whenever the hashish ran out, someone stuck a fork between the timbers of the farmhouse table. Any discarded herb was uprooted with a bit of gentle manoeuvring, and the chillum pipes were filled again. Once replenished, the band picked up their instruments and started playing.

Welcome to Fleetwood Mac's fourth album, *Kiln House*, an LP enveloped in the scent of hash smoke, old hops and an absent Peter Green. The group started living together in summer 1970 when it became too challenging to rehearse with four musicians scattered around London. Also, Mick Fleetwood wanted to conjure the same magic as Traffic after they moved into a communal cottage together. 'Getting it together in the country,' was all the rage.

Fleetwood was recommended an oast house property to rent near the Hampshire village of Alton. The house comprised two adjoining kilns converted for domestic living and a hops drying room, perfect for a rehearsal space.

Fleetwood Mac arrived *en masse*: Mick and his pregnant fiancée Jenny; John and Christine McVie, Jeremy and Fiona Spencer and their young son; Danny Kirwan and his partner Clare, and road managers, Dinky Dawson and Dennis Keane. But no Peter Green.

'Peter was gone,' said Fleetwood, 'But we just blunderingly kept going. It was like a form of shock – "Doesn't that guy know he's lost his leg? He still thinks he's fucking walking!"'

Soon after, everybody else told Fleetwood they wanted to leave too. Kirwan and Spencer didn't fancy fronting the group, and John McVie was done with music and wanted to become a roadie instead. 'They were all petrified,' said Fleetwood, who recalled 'long evenings spent quelling mutinies and threats of disintegration.'

Fleetwood Mac wrote and rehearsed in the hops drying room before recording at London's De Lane Lea Studio in June and July. *Kiln House* sounded like a group in transition. Three of its ten songs were covers, and while Kirwan's compositions had clarity, Spencer's lacked inspiration.

Spencer had barely contributed to its predecessor, *Then Play On*. But he'd just released a solo album, *Jeremy Spencer*, and brought its retro rock 'n' roll feel to *Kiln House*. Spencer's 'This is the Rock' was an affable '50s throwback. But his Elvis-mimicking 'Blood on the Floor' and 'Buddy's Song' (written by Waylon Jennings but credited to Buddy Holly's mother, Ella) sounded like pastiches. Only Spencer's wistful 'One Together' acknowledged his roots without slipping into parody. Bizarrely, he wanted the song dropped from the album, but the others insisted it stayed. Elsewhere, he boldly sang a version of Big Joe Turner's 'Hi Ho Silver' and made light work of Donnie Brooks' 1960 hit, 'Mission Bell'. '*Kiln House* had positive moments of experimentation and fun,' he said. 'But I was desperately lacking original inspiration.'

Danny Kirwan's songs, some of which he co-wrote with his bandmates, were more assured. On stage at the Peter Green tribute concert in London in 2020, Pete Townshend cheerily announced that he'd ripped off the gonzo riff to 'Station Man' for the Who's 'Won't Get Fooled Again'. Kirwan softened up for the instrumental 'Earl Gray' before bringing some grit to 'Jewel Eyed Judy' and the album's strongest song, the urgent-sounding 'Tell Me All the Things You Do'.

Kiln House was released in September 1970 and became the first Fleetwood Mac LP not to make the UK top ten or even the top forty. 'It's a really charming album,' insisted Fleetwood, 'but we were quietly aware we had a challenge ahead without Peter.'

In 1969, after a problematic solo tour, Christine McVie announced her decision to become a housewife instead. She'd spent the summer at Kiln House cooking, cleaning, rolling joints, tie-dyeing T-shirts, forking hashish out of the kitchen table and drawing a kid's book-style illustration for the LP cover. Christine played piano and Wurlitzer somewhere on the LP, and it sounds like her voice is in the background on 'Mission Bell'. But she wasn't asked to join Fleetwood Mac until just before an American tour in August.

'Literally, days before,' said Fleetwood. 'The sound was a bit empty, and we told Chris, "We need the extra voice, and we want the piano."'

'They said, "What do you think about joining the band?"' recalled Christine. 'I said, "You must be mad, but yes."'

Fleetwood Mac replaced Peter Green with a vocalist and keyboard player rather than another guitarist. This was born out of necessity, even desperation, but Christine's impact on the group was profound. It just took further upheaval to realise it.

Jeremy Spencer became even more disillusioned during the US dates. He was twenty-two years old, a husband and father, and his head was spinning. Spencer's exuberant stage act included changing into a gold lamé suit to perform Elvis's 'Viva Las Vegas', but he claimed the impersonation was another sign of how creatively spent he was.

Spencer stayed with Fleetwood Mac until February 1971, when he disappeared to join the Children of God religious movement in LA. In an absurd twist, his replacement for the rest of the tour was Peter Green, who arrived with his manager's conga-playing brother-in-law, Nigel Watson, in tow. The message was clear: no Nigel, no Peter. Watson lasted a few shows, before, according to Fleetwood, 'he freaked out and went home'.

Worse still, much of the rest of the set was given over to freeform jamming. 'We'd walk on stage some nights,' said Fleetwood, 'and not have a clue what we would play.'

Dreams

Spencer departed just as *Kiln House* became Fleetwood Mac's highest-charting US album. Six months after they arrived, the lease on the property was up. The group packed their bags and moved seven miles down the road to another communal residence. The hash-filled kitchen table and their Elvis impersonator were consigned to history.

'Dragonfly'

Peter Green's Favourite Non-Peter Green Song

In March 1971, 'Dragonfly', Christine McVie's first single as a member of Fleetwood Mac, reached number fifty-two, a catastrophe after its predecessor, 'The Green Manalishi (With the Two Prong Crown)' went top ten. Critics claimed its failure proved that they couldn't cut it without Peter Green. Truthfully, 'Dragonfly' might have been better bolstering the *Kiln House* or *Future Games* LPs, instead of creeping out as a non-album single.

Written by guitarist Danny Kirwan, 'Dragonfly' was based on a poem of the same name by the Welsh author W. H. Davies. Kirwan had previous in this area (see 'Dust', his song based on a Rupert Brooke verse). Davies was a Victorian-era man of letters turned wayfarer, who spent most of the late 1890s roaming the British countryside, living in the United States, and recounting his adventures in a best-selling memoir, *The Autobiography of a Supertramp* (whose title inspired the name of Fleetwood Mac's contemporaries Supertramp). Davies and Kirwan shared a mutual fascination with the natural world. But in some cultures, the dragonfly was also a symbol of rebirth and good luck: two things Fleetwood Mac were in urgent need of.

Lyrics such as 'He rested there upon an apple leaf/A gorgeous opal crown sat on his head' also reflected the stoned, pastoral vibes around the group's communal Kiln House residence. However,

107

Christine McVie later suggested that Kirwan was less relaxed and easy-going in person than some of his songs suggested.

Separating the art from the artist, though, 'Dragonfly' is still a peerless example of Fleetwood Mac's hazy, bucolic period – all shimmering, 'Albatross'-style guitar and whispered vocals. Peter Green later declared it the best song Danny Kirwan ever wrote. Meanwhile, Christine compared its failure to being 'beaten about the head with a giant club' as 'Dragonfly' divebombed out of the charts, like the titular insect swooping down on its prey.

Bob Welch

The Curse of the Fleetwood Mac Guitarist, Part III

Guns N' Roses' ex-drummer Steven Adler, as heard on the hit single 'Sweet Child O' Mine', never forgot the first time he smoked crack cocaine. It was the spring of 1985 at Bob Welch's place in the Hollywood Hills.

Adler's girlfriend at the time had told him about a 'fun dude' she knew. When they arrived at Welch's house, they discovered he was recovering from a heroin overdose in Cedars-Sinai hospital. Nevertheless, Welch's housemate let them in, fired up a glass pipe on the living room table and offered Adler a taste. 'I inhaled, and had never experienced such a dire need to get high again, right away, *now*,' he wrote in his autobiography, *My Appetite for Destruction*.

Adler soon joined the other waifs and strays at the property and moved his drum kit into the garage. Bob Welch re-joined the party as soon as he was out of hospital. But the twenty-year-old glam-rock wannabe and forty-year-old former Fleetwood Mac guitarist made an odd couple.

The pair would sit up at night, playing music and watching videos of Welch performing at the 1978 California Jam, with Stevie Nicks waving her tambourine and singing backing vocals. Bob, whippet-thin and hollow-cheeked, fired up the pipe and shared tales of the pre-superstar Mac and his solo hits, 'Sentimental Lady' and 'Ebony Eyes'.

Other future members of Guns N' Roses were soon rehearsing in the garage, with Welch as their landlord/mentor. The party stopped six months later when the Los Angeles Police Department arrested Welch for drug possession. 'I was smart enough to see the writing on the wall and changed all my friends,' he said years later. 'I was being a very bad boy. It was not a good time.'

It was also a comedown for a musician who'd sung, written and played on five Fleetwood Mac albums. 'People forget,' said Mick Fleetwood after Welch's death. 'Bob became part of a band that could have drifted into oblivion and was hugely important in keeping us going.'

Robert Lawrence Welch Jnr was born in 'Old Hollywood' in August 1945. His father produced movies starring Bob Hope, his mother Templeton Fox was an actress, and the family lived across the street from Yul Brynner. Bob spent his childhood being chauffeured to school in a limousine and acting older than his years at ritzy Beverly Hills parties. 'People over the years have sung about how decadent LA is, but they're all transplants,' he said. 'I'm a native. I was born right here. I'm the real deal.'

After graduating, Welch moved to Paris to study art. But he was distracted by the nightlife and returned to LA in 1964. Soon after, he joined his first group, a soul revue-style band, Seven Souls. They never had a hit, but their sponsor, a wealthy German hotelier, booked them to play at exclusive resorts in Saint-Tropez and the Italian Riviera until they split in 1969.

Welch stayed behind in Paris and formed a funk-rock trio, Head West, who made an album but ended up destitute after bailiffs repossessed their equipment. Then Welch's old high school friend and Fleetwood Mac's *aide-de-camp* Judy Wong rang to tell him Jeremy Spencer had left, and there was an opening in the band. 'I didn't know what to do,' said Welch. 'I had no money for an air ticket to Los Angeles, and I was getting very depressed.'

Fleetwood Mac bought him a ticket to England, and Welch scavenged enough for the train fare from London to Guildford. He was waiting outside the station with his acoustic guitar and a bag of clothes when Mick Fleetwood pulled up in a Volkswagen Beetle. 'He was 6'6" and weighed about 120 pounds,' Welch recalled. 'He was a strange-looking human being.'

Welch moved into their communal house, Benifold, and formally joined the group in April 1971. 'Bob never played a note,' recalled Christine. 'All we did was sit around and talk until dawn. We just thought he was an incredible person.'

Having lost Spencer and Peter Green in strange circumstances, they wanted to be sure Welch wouldn't abscond, too. 'I wasn't being scrutinised for my musical talents as much as my psychological soundness,' he said. Welch described his new bandmates as 'like the British royal family'. Nevertheless, he made his mark on the poetic title track of their next album, *Future Games*, and composed one of Fleetwood Mac's most straightforward love songs, 'Sentimental Lady'. It wasn't a hit in 1972 but would later become his signature song.

Welch came from a different place to his predecessors. Jazz guitarist Wes Montgomery was his primary influence; he had a languid, very Californian vocal delivery and channelled some recherché interests into his songwriting. Welch's 'The Ghost', 'Miles Away' and 'Hypnotized' dabbled in esoterica. His lyrics were inspired by unexplained phenomena; by Carlos Castaneda, the works of French novelist André Malraux, who'd embarked on a quest to find the lost city of the Old Testament Queen of Sheba.

Welch shored up his position after Danny Kirwan was fired in 1972. But not everybody was a fan. Clifford Davis didn't rate the American interloper, and Welch couldn't understand why the group didn't ditch their bluff cockney manager.

Davis also encouraged Fleetwood Mac to hire lead singer Dave Walker because he didn't think Welch was a convincing frontman. In fairness, Bob, with his bug-eyed spectacles and troublesome hairline, did resemble the class geek who'd become a guitar prodigy. Dave Walker looked the part, but Welch and McVie's songwriting and harmony vocals didn't suit him.

Welch had become accustomed to the royal family's eccentric ways by now. When Peter Green arrived at London's Air Studios to play on 1973's *Penguin*, he had a piece of cheese stuck in his hair. 'I don't know if it was Caerphilly or Cheddar,' Welch recalled. 'But when he left, Peter still had the same piece of cheese in his hair.' Nobody thought to mention it.

However, Fleetwood Mac were about to face their greatest challenge yet. When Fleetwood pulled out of an autumn 1973 US tour because of marital problems, Clifford Davis assembled a new Fleetwood Mac, minus any existing members, to tour in their absence. Welch hired a lawyer and was instrumental in keeping the real group together. He'd invested three years of his life in this dysfunctional bunch and wasn't going down without a fight. He persuaded the others to relocate to Los Angeles and see off Davis and his counterfeit group. It worked.

In early 1974, the real Fleetwood Mac received an advance of $100,000 for a new album, *Heroes are Hard to Find*. Welch agreed to pay it through his bank account, as he was the only one with US citizenship, which led to huge problems with the Internal Revenue Service (IRS) for years to come.

Heroes are Hard to Find showcased Welch's topically spooky 'Bermuda Triangle' and the drily witty 'Silver Heels', and was their biggest-selling US album yet. But Welch quit at the end of the year. The drugs, the IRS and the legal battles had all taken their toll, but there was more. 'Musically speaking, I wanted to do things they didn't want from me,' he said.

This was evident in Paris, the trio he formed with ex-Nazz drummer Thom Mooney and lapsed Jethro Tull bassist Glenn Cornick. 'Black Book', the first song on their self-titled debut, was almost a Led Zeppelin pastiche, with the rest of the LP in a similar vein.

Welch hadn't abandoned his love of esoterica either. During Paris gigs, he'd throw old books into the audience, inscribed with bizarre messages, which confused his bandmates as much as their fans. Paris replaced Mooney with future David Bowie's Tin Machine drummer Hunt Sales (also responsible for *that* walloping rhythm on Iggy Pop's 'Lust for Life') and expanded their sound on a second LP, *Big Towne, 2061*. But Paris struggled to sell records.

Before the group split, Welch composed a bunch of idiosyncratic but more radio-friendly songs for a third album. Mick Fleetwood heard them and was so impressed he signed Welch to his Limited Management company as a solo act. 'There was no doubt in my mind, Bob could have a hit record,' said Fleetwood. 'We felt like we were on the coaster heading up, and I wanted Bob in on this ride.'

Welch's solo album, *French Kiss*, arrived after *Rumours* in the summer of 1977. It included Fleetwood, Christine and Lindsey Buckingham guest spots and songs skirting hard rock, album-oriented rock and orchestral disco. The LP and the singles 'Sentimental Lady' and 'Ebony Eyes' cracked the US top twenty. By the following summer, Welch was opening for Fleetwood Mac and flying between shows on their chartered plane. Mick escorted him to radio interviews as his manager and was then interviewed by the same host talking about Fleetwood Mac. Welch was having hits, but his old band had become rich and famous without him.

'I didn't feel like I was missing the boat because it's a different group,' he insisted. 'But I contributed something to the group's sound and felt very proud that they were making it.'

The follow-up to *French Kiss*, 1979's *Three Hearts*, was another hit but still indulged Welch's left-field influences and conspiracy theories. 'Danchiva' was inspired by Hindu philosophy and 'The Ghost of Flight 401' by the Bermuda Triangle.

Visually, the two LPs were very much of their time. Welch appeared on both sleeves flanked by underdressed female models pulling aroused facial expressions. In his beret and tinted shades, Bob looked like the Bee Gees' imaginary older brother dispensing Class As in the back office of a Malibu nightclub.

Life was starting to imitate art. In 1980, Welch began hosting *Hollywood Heartbeat*, a music video TV show, where he interviewed Mick Fleetwood. The pair joshed around like old pals, but Welch's skeletal appearance suggested some ruinous lifestyle choices.

Most of Fleetwood Mac guested with Welch at the Roxy in Hollywood in 1981. By then, Bob had acquired new hair and a silk kimono embroidered with Chinese dragons. He played out of his skin on 'Hypnotized' and 'Rattlesnake Shake'. But without his old group's patronage, he struggled to sell records. Welch turned down the offer to sing in Mick Fleetwood's Zoo, but his solo albums all missed the charts. The failure of 1983's *Eye Contact* was a tipping point. Welch had a house in the Hollywood hills, a studio and gold discs on the wall, but his marriage was over, and he'd just lost his record deal.

It took an overdose, a drugs bust and members of Guns N' Roses using his garage as a junkies' shooting gallery for Welch to come to his senses. However, soon after his hospital stay, Welch was in the Viper Room nightclub when he was introduced to the woman who'd become his second wife, film assistant Wendy Armistead.

Welch married Wendy in December 1985 and, in the parlance of recovering addicts, 'did a geographic' and moved to Phoenix, Arizona. Welch explained his lifestyle change: 'I was able to pull out of a major depression, drug addiction and extreme negativity, thanks to the LA Sheriff's Dept – I was busted – the hospital where I was rehabilitating, and, especially, a lovely lady who helped me stop beating my head against a brick wall. Wendy helped me to get back into reading music again, to want to do a band again, and to regain my musical and personal identity.'

Welch's next band, Avenue M, didn't last, and he and Wendy later settled in Nashville, where he focused on writing songs and launched a lawsuit against Fleetwood Mac. Welch claimed they'd signed a contract with Warners agreeing to an equal share of royalties for the records they'd made together. Welch believed the other three members had renegotiated the deal with a higher rate for themselves, and he was being underpaid.

In 1988, Fleetwood Mac were inducted into the Rock & Roll Hall of Fame, and Welch's name was missing from the roll call of past members. 'Mick Fleetwood dedicated a whole chapter of his biography to my era of the band,' Welch told the press.

'He credited me with "saving Fleetwood Mac". Now they want to write me out of the history of the group. Mick treats most past band members as if they didn't really have anything to with Fleetwood Mac, with the exception of the *Rumours* band, Peter Green and, rarely, Jeremy Spencer. Everybody else he shuts out of his mind.'

Fleetwood Mac eventually settled out of court in 1996, and Welch revised his story, blaming Warner Bros for the financial mismanagement and the Hall of Fame for the snub. By now, Welch was making music again, including two albums of re-recorded Fleetwood Mac songs.

Welch was still fascinated by the paranormal and left-field science. In a rare interview, he was asked what he did besides music and replied 'UFO-watching'. His website linked to articles about extraterrestrial visitation, anti-gravity technology and bio-mind superpowers. By the 2000s, though, he was, in his words, 'semi-retired' but still playing a few dates a year. 'Two shows at a time and then go home,' he said. 'At my age, that's all that I want to do.'

Welch maintained his sobriety after leaving Los Angeles. But he underwent spinal surgery in March 2012 only to learn his chances of recovery were slim and he'd eventually lose all mobility. Welch was in great pain and wrote a letter to his wife, explaining how he'd seen his mother caring for his invalid father and didn't want Wendy doing the same for him. Welch took his own life on 7 June, dying from a self-inflicted gunshot wound to the chest.

'Like Stevie and Lindsey later on, Bob came out of the ether when we needed someone just like him,' explained Fleetwood, a few months after Welch's death. 'I would have hated the thought of him becoming like that guy, Pete Best, who left the Beatles and was thinking, "I was right there, then I left and then *this* happens."' At the time, Fleetwood paused and furrowed his brow. 'I do so hope he felt identified and not just left on the sidelines.'

'Tell Me All the Things You Do'

The (Almost) Great Lost Single

Had 'Tell Me All the Things You Do' been recorded by one of Fleetwood Mac's American peers – Creedence Clearwater Revival, perhaps? – it might have gone higher than nowhere in the charts.

Culled from *Kiln House* and released as a single in early 1971, it was the second in a long run of commercial duds, beginning with 'Dragonfly' and only ending when 'Over My Head' cracked the US top twenty, by which time Buckingham and Nicks were in the band.

The whole song sounds like engineer Martin Birch pressed 'record' during a lengthy jam session at London's De Lane Lea studio, then switched the tape machine off 4:15 minutes later. Really, it's an instrumental on which composer Danny Kirwan grafted some vague lyrics. 'Danny was a producer of music,' explained Mick Fleetwood. 'He never really felt comfortable singing anything.'

The vagueness of Kirwan's lyrics never detracts from the mantric blues, with its whinnying guitar and Fleetwood's rolling groove (as the song went on, he started whacking his cowbell at increasingly random intervals). The unsung hero, though, is Christine McVie, still then a mother and not yet a band member, peeling off some piano licks in the background.

There's a recording online of the Buckingham Nicks line-up rehearsing the song for their 1977 tour. Halfway through, everyone stops, and Buckingham plays the riff to what became 'Tusk' instead. It just wasn't their song anymore.

During the 2018 world tour, Fleetwood Mac exhumed 'Tell Me All the Things You Do' at new guitarist Mike Campbell's request. It was a brave choice. But the queue for the bars suggested that around 90 per cent of the audience had never heard it before. 'That's the trouble,' said Mick Fleetwood. 'People forget there was *another* Fleetwood Mac after Peter, but before Lindsey and Stevie.' 'Tell Me All the Things You Do' was quietly dropped from the set soon after.

'Future Games'

Cameron Crowe's Favourite Fleetwood Mac Song

What must it have been like for native Californian Bob Welch to swap sunny LA for a dilapidated country house in rural Hampshire? In 1971 Welch came to England to replace Jeremy Spencer. He also became another vocalist, guitarist, composer, lyricist and creative mind.

Welch's first impression of his new group was confusion. 'It was like they were on some sort of mystical quest, by appointment to her majesty,' he said. Welch would spend four years and four albums trying to figure it out before giving up.

His title track to 1971's *Future Games* sounded like part of the quest. 'When I wrote "Future Games", the Vietnam War was still going strong, they had the riots at the Democratic Convention two years before, Nixon was in the White House,' said Welch. 'They were giving people eighty-year jail sentences in Texas for possession of one marijuana joint, and the FBI was wiretapping your grandmother.'

Musically, 'Future Games' glided in a way Fleetwood Mac had only managed before on 'Albatross'. Welch's jazz-guitar flourishes and Christine's regal-sounding organ decorated its unbroken eight-minute groove. When Stevie Nicks and Lindsey Buckingham replaced Welch, they had to perform some of his songs live. Not this one, though.

'Future Games', like many Welch-era songs, was forgotten after Fleetwood Mac's gold rush. Then former *Rolling Stone* writer turned film-maker Cameron Crowe used it in his 2000 movie, *Almost Famous*, a semi-autobiographical story about a teenage music critic's adventures with a fictional rock band called Stillwater. 'Future Games' accompanied a scene where Stillwater's self-regarding lead guitarist, 'Russell Hammond', delivers a stoned soliloquy to a bunch of high school kids at a house party.

'You are what it's all about,' he implores, as Bob Welch's voice and guitar glides by in the background. 'You are real . . . Your room is real . . . In eleven years, it's gonna be 1984! Think about *that*!'

His audience listens in rapt silence until one of the teenagers pipes up: 'Er, wanna see me feed a mouse to my snake?'

'Yes!' replies Hammond, as if he's just been told the meaning of life.

A few minutes later, Hammond reappears on a garage roof and proclaims himself 'a golden god', a scene based on a real-life incident when Led Zeppelin's Robert Plant made the same wild proclamation at a party in Los Angeles.

The soundtrack to *Almost Famous* didn't do for 'Future Games' what it did for Elton John's 'Tiny Dancer', another '70s deep cut ripe for rediscovery. The film grossed $47.4 million, and hopefully landed Bob Welch a long-overdue payday. Perhaps for a few precious minutes, he felt like a golden god too.

Future Games and Bare Trees

The Anti-Rumours

Before some enterprising soul invented the internet, *Future Games* and *Bare Trees* spent most of the '80s and '90s languishing in the racks of second-hand record shops. Neither were big hits in the '70s, and the impression was that they'd been offloaded by two different demographics. First, by their original audience, who'd sold their record collections to make space in the family home, and, second, by those who loved *Rumours* and thought they'd investigate some of Fleetwood Mac's 'earlier stuff'. This second group wondered what on earth they were hearing and where was Stevie Nicks?

Future Games and *Bare Trees* were released seven months apart (in 1971 and 1972). With some judicious editing, you could create an excellent single-and-a-half album out of the two.

By the summer of 1971, Jeremy Spencer had run away to join a religious commune, so fellow guitarist Danny Kirwan composed most of *Future Games* sequestered in his attic room at the group's communal Hampshire home, Benifold. He gave his bandmates the fragile, folky 'Sometimes' and the pastoral 'Woman of 1000 Years' and 'Sands of Time'. '"Sands Of Time" was a killer song,' said Christine, who recalled making *Future Games* at London's Advision Studios. 'We had to do that in one take, beginning to end.'

Bob Welch soon realised his bandmates didn't just want a Jeremy Spencer understudy and needed his songs to progress. 'Because we didn't want to be a purist blues group or an acid rock band any-more,' explained Fleetwood. Welch came up with *Future Games'* hymn-like title track, which was Fleetwood Mac's best work since 'Oh Well'.

It wasn't all new brave new worlds. Christine's 'Morning Rain' was a standard drivetime rocker, and 'What a Shame' (with her brother, John Perfect, on saxophone) was a trundling instrumental written to fill some empty grooves. Christine outshone both though with 'Show Me a Smile', templating the graceful ballad style she'd later deploy on *Rumours*. The lyrics read like she was urging a child not to grow up too fast. Aptly, the LP sleeve showed a photograph of Fleetwood's sister Sally's kids paddling in the River Nadder.

Future Games arrived in September 1971, in time for a US tour opening for Frank Zappa and Deep Purple. It sneaked into the US top 100 but didn't trouble the UK charts. Future food critic and pasta-sauce maker, Loyd Grossman, described it as 'thoroughly unsatisfactory' in *Rolling Stone*.

Fleetwood Mac went on the road for almost a year and only returned to make *Bare Trees*. The group were match fit. Less so De Lane Lea's new studio in Wembley, north London. The owners had just discovered inadequate soundproofing after they booked an unknown group called Queen to test the rooms. Undeterred, Fleetwood Mac and their producer Martin Birch emerged a few weeks later with a new LP.

'Heavy country blues keep-a-rockin,' implored Kirwan on 'Child of Mine', a song written to get the kids at Salpointe High School, Tucson, Arizona, and other venues on the circuit, up off the bleachers and dancing. Similarly, 'Homeward Bound' had Christine singing 'I don't wanna see another aeroplane seat,' in a cut-glass English accent.

Bare Trees was better when it dialled down the road-hog rock. 'Sunny Side of Heaven' suggested the Allman Brothers Band play-ing 'Albatross', and 'Danny's Chant' was a wah-wah pedal stomp crying out to be sampled by some enterprising DJ this millennium. Kirwan raised the stakes elsewhere with a title track that placed his

half-scatting over a stately English blues, and 'Dust', a contempla-
tive folk song based on a poem by First World War soldier poet
Rupert Brooke.

McVie and Welch had the LP's best tunes, though, with the
gospel-flecked 'Spare Me a Little of Your Love', 'Sentimental Lady'
and 'The Ghost'. Welch was fascinated by UFO-logy, and 'The
Ghost's chiming chorus and Mellotron fills soundtracked lyrics
about extra-terrestrials sizing up planet Earth for invasion.

Welch wrote 'Sentimental Lady' for his wife, Nancy, and Christine's peeling harmonies helped elevate the chorus. In 1977,
Welch's re-recorded 'Sentimental Lady' became a US solo hit just
as *Rumours* conquered the world.

Bare Trees ended with 'Thoughts on a Grey Day', a poem read by
their elderly neighbour, Mrs Aileen Scarrott. 'God bless our perfect, perfect grey day, with trees so bare,' she said. It was a very
English finale, which inspired John McVie to take the cover photo
but must have baffled the kids at Salpointe High School when they
heard the record.

The album was released in March 1972, after a near disaster.
Fleetwood Mac took the master tapes to New York, but they were
erased after being put through the new-fangled X-ray machine at
JKF Airport. The whole record had to be remixed in a few days
before another tour.

Danny Kirwan soon joined the ranks of other ex-Fleetwood Mac
guitarists after having a breakdown on tour. Meanwhile, *Bare Trees*
sold fractionally better in the US than *Future Games* but flatlined in
the UK.

'It does feel lonely,' admitted Welch. 'I don't know how that happened. But there was no overall plan to make *Bare Trees* sound quite
so bleak.'

Dave Walker

The Lead Singer that Time Forgot

Dave Walker moved to Gallup, New Mexico in 1987. His most recent venture, the Dave Walker Band, had failed to land a record deal, and he'd taken a job in construction. Gallup was on Route 66; the highway celebrated in many rock 'n' roll songs and a permanent reminder of its new resident's musical dreams. Not that Walker had stopped dreaming. The ex-Fleetwood Mac vocalist had been hustling since the early '60s and wouldn't stop now.

David Walker was born in January 1945 in Walsall and grew up in the same milieu as future members of the Electric Light Orchestra and Black Sabbath. In 1970, he replaced the Idle Race's guitarist Jeff Lynne when he went off to form ELO. A year later, Black Sabbath's Tony Iommi recommended Walker for a job with blues-rockers Savoy Brown.

Walker first came onto Fleetwood Mac's radar when they opened for Savoy Brown in 1972. Walker had the requisite gravel to his voice but also threw some rock-star shapes on stage. Fleetwood Mac's manager, Clifford Davis, was impressed. 'He said, "What you need is a guy out front like a cheerleader,"' recalled Fleetwood. 'And like an idiot, we did it. It was a big mistake.'

Walker accepted the offer to join Fleetwood Mac under false pretences. John McVie had told him their guitarist/vocalist Bob Welch was leaving. Except Welch stayed on, and Walker discovered

123

they'd hired another guitarist, Bob Weston. On stage, Walker wore snakeskin boots and Native American jewellery, tossed his hair and implored the audience 'to boog-i-i-e-e!' But finding his place in the studio was impossible. Bob Welch and Christine McVie monopolised the writing and struggled to compose for his voice, meaning Walker was barely present on 1973's *Penguin*. Mick Fleetwood also claimed he spent more time in the local pub than he did working. 'I was always down the pub because they sent me to the pub,' Walker protested. 'They'd say, "Go down the pub, Dave, and we'll call you when we're ready."'

There was also tension between Walker and Bob Welch. Bob considered their latest recruit 'a stereotypical lead singer' and 'a little too flash with the jewellery and snakeskin boots.' Meanwhile, Dave dismissed Bob's songs as 'crap'. 'Fleetwood Mac were always a good blues rock band,' he grumbled. 'Why they quit playing it, I'll never understand.'

Fleetwood Mac fired Walker during the making of 1973's *Mystery to Me*. Only Clifford Davis and Walker's drinking buddy, John McVie, were sorry to see him go. Both parties used the traditional excuse of 'musical differences'. Walker later admitted to having marital problems and drinking too much but was still devastated. 'It undermined my confidence immensely,' he admitted. 'I couldn't even sing for six months and didn't do anything musically for about four months. But it was difficult for anyone to come into a band like Fleetwood Mac and start throwing their weight around.'

Walker moved to the US, eventually assembling a new group, but progress was slow. Then, in November 1977, Tony Iommi called. Black Sabbath's lead vocalist, Ozzy Osbourne, had quit, and would Dave like the job? Walker accepted, only to be fired two months later when Ozzy decided he wanted to re-join.

Dave Walker currently lives in Montana, playing gigs, making the occasional album and talking about his past employers. He's not bitter. 'My claim to fame,' he said, 'is I have been fired by some really famous people.'

Penguin and Mystery to Me

Fleetwood Mac Go Wild in the Country

'Dysfunctional' is frequently used to describe Fleetwood Mac. But the drama of the Buckingham/Nicks era often obscures the fact that the band were having bust-ups and clandestine affairs long before those two arrived. *Mystery to Me* is an apt title: it's surprising that this album or its predecessor, *Penguin*, were ever made.

The band released them seven months apart in 1973, during which time they hired and fired a lead singer, Christine ran off with their sound engineer and their new guitarist had an affair with Mick Fleetwood's wife. Buckingham and Nicks had nothing on this tumultuous, cuckolding version of Fleetwood Mac.

At the time, Britain was besotted with glam rock. Bowie and Roxy Music were in the ascendant, but Fleetwood Mac didn't do glittery stack heels and face paint. The group still played the UK college circuit but did better business in America. However, a US tour with Deep Purple highlighted a perceived shortcoming. Purple's lead singer, Ian Gillan, shook his waist-length hair and worked the audience like a circus barker. In contrast, Fleetwood Mac had bespectacled jazz guitar-playing Bob Welch and Christine McVie stuck behind an organ.

So, with Danny Kirwan gone, Fleetwood Mac hired lead vocalist Dave Walker. He was joined by another new recruit, ex-Long John Baldry guitarist Bob Weston. Mick Fleetwood described the

125

bearded, be-denimed Dave Walker as 'a rabble rouser', and he roused the rabble at backwater venues from Trenton, New Jersey, to Hartford, Connecticut. But it was difficult to accommodate him on record.

Fleetwood Mac recorded *Penguin* at their communal house, Benifold, using the Rolling Stones' mobile studio. The scrum of egos and styles resulted in an LP which zigzagged between Christine's chipper country rock ('Remember Me'), Bob Welch's tales of biblical reckoning and flying saucers ('Bright Fire', 'Revelation') and the McVie/Weston duet 'Did You Ever Love Me', the only Mac song ever to include steel drums. Peter Green also reappeared, like Marley's ghost, to play on 'Night Watch'.

Welch and Christine McVie's musical bond had grown strong over the past year. This wasn't an issue for Weston, but it was for Dave Walker, who was only permitted one original song, 'The Derelict', and a cover of '(I'm a) Roadrunner'.

'Dave was great in Savoy Brown,' said Christine later. 'But you try and get a guy like Dave Walker singing anything other than Howlin' Wolf or Freddie King or rock 'n' roll boogie-woogie.'

Penguin, released in March 1973, was a stylistic mess but their highest-charting US release yet. Meanwhile, CBS reissued 'Albatross' as a single in the UK. The exasperated band watched it become a top-five hit and winced as radio DJs speculated on their current whereabouts.

On the road, Dave Walker's rabble-rousing irritated Bob Welch, and tensions continued to simmer while making *Mystery to Me*. Walker barely featured on the album and was let go before the recording was finished.

The LP arrived in October in a knuckle-suckingly awful sleeve – a cartoon gorilla eating a cake. The highlights, Welch's 'Hypnotized' and 'Emerald Eyes', and McVie's 'Why', showcased his laconic white funk and her posh home-counties blues. Some of it wasn't that distant from Steely Dan's upcoming second album, *Countdown to Ecstasy*. 'I love Steely Dan,' said Christine. 'But, of course, we were making that sound before them.'

Welch later divulged that the album's chemistry was improved by 'the extreme sexual zingers going on between Christine and engineer, Martin Birch.' Chris and Martin were having an affair, which didn't please John, 'But was great for musical creativity.'

Despite a fruitless version of the Yardbirds' hit 'For Your Love', it looked like Fleetwood Mac had found a clear direction. Then it all went wrong – again. Just a few dates into another US tour, Fleetwood discovered his wife was having an affair with Bob Weston. 'I had no idea,' he said, 'apart from the feeling something wasn't right.' Fleetwood refused to speak to Weston but insisted the show go on. But the guitarist was fired after a couple of weeks, and the remaining dates were cancelled. This was Clifford Davis's cue to assemble a new group and try to pass them off as 'Fleetwood Mac'. The ensuing lawsuits took up all their time, and *Mystery to Me* dive-bombed out of the charts.

Not that any of this dented Christine's appreciation. '*Penguin* was our worst ever album,' she said. 'But I have a bit of a penchant for *Mystery to Me*. In fact, it's my third favourite Fleetwood Mac album.'

'Hypnotized'

A Close Encounter

Benifold, the house where Fleetwood Mac lived in the early '70s, is a Victorian pile near the Hampshire village of Headley. It was where they had affairs, raised children, fell out, made up and composed music, including the hit-single-that-never-was, 'Hypnotized'.

In late 1970, the six-month lease expired on the group's first communal residence, Kiln House. Mick Fleetwood's sister Sally recommended Benifold, seven miles away. The building belonged to a religious group that'd converted it into a prayer house for Christians of every denomination. Fleetwood Mac acquired the property for £23,000 from a record company advance, and moved in with their partners, roadies and dogs that winter.

Benifold was dilapidated but had twenty rooms (one of which became a rehearsal space) and a tennis court flanked by acres of woodland. Mick and his wife Jenny commandeered the servants' quarters, and John and Christine McVie took a self-contained suite of rooms opposite. Jeremy Spencer and his wife, Fiona, moved upstairs, and Danny Kirwan and his partner, Clare, took over the attic space.

'It was a strange way to live,' admitted Christine, years later, 'all in the same house but in our own sections – like a big apartment block with no privacy.'

On any given night, too, random musicians and acquaintances could also be found in the house, skinning up and nodding along with the music. 'It was heaven on earth,' said Fleetwood. 'At least for the first year and a half.'

In January 1971, Jenny gave birth to a daughter, Amelia. The band were playing in Scotland, and Fleetwood dashed back to briefly see his wife and child before finishing the tour. But Jenny soon spent weeks alone with a tiny infant while her husband and housemates toured the US. 'And when I came back, I used to spend most of my time talking about the band,' Fleetwood admitted.

Then fellow Mac member Bob Welch channelled Benifold's psychic tension into their music. Welch had arrived at the house in late 1971. Two years later, he composed 'Hypnotized' for their new album, *Mystery to Me*. The song began as a straight blues shuffle. But when the Mac's then-lead singer, Dave Walker, was fired, Welch re-purposed it to suit his voice and personal obsessions. Welch was fascinated by paranormal phenomena. The line 'a place down in Mexico, where a man can fly over mountains and hills' was inspired by author Carlos Castaneda, whose books explored the teachings of an astral-travelling Yaqui Indian shaman named Don Juan Matus.

The 'strange, strange pond' with 'sides like glass' came from Welch's motorcycle gang friends in the US. While dirt-biking in a forest near Winston-Salem, North Carolina, they'd discovered a rain-filled crater, miles from any caterpillar tracks or access roads. 'A strange crater in the ground with smooth sides like melted glass,' recalled Welch, who thought it was evidence of a UFO craft landing.

Benifold also found its way into the song's opening verse. The band were recording *Mystery to Me* with the Rolling Stones' mobile studio. Nobody had to venture beyond the house or its neighbouring woods. They were cohabiting and working in a bubble.

Welch wrote about 'two friends' seeing an object fly past their window – 'it might be out on that lawn, which is wide, at least half of a playing field.' 'Benifold was spooky and strange, even in the summertime,' he explained. 'There was an odd, ethereal mood around those grounds. One night I had a vivid dream that a UFO piloted by a Navajo shaman landed on our overgrown grass tennis court.'

Welch completed the song with Christine McVie, whose backing vocals drifted throughout like a distant echo. At its core, though, was the sound of Mick Fleetwood impersonating Welch's Maestro Rhythm King MRK-1 drum machine. Fleetwood's mesmeric shuffle conjured up the stillness of the Chihuahuan Desert with or without Don Juan Matus floating overheard.

'Hypnotized' was released in November 1973, on the B-side of Fleetwood Mac's cover of the Yardbirds' hit, 'For Your Love'; a decision as baffling as Welch's Navajo-piloted flying saucer dream. Nevertheless, 'Hypnotized' became a staple of the setlist even into the Buckingham Nicks era. There's footage online of them performing it onstage at LA's Capitol Theatre in October 1975. Sadly, Lindsey Buckingham couldn't do the song justice. It needed Benifold's strange juju or a Yaqui shaman for that.

Fleetwood Mac remained in their mansion until the summer of 1974 when they decamped to Los Angeles. The house was last put up for sale in 2021, with estate agent Knight Frank making much of its musical history. 'Located on a quiet tree-lined road in East Hampshire, you definitely won't want to "Go Your Own Way,"' they joshed. Benifold eventually sold for £4 million.

'The Fake Mac'

When is Fleetwood Mac Not Fleetwood Mac?

Case No 1

'I don't know if the audience were really stoned or didn't know what Fleetwood Mac looked like.'

In January 1974, Mick Fleetwood's wife, Jenny Boyd, visited a psychic. Her affair with Fleetwood Mac's guitarist Bob Weston had sent shockwaves through the group. So much so that Fleetwood had put the band on ice and gone to Africa 'to get my head together'.

The psychic studied Jenny's wedding ring, and then claimed her new lover was using her 'as a pawn' and that she should be with her husband. Unfortunately, the psychic didn't foresee that a new line-up of Fleetwood Mac, without any of its current members, were about to tour in their absence.

Fleetwood Mac had managed a fortnight on the road promoting their new album, *Mystery to Me*. But Mick couldn't bear sharing a stage with Weston and cancelled the remaining dates. Clifford Davis was furious, as many of the outstanding shows had been postponed once before, and he was at risk of being sued.

The Mac's lead singer/guitarist Bob Welch told Davis that the group weren't splitting, only taking a break while Fleetwood attended to his marriage. However, Davis claimed he owned the name 'Fleetwood Mac'.

'He sent me, Mick, John and Chris a letter saying that "he was not going down because of the whims of irresponsible musicians,"' recalled Welch. 'He also said that he intended to put together a "star-quality headlining act" and that he was offering us jobs in this band, and we could take them or not.'

Welch and the others called Davis's bluff. Then he called theirs and assembled a new band. On 16 January 1974, the new Fleetwood Mac arrived at Syria Mosque in Oakland, Pittsburgh, to play their debut show. 'This is not Fleetwood Mac,' declared promoter Rich Engler, as he watched the new members file past him into the dressing room. Davis, who'd heard this several times already, insisted it was and allegedly threw a punch.

Nevertheless, the fake Mac wowed most of the audience, and only a dozen people asked for their money back. 'They were really good,' wrote Engler in his memoir, *Behind the Stage Door*. 'But I don't know if the audience were really stoned or didn't know what Fleetwood Mac looked like.'

This new line-up included two of Davis's other management clients, vocalist Dave Terry (better known as Elmer Gantry, ex of Elmer Gantry's Velvet Opera) and former Curved Air guitarist Kirby Gregory, alongside bassist Paul Martinez, keyboard player Dave Wilkinson and drummer Craig Collinge. Promoters were told that Collinge was understudying for Mick Fleetwood, who planned to join the new Mac as soon as he was back in the US. It never happened, though, and word spread about the fake group before the second date at New York City Academy.

That night, Davis walked on stage and informed the audience that *he* was Fleetwood Mac and *he* alone chose who was in the group. However, Gantry had lost his voice, forcing the others to play an instrumental set without him. 'They were convinced if they didn't go on at all there'd be a real crowd problem,' reported *Rolling Stone*, 'and the audience had already sat through [support act] Kiss.'

This time, 800 people asked for their money back and Fleetwood and his bandmates filed a lawsuit against Davis, preventing the pseudo-Mac from touring. Davis counter-sued and tried to freeze the band's assets. 'That was the only time I got really panicky,' said Christine. 'Because we couldn't work until we'd proved we owned the name.'

Eventually, the matter was resolved out of court in what was described as 'a reasonable settlement not unfair to either party'. Fleetwood and Co. were permitted to continue as 'Fleetwood Mac' but Davis retained a piece of their earnings in the short term. He continued to manage both Peter Green and Danny Kirwan, before leaving the music business for a new career as a property developer.

In the meantime, Bob Welch had pleaded with the others to join him in Los Angeles. They agreed, and a new Fleetwood Mac album, *Heroes are Hard to Find*, appeared in the summer of 1974.

The understudies weren't done yet, though. Gantry, Gregory and Martinez reappeared in a new group, Stretch, and scored a UK top-twenty hit, 'Why Did You Do It?', in November the following year. The fake Fleetwood Mac experience inspired its reproachful lyrics. 'The damage is much deeper than you'll ever see,' sang Gantry. 'Hit me like a hammer to my head/I wonder were you pushed or were you led?'

An alternative version of events has emerged since 1974, though. Clifford Davis and band members Gantry, Gregory and Martinez have all insisted that Fleetwood sanctioned the alternative band. 'Mick came to my house and said he couldn't rehearse with us, "But if you get a drummer, I will join you later when I can on the tour,"' Gantry told the BBC's Johnnie Walker in 2017. 'We turned up in the States, but Mick didn't, and then we heard stories about people not knowing who we were.'

Gantry also said he'd received court documents from an anonymous source in which Fleetwood admitted to meeting with the new band before the tour. Others inside the Mac camp claim John McVie also gave them his blessing. McVie was hurt by Christine's blossoming relationship with their engineer Martin Birch and told Davis that he was retiring from the road to live in Hawaii. Davis also claimed that Christine informed him she was leaving the group to work on a solo project with Birch. In fact, the only member of the real Fleetwood Mac still flying the flag was Bob Welch, who was aggrieved about being left band-less.

In this alternative account, Mick Fleetwood agreed to join the new Mac on their third date in Baltimore. When he didn't arrive, Davis became suspicious. Fleetwood rang to tell them he couldn't make it because he was still having problems at home and trying to get his daughter settled in a new school. Fleetwood's party line, though, is that none of this happened. 'Clifford had been specifically told, "Don't worry, we're not breaking up,"' he wrote in 1990's *Fleetwood*. 'But he thought he'd take this thing over and registered the name "Fleetwood Mac". To this day I don't know the name of the musicians involved and I don't want to know.'

Fleetwood stuck to this story in his second memoir, 2014's *Play On*. '"Why Did You Do It?" was a direct attack on me for not showing up for the bogus Fleetwood Mac tour, which I'd never promised to do,"' he huffed. However, Davis and members of the road crew have since claimed that the real Mac regrouped because their livelihoods were threatened. Christine's relationship with Birch ended when he went back to his wife, and Fleetwood didn't want to start over again with a new band.

Whatever its provenance, the bizarre episode prompted Fleetwood to take charge of his affairs. After Davis's departure, the band formed their own company, Seedy Management, and by locating to the US were a step closer to discovering Stevie Nicks and Lindsey Buckingham.

Case No 2

'The man is a liar and an imposter!'

On 1 November 1982, London's *Evening Standard* newspaper ran an interview with a man they believed to be guitarist Jeremy Spencer, who'd left Fleetwood Mac over a decade earlier to join the Children of God commune.

Spencer told *Ad Lib* columnist Peter Holt that he'd fled the cult against their wishes and had been living in Switzerland before returning to London. 'I've been trying to keep a low profile,' he explained. 'I've got ten safe houses into which I can disappear if [the Children of God] come looking for me. They can turn very nasty.'

Holt also announced that Spencer had joined ex-Fleetwood Mac bassist Bob Brunning's De Luxe Blues Band and would be headlining the London Blues Festival at Wimbledon Theatre the following night. Sadly, it was all a hoax. 'The man who played at the London Blues Festival under the name "Jeremy Spencer" is *not* the ex-Fleetwood Mac guitarist Jeremy Spencer,' wrote Holt in a lengthy retraction on 5 November. 'The man is a liar and an imposter!'

Two days after the interview was printed, one of the real Spencer's girlfriends contacted Holt with conclusive evidence of fraud. The trouble is everyone wanted to believe this Jeremy Spencer was *the* Jeremy Spencer.

By day, Bob Brunning was the headmaster of Clapham Manor Junior School and considered himself a shrewd judge of character. He'd not only played in Fleetwood Mac with Spencer, but he'd also shared a flat with him. Brunning was suspicious when he reappeared but agreed to meet him in a pub.

'He bore more than a passing resemblance to Spencer,' Brunning insisted. 'I wasn't wholly convinced, but he went a long way towards convincing me with his astonishing recollection of early Fleetwood Mac experiences.'

Brunning performed with 'Spencer' at the Wimbledon Theatre, but noticed he was playing with his back to the audience. The reason became apparent when the real Spencer's parents confronted Brunning after the show. 'Jeremy is still with the Children of God in Sri Lanka,' explained his father, Gerald. 'The person playing guitar is not him.'

The next day, the *Evening Standard* summoned the imposter back to their offices. Under interrogation, 'Spencer' finally confessed that his real name was 'Andrew Clarke' and he'd spent the past decade impersonating Jeremy Spencer, including jamming with Irish guitarist Rory Gallagher at the Montreux Jazz Festival. To enable this, he claimed to have a passport and driving licence in Spencer's name (though the real Spencer had never learned to drive).

Clarke also said he'd once been a member of Jeremy Spencer's pre-Mac trio, the Levi Set, and had also joined the Children of God, who'd instigated the whole con. 'They talked me into doing this, and it's got out of hand,' he told the *Evening Standard*. 'I'm skint and it's all become a nightmare.'

However, Spencer's parents insisted this imposter was never a member of the Levi Set, but that their son had been at school with an 'Andrew Clarke' who'd played in another group on the Midlands circuit. Perhaps it was him, they speculated. The police intervened, Scotland Yard's fraud squad interviewed Bob Brunning about the deception, but charges were never brought.

The most remarkable aspect of the story was that the fake Jeremy Spencer was a genuinely accomplished musician. 'His guitar playing was much better than the real Jeremy's,' confided Brunning. Yet 'Andrew Clarke' was never heard of again.

Case No 3

'Most of our conversation was, "Is he up to it? Can he do it?" It wasn't, "Is he Peter Green?"'

Sometime in the early '90s, a softly spoken and rather dishevelled gentleman started appearing in guitar shops and at music fairs. He often introduced himself to the staff as 'Beetroot' or 'Jimi Hendrix', before telling everybody he was Peter Green.

As the real Peter Green was rarely seen in public but known for his down-at-heel appearance, many took him at face value. But this 'Peter Green' was actually an Essex farmer named Patrick Himfen, known to his customers in Rochford and its surrounding towns and villages as 'the Egg & Potato Man'.

Incredibly, Himfen managed to deceive several journalists, music shop owners and musicians up until 1994. Among them was

David Edwards, an Ilford guitar shop manager and guitarist in an unsigned blues-rock group called National Gold. Edwards had met the real Green in 1982 and claimed Himfen had the same large hands and toothy smile.

Himfen offered to play with National Gold and help them get a record deal. He approached Eric Clapton, Led Zeppelin's Jimmy Page, former Shadows drummer Tony Meehan and Queen drummer Roger Taylor to collaborate. Most cited prior commitments, except Taylor, who offered the group free studio time. In truth, Himfen was barely audible on the tape he'd sent to his rock-star 'friends'. But they all presumed David Edwards' lead guitar playing was Peter Green's.

Himfen was highly convincing. He had a forensic knowledge of Green's early life and guitars, and a garage full of vintage amps and original John Mayall's Bluesbreakers setlists. He even gave the American blues guitarist Ben Fisher permission to record 'his' material for a tribute album, which resulted in Fisher landing a record deal.

There were red flags along the way, though. Some who heard him play thought Himfen sounded like 'a bad Peter Green impersonator'. But they indulged him, arguing that Green probably wouldn't play as well as he had in the old days.

In 1993, Himfen was asked to write the foreword to a new guitar book, *Burst 1958–1960 Les Paul Standard*. He delivered a paragraph of nonsense ('Depend on your own ear, fuck everybody else . . .'). But it was published anyway because the authors believed he was the real deal.

Himfen was finally caught out when he asked to borrow a guitar from a music shop in Southend. The salesman happened to be married to former Fleetwood Mac guitarist Danny Kirwan's ex-wife, Clare, and refused. He'd also met Peter Green numerous times and knew this wasn't him.

David Edwards learned about the deception and confronted Himfen, who insisted he was Green but was using a new name because his family were trying to steal his money. He also told

Edwards the Mafia had arranged the name change, as they now owned his back catalogue and paid him royalties.

It was Green's brother, Michael, who ended the ruse by simply phoning up the imposter. Himfen cracked under interrogation and told Michael he was 'a big Peter Green fan' but admitted he'd been impersonating him since the mid-'80s. No criminal charges were brought, but National Gold had to return the equipment Himfen had acquired on their behalf and Ben Fisher's tribute album was put on hold.

Understandably, there was widespread embarrassment and anger among those who'd been conned. Some still wondered whether it wasn't an elaborate hoax masterminded by the real Peter Green, who, according to his family, was baffled by the whole affair.

In October 2000, BBC One broadcast a documentary, *Fake*, in which Himfen's story was recounted alongside those of bogus Formula One racing drivers and professional footballers. There was a common thread: these imposters all become overwhelmed by a lie that was encouraged to grow because people wanted to believe it. 'Most of our conversation was, "Is he up to it? Can he do it?"' explained Tony Meehan in the show. 'It wasn't, "Is he Peter Green?"'

At the time of writing, the Egg & Potato Man is still living and trading from his farm in Rochford, Essex, but not answering any questions about the time he pretended to be Peter Green.

Zambia

Mick Fleetwood's Great Epiphany

In the winter of 1974, Mick Fleetwood was in a fix. He'd just cancelled a US tour after his wife, Jenny, had a fling with one of his
bandmates. Now, his manager was putting a new line-up of Fleetwood Mac together without him – and lawyers were circling.

Mick poured out his woes to his father. Retired wing commander
Mike Fleetwood suggested that he go somewhere where nobody
knew who he was. A week later, Fleetwood flew to Lusaka in the
south-east African country of Zambia. Fleetwood planned to visit a
family friend studying at the local university. Really, it was an excuse
to get away from the legal letters and embittered phone calls.

Fleetwood rented a house in town but was soon bored. On a
whim, he caught a bush plane to the national park and checked into
a hunting lodge on an out-of-season game reserve. He was one of
just three guests and a couple of safari guides.

Fleetwood had plenty of time to gather his thoughts. At night,
guests and guides alike sat together drinking the local grog while
Fleetwood drummed on a pile of tin cans or any other percussive
object he could find. He was miles from civilisation and cut off from
his family and his bandmates. But he quickly discovered how insig-
nificant he was in his new surroundings.

After wandering too far into the bush alone, he realised that the
vultures circling overhead were like his manager's lawyers back at

139

home: they were waiting for him to give up and die. On another occasion, he watched a bull elephant charge a group of disrespectful tourists who'd wandered too close. One night, Fleetwood heard low, heavy breathing outside the door of his lodge. He lay in bed, too scared to move, until whatever he'd heard disappeared into the night. The following day, Fleetwood discovered that he'd been visited by an elderly lion cast out by the pride, who now roamed the bush alone. 'I felt some empathy for the beast,' he said later, 'as I too felt cast out into the wilderness.'

It was time to go home. Fleetwood caught the next plane to Lusaka to find a telegram from Jenny asking him to return. 'Something in my soul felt cleansed,' he said. 'I felt recharged and better prepared for the battles awaiting me just over the horizon.'

Fleetwood reconciled with his wife and reassembled the band. The legacy of his trip was a life-long love affair with Africa. He later visited Ghana, where he recorded local musicians and made his first solo album. The journey to Zambia was the turning point, though. After that, Fleetwood would never let anyone or anything get between him and his beloved Fleetwood Mac again. Their future was now assured.

The Great Lost Jam Session

Peter Green and Friends, Autumn 1974

Graham Whyte suspected that this wasn't going to be an ordinary session when he arrived outside Peter Green's house. Whyte, a former road manager for 'All Right Now' hitmakers Free, had been asked to drive Green to a nearby rehearsal studio.

'Peter was sitting on the front lawn when I arrived,' he recalled. 'The front door was open, but he still went in through the window and came back through the same window with his guitar.'

At the time, Fleetwood Mac had moved to the US, and Green was in personal and professional limbo. Meanwhile, Free had broken up and their guitarist Paul Kossoff was looking for a new gig. Which is when Green suggested that the two of them try playing together. Both were talented musicians wrestling with multiple demons, though. In Kossoff's case, a growing drug dependency.

Not that any of this impacted on their great lost jam session in autumn 1974. At least not for an hour. The musical summit took place at a half-built studio in Lots Road, Chelsea, around the corner from where Ian 'Lemmy' Kilmister of future Motörhead fame was squatting. Green and Kossoff were joined by ex-Spooky Tooth drummer Mike Kellie and an unnamed bass guitarist, possibly Kossoff's schoolfriend, Nic Potter of knotty progressive rockers, Van Der Graaf Generator.

The Green/Kossoff love-in made sense on paper. Both were intuitive, emotional players who understood the importance of space and the concept of 'less is more'. The session didn't get off to a good start, though. Green had forgotten to bring a guitar strap, any additional strings or an amp. So, Kosoff leant him his spare instrument and plugged it into a Marshall stack.

All the musicians involved have since passed away, but Kossoff's former tour manager, John Taylor, remembers the night. 'They were on great form, all trading off each other,' he said. 'After a few minutes, Mike Kellie made a sign with his drumstick in the air as if to say, "Is there a tape? Are we recording this?"

'It was weird because it was great and then all of a sudden it just fell apart,' he recalled. 'I tried to lighten the mood and said, "Does anyone want a cup of tea? . . ." But Peter had gone off and was sat on his own in the corner, with his back to everyone. Every time anyone tried to talk to him, he turned his back on them. It was as if he'd just switched off and gone to another place – and that was it.'

A driver was supposed to collect Green after three hours, but Graham Whyte took him home after an hour. Kossoff never heard from Green again. Instead, he began piecing together his next group, Back Street Crawler, and Mike Kellie went on to enjoy some chart success with the new wave group the Only Ones.

Meanwhile, Green climbed back through the metaphorical window and disappeared into the shadows. 'That session was the most sublime thing I ever heard,' said Taylor. 'And then it was gone, over.'

Heroes are Hard to Find

The Almost But Not Quite Great Lost Album

There's something unsettling about the cover of 1974's *Heroes are Hard to Find*. Fleetwood Mac's ninth album shows a topless, skinny-ribbed Mick Fleetwood wearing lace underwear and clasping hands with his young daughter, Amelia. The photograph was taken in front of a three-way mirror, and the knickers belonged to the art director's wife.

The image suited the album, though, which was full of what Fleetwood called 'Bob Welch's kooky songs'. But it would be Welch's final Mac LP and the last of the post-Peter Green, pre-Buckingham Nicks albums.

After firing Bob Weston for his fling with Jenny Fleetwood, the group began 1974 in flux – and when they refused to tour, their manager insisted that he owned the name 'Fleetwood Mac' and put an alternative version of the band on the road. 'So for six months, we did nothing but try and extricate ourselves from the legal mess,' explained Welch.

Welch begged them to move to Los Angeles to help fight the case, but the McVies were reluctant. 'I hated the idea,' said Christine. 'My life was here, my family were here . . .' She finally agreed with the caveat that they only stayed for six months.

Fleetwood Mac arrived in California in April 1974 with $7,200 to their name but unsure if they could legally continue working. They swiftly formed a management company and renegotiated their deal with Warner Bros. Despite a chronic lack of hits, the band shifted enough records to convince Warners to fund another.

Heroes are Hard to Find was recorded at LA's Angel City Sound Studios in just four weeks and the throes of a lawsuit. 'In the middle of recording, we'd get twenty-page letters from our English lawyers which had to be answered immediately,' recalled Welch. 'The situation was nightmarish.'

Welch wanted Fleetwood Mac to make 'modern, no cliché music'. Which Warners probably interpreted as 'no hits'. They succeeded, as the album's lone single, Christine's brass-driven title track, didn't get near the charts. Elsewhere, though, she took their ex-manager to task on 'Bad Loser', while her soft-rock compositions 'Come a Little Bit Closer' and 'Prove Your Love', were like signposts reading, 'This way to *Rumours*'.

Welch's 'kooky songs' dominated the rest, though. Pedal steel ace 'Sneaky' Pete Kleinow helped make 'She's Changing Me' sound like a scuzzier Eagles, and even cracked a smile on the sunny country-rocker 'Silver Heels'. 'If I could sing like Paul McCartney, get funky like Etta James,' he implored.

But most of the time, Welch sounded like his nose was buried in the latest issue of *Fortean Times*. 'Coming Home's phased sound effects and blurred vocals suggested a pharaoh's ghost mumbling inside the Great Pyramid, while 'Bermuda Triangle' balanced its conspiracy-theory lyrics with a great swinging shuffle. Fleetwood's drumming is a high point of the album. He plays like a man trying to forget, presumably, his wife's infidelity and his band's legal nightmares.

Released in September 1974, *Heroes are Hard to Find* gave Fleetwood Mac their first US top-forty LP. But Bob Welch was done after three years in a band whose career resembled M. C. Escher's staircase. 'He'd had enough,' said Fleetwood. 'He didn't think it was going anywhere. But, of course, he didn't know what was coming next.' None of them did.

Part Three

'Look, we're starving to death here'

How a trip to a Laurel Canyon grocery store and dinner and margaritas in a Mexican restaurant stopped Fleetwood Mac from breaking up (again).

Lindsey Buckingham

'I've Always Been the Troublemaker'

'Lindsey takes a song, and treats it like a painting.'

Christine McVie

'I loved him before he was a millionaire. I washed his jeans and embroidered stupid moons and stars on them.'

Stevie Nicks

'We had a couple of run-ins.'

John McVie

'He's brilliant but difficult, God love him.'

Mick Fleetwood

'Extraordinarily talented . . . extraordinarily annoying.'

Ken Caillat

Lindsey Buckingham's Greatest Fleetwood Mac Moments

'Monday Morning'
'I'm So Afraid'
'Second Hand News'

'Never Going Back Again'
'Go Your Own Way'
'I Don't Want to Know'
'What Makes You Think You're the One'
'Walk a Thin Line'
'Tusk'
'Oh Diane'
'Big Love'
'Tango in the Night'
'Family Man'
'Say Goodbye'

A journalist from the *New York Times* once interviewed Lindsey Buckingham and noticed that he was wearing the same ensemble as the previous occasion they'd met: a black V-neck T-shirt and slim-fit jeans. 'As though, like a rock 'n' roll Steve Jobs, he long ago selected an optimal outfit,' they wrote, 'and cleared more space in his mind for what is still his central concern: music.'

During his off-on four-decade relationship with Fleetwood Mac, Buckingham's central concern was always the music. At times, he was their principal writer, arranger and producer. But it wasn't easy for Buckingham or the rest of Fleetwood Mac. God knows, both parties suffered for his art.

Lindsey Adams Buckingham arrived in the world, via Palo Alto, California, on 3 October 1949, and never understood why his parents called him 'Lindsey'. His older brothers were named Jeff and Greg: 'So maybe my mother had some intuition that I was going to be weird.'

Morris and Rutheda Buckingham moved the family to the upper-middle-class San Franciscan town of Atherton. Morris ran a coffee-making plant, and Lindsey initially followed in the footsteps of brother Greg, a 1968 Olympic medal-winning swimmer. There's a photograph of the teenage Lindsey in the Menlo-Atherton High School swim team, modelling a sensible haircut and chiselled abs. However, he also inherited his other brother Jeff's love of rock 'n' roll and learned to play the guitar. Lindsey listened to Elvis, Peter, Paul and Mary, and the Everly Brothers, and by 1966 he was playing bass in the high school's Fritz Rabyne Memorial Band.

One night, Buckingham was singing the Mamas and the Papas' 'California Dreamin' at a school music group, when Stephanie Nicks, a student who'd transferred to Menlo-Atherton for her final year, joined in. 'I thought he was a darling,' Nicks recalled.

But the couple didn't see each other again until months later when the Fritz Rabyne Memorial Band offered Stephanie a job. It was 1968, the group had embraced psychedelia and abbreviated their name to Fritz. Buckingham and Nicks were team players but weren't romantically involved. She sang; he sang and played bass, and the songs were written by their keyboard player.

'It was a lot of folk and acid rock,' recalled Buckingham. 'We were a fairly popular band in the Bay area, and we latched on to a guy who was at Stanford University and booking gigs on campus. He did us favours by getting us opening slots for Jimi Hendrix, Janis Joplin and the Moody Blues.'

In 1971, producer Keith Olsen brought Fritz to LA's Sound City studio to make a demo, but the group were falling apart. Olsen was struck by the combination of Buckingham and Nicks' voices and chemistry, and suggested that they leave the band and move to LA.

After receiving a family inheritance, Buckingham bought a car, a guitar and an Ampex reel-to-reel tape recorder, and started writing songs. But the LA move was put on hold when he contracted glandular fever and was forced to stay home for several months.

The enforced rest gave him time to practise the guitar, inspired by the British folkie Cat Stevens, and Jimmy Page's acoustic playing on those early Led Zeppelin albums. 'That finger-picking technique had been dormant in Fritz,' said Buckingham. 'I had to re-tool my whole approach.'

Lying on his back in bed, Buckingham learned to play the bass part with his thumb on the lower strings while using his fingers to pick out the melody on the higher strings. It was Elvis's guitarist Scotty Moore meets bluegrass banjo players meets country picker

Chet Atkins, and a distinctive style that Buckingham later brought to Fleetwood Mac.

Once Buckingham had recuperated, the couple finally moved into Olsen's place in Coldwater Canyon, and were soon demoing songs that would appear on later Fleetwood Mac albums. But every record company and manager passed on the boy-girl duo, Buckingham Nicks. Carole King's producer and label boss Lou Adler apparently listened to half a song before turning the tape off and saying 'no'.

Neither Buckingham nor Nicks wanted to go home and admit defeat. Instead, they found a new apartment with Sound City's young engineer Richard Dashut and scavenged free studio time after hours.

They did what it took to get by. Accompanied by Nicks' future solo band guitarist, Robert 'Waddy' Wachtel, they played Dolly Parton songs and other country tearjerkers in clubs around LA and bounced cheques at the House of Pancakes restaurant when the money ran out.

It was also a chauvinistic setup. Buckingham and Dashut stayed at home, smoking weed and writing music, while Stevie waited on tables. Then, finally, somebody said 'yes'.

Buckingham Nicks landed a contract with the independent Anthem Records, and a distribution deal with Polydor. They spent six months recording their debut at Sound City, with some of LA's top session musicians, among them Elvis's bass player Jerry Scheff and drummer Ronnie Tutt.

Released in September 1973, *Buckingham Nicks* was a fine folk pop-rock record, some of which sounded like Fleetwood Mac-in-waiting. The group later re-recorded 'Crystal' and used part of 'Lola (My Love)' in 'The Chain'. The Buckingham Nicks group took the album out on the road, but reviews were poor, and it failed to sell. The Anthem/Polydor contract lasted until the winter of 1974 before the duo were let go.

Olsen allowed them to use Sound City during downtime until they found another deal. Buckingham was determined to carry on, but Nicks wavered. The pressure of being in a romantic and working relationship was stifling. 'I couldn't support Lindsey when he'd had a bad day in the studio, because I had been there too,' she said.

The story of how Mick Fleetwood met the pair by chance at Sound City has become folklore. Likewise, Stevie telling interviewers Buckingham didn't want to join Fleetwood Mac.

'I hesitated,' he admitted, 'because I wasn't sure what the band was anymore. They'd gone from incarnation to incarnation. What they needed was someone who had a vision, and take them places, which they hadn't had since Peter Green. Danny Kirwan was a wonderful writer and player but he was not a big-picture guy. I came in as a conceptualist – and that's what they needed.'

Imagine the culture clash when twenty-five-year-old Californian Lindsey Buckingham arrived in Fleetwood Mac. Buckingham drove them all crazy, but probably John McVie the most. McVie was barely thirty, but middle-aged in '70s pop years. While Lindsey was impressing Stephanie with 'California Dreamin' at a high-school music club, John was playing the blues alongside 'Harold the Dildo'.

Not that Buckingham let his age or inexperience interfere with his mission. 'Part and parcel of having an idea is how someone should play bass,' he explained. 'I had so many ideas and so much energy I wanted to get the band to a different place.'

There were disagreements and compromises on both sides: McVie quickly took Buckingham aside and reminded him *he* was the Mac in Fleetwood Mac, and Lindsey stopped playing his Fender Strat because it jarred with Christine's piano. But he moved the band forwards. The difference between 1974's *Heroes are Hard to Find* and the following year's *Fleetwood Mac*, aka the '*White Album*', was like night and day.

It helped that the new kids arrived with 'Monday Morning', 'I'm So Afraid', 'Rhiannon' and 'Landslide'. But Buckingham also unintentionally helped empower Christine, who composed the LP's first single, 'Over My Head', as a cautious homage to her pushy new bandmate.

On tour, Fleetwood Mac sold the new album hard, but still had to perform the old stuff. The 2017 deluxe edition of the '*White Album*' includes Buckingham singing 'The Green Manalishi . . .' and his predecessor Bob Welch's 'Hypnotized', live in Connecticut. 'I felt like I was in a covers band,' he grumbled. 'I wasn't doing me, I was doing the history of Fleetwood Mac.'

However, albums that sell 10 million copies worldwide in a month re-write history, and everything changed after *Rumours*. Buckingham and Nicks' relationship disintegrated, encouraged, said Lindsey, by Christine leaving John: 'I won't go as far as to say they created a wedge between us. But there was the interplay between band members that acted as a catalyst.'

Buckingham's *Rumours* songs were more closely linked to Fleetwood Mac's past than history suggests. 'Second Hand News', 'Never Going Back Again' and 'Go Your Own Way' were his version of the blues – just more uptight, jittery and hurt sounding.

'But I still had to see Stevie every day and never got a chance to get any closure. I still had to try to do the right thing for her and, in some ironic sense, help her to move away. We were also aware there was this calling – this destiny – that we needed to fulfil. What was going on with one's personal life was secondary to that calling.' Or as Christine put it: 'The band had a responsibility not to break that up for anything as trivial as a divorce.'

However, Buckingham hasn't given an interview since 1977 in which the writer hasn't mentioned his ex-girlfriend. He can't escape their past and shared history. He still *really* cares about the music too. Speaking in 2012, Buckingham laughed about his younger self calling up the Los Angeles radio DJ, B. Mitchel Reed, after he'd dismissed their new single, 'Go Your Own Way', on air.

But one can imagine the 1976-vintage Lindsey, scowling under his afro, the phone jammed to his ear, interrogating Reed: 'What don't you like about it?' It was Mick Fleetwood's drumming, apparently. With *Rumours* having now sold more than 40 million copies, who cares? Buckingham does.

Also, while Lindsey had the studio Midas touch, Stevie became the group's frontperson. On stage, it was all about her. Buckingham disliked Nicks' whirling-dervish routine during 'Rhiannon' but learned to accept it: 'This thing is bigger than all of us.'

After *Rumours*, everybody compromised for Lindsey, too. He was listening to new music by the Clash and Elvis Costello, chopped off his long hair as part of a musical and stylistic makeover, and filled their next album, *Tusk*, with songs that sounded nothing like *Rumours*. *Tusk* was Lindsey's Trojan Horse: especially when he sequenced one of his 'rockabilly on acid' numbers straight after one of Christine's or Stevie's ballads.

This musical *volte-face* drove his collaborators to distraction. But Buckingham took a perverse pleasure in doing the unexpected. He shocked the others by arriving for the first night of the *Tusk* tour wearing black eyeliner and an Armani suit. Mick Fleetwood was so shocked that he dropped his bottle cap of cocaine on the tuning room floor. Christine apparently tottered over, peered into Buckingham's eyes and roared, '*Christ!* Are you wearing make-up?'

Buckingham became the scapegoat when *Tusk* sold less than *Rumours*. Ultimately, though, it saved the band. Without Lindsey subverting from the inside, *Tusk* would have been to Fleetwood Mac what *The Long Run* was to the Eagles after *Hotel California*: a cop-out. Instead, it cued them up for the 1980s.

In the meantime, he had to watch Stevie have relationships with the Eagles' singing, songwriting drummer Don Henley and their guitarist, Joe Walsh. 'Being in this band fucks up relationships with chicks,' he complained in 1977. 'Since Stevie, I have found that to be true. I could meet someone that I really like, have maybe a few days to get it together and that's it. The rest of the time I'm too into Fleetwood Mac.'

Studio assistant-turned-costume designer Carol Ann Harris became Buckingham's partner after *Rumours* and witnessed his obsessiveness. 'He entered into another world where nothing mattered but the music,' she complained.

153

'You have to allow yourself to get drawn into the music,' explained Buckingham. 'I'd come out of a basement studio after six hours, and Carol would be sitting in the living room watching TV, and I just wouldn't have much to say. My mind would be racing.'

Buckingham's 1981 solo debut, *Law and Order*, included the US top-ten hit, 'Trouble', but stalled outside the top thirty, while Stevie's debut, *Bella Donna*, reached number one.

'I would have never started making solo albums if it hadn't been for *Tusk*,' he said. 'I've always been the troublemaker in Fleetwood Mac – "Oh God, what's he doing now?" So to indulge that left side of the musical palette, I had to go away and make these records.'

Running parallel to that left side, though, was a deep love of classic pop. Buckingham adored the Everly Brothers, the Beach Boys, and American folkies the Kingston Trio. He's never been shy of a blatant hook or melody either. 'Holiday Road', his theme song for the comedy movie, *National Lampoon's Vacation*, spliced an earworm chorus with the sound of barking dogs. But the record-buying public found him a bit odd and intimidating on his own.

There was less of what Mick Fleetwood called 'Lindsey's weird shit' on the next LP, 1982's *Mirage*. But it demonstrated Buckingham's skill in fine-tuning other people's songs. Both Christine's 'Hold Me' and Stevie's 'Gypsy' would be duller without his guitar solos and electronic squiggles.

After *Mirage*, though, Stevie became a solo star, and Lindsey tried to catch up. It cost him a relationship. 'I'd had to learn how to deal with a tortured genius, a spoiled rock star, a man who could be so generous at one moment and a frightening stranger the next,' wrote Carol Ann Harris in 2007's *Storms: My Life with Lindsey Buckingham and Fleetwood Mac*. Nobody, least of all Buckingham, came out of the book well.

Lindsey dedicated his second solo album, 1984's *Go Insane*, to Carol. The back cover showed him gazing at a naked woman hanging her head in, presumably, shame or despair. When Harris heard the album, she said she felt violated.

Go Insane failed to reach the US top fifty, but some of the songs might have been hits if they'd been Fleetwood Mac. As if to prove the point, Buckingham donated his next batch of solo works to 1987's hit *Tango in the Night* but left the band straight after.

He then spent five years re-acclimatising before releasing *Out of the Cradle*. Songs such as 'Soul Drifter' and 'You Do or You Don't' were superior to anything Fleetwood Mac managed in his absence, while 'Wrong' attacked Mick Fleetwood for his memoir, *Fleetwood: My Life and Adventures in Fleetwood Mac*. 'Mick was always trying to do things that would bring in some income,' grumbled Buckingham. 'As much as I loved Mick and I still love Mick, I couldn't love that part of him.'

However, *Out of the Cradle* flopped, and there was now something of Shakespeare's Henry V about Buckingham's solo ventures: 'We few, we happy few . . .' etc. 'My solo work is more esoteric,' he admitted. 'You lose nine out of ten listeners because you're disconnecting from their idea of what Fleetwood Mac is.'

No longer in the band, Buckingham was at an airport in North Carolina in 1992 when he met the young actor, Anne Heche. 'I played the game of "Who's the cutest person in the airport?"' she recalled. 'My eyes were gazing when I came upon a guy all in black – black from head to toe. Black was way too mod in these parts. He got my vote – if not for looks, at least originality.'

The couple were together for a year before Anne landed a part in John Frankenheimer's *Against the Wall* and moved on. After which, his life changed in ways he'd never imagined. He married photographer Kristen Messner and started a family at the age of forty-eight. 'I'm glad I waited. I saw a lot of people I knew try to be parents and spouses and rock 'n' rollers and get so screwed up.'

According to Stevie, the arrival of Buckingham's son, William, and daughters, Leelee and Stella, ushered in a new Lindsey Buckingham. For a time, anyway. 'He has two daughters, so he really lives in girl world now,' said Stevie in 2012. 'His house is full of little girls running around and doing ballet. That's good for me too.'

Nevertheless, Stevie and Lindsey picked away at the old wounds on reunion tours and 2003's *Say You Will* reunion album. They'd walk on stage holding hands, cast both doting and angry looks at each other, and behave like two people revisiting an ancient love affair to sell concert tickets.

'We are aware that's part of the appeal, and we're playing off it,' admitted Buckingham. 'But it's also real. Who's to say where the line is, where the show stops and reality starts? We always brought out the voyeur in everyone.'

The documentary *Destiny Rules* captured Fleetwood Mac making *Say You Will* at Buckingham's home studio. It showed Lindsey and Stevie niggling each other over the tenses in one of her songs and having a row about her manager. The pitch of Buckingham's voice became higher and whinier when he was upset or keen to make a point. But the film also showed how far he was prepared to go for the sake of the music. He shocked the others by offering to take fewer royalties if the band would make *Say You Will* a double album and tried to persuade the others to pay for several mixing engineers.

'How much is this gonna cost me?' asked John McVie.

'Er . . . nine grand divided by four,' Buckingham replied.

'That's too much.'

'Okay, we just won't mix your bass parts in.'

'You've done that for years anyway,' McVie laughed.

The record industry was in a post-Napster panic, and Warner Bros didn't want a double album. Also, Buckingham was having a new house built and quietly backed down.

Once again, he'd donated songs intended for a solo LP to Fleetwood Mac. *Say You Will* was a UK and US top-ten hit. Buckingham's next work, *Under the Skin*, wasn't. Neither his *Gift of Screws* nor *Seeds we Sow* troubled the top forty either.

Buckingham now accepted 'the big machine' versus 'the little machine', as he called Fleetwood Mac and his solo career. Publicly he compared himself to the left-field filmmaker Terrence Malick, and Fleetwood Mac to Steven Spielberg. But Fleetwood Mac funded his indulgences.

Inevitably, 2017's *Lindsey Buckingham Christine McVie* collaboration was a bigger hit, because it was a Fleetwood Mac album, minus

Stevie Nicks. But a year later, the band dismissed Buckingham after Nicks issued her 'either he goes or I do' ultimatum.

Buckingham's health and personal life ran into trouble soon after. In February 2019, he suffered a heart attack; a grim reminder that his father, Morris, had died of heart failure and his brother Greg had passed away after a heart attack aged forty-five. Buckingham made a full recovery and released a long-delayed solo album in 2021. *Lindsey Buckingham* was full of gorgeous, literate pop songs many of which predicted the breakdown of his marriage. 'A lot of these songs are celebrating long-term relationships, but doing it in a non-romanticised way,' he said. He and Kristen announced their separation but later reconciled.

Buckingham returned to the fray, usually wearing a black or white V-neck T-shirt, and with a shock of silver hair exploding upwards like David Lynch's Eraserhead meets Marge Simpson. His exit from Fleetwood Mac dominated every interview, and he was amusingly candid. 'In all the time Irving Azoff managed me, he only came to one solo show,' he revealed. 'The only thing he said after was, "The balcony wasn't full."'

The not-full balcony is a metaphor for Buckingham's solo career. He'll always be known for 'Go Your Own Way' rather than any of his solo records. Someone's listening, though. In 2023, 'Holiday Road' and 'I Want You' (from *Go Insane*) showed up in the soundtrack to Disney's dark comedy-drama *The Bear*. They both sounded magnificent.

'Lindsey's all about the music, man,' grumbled John McVie once. He wasn't wrong. Fleetwood Mac wouldn't have become *the* Fleetwood Mac without him.

Buckingham Nicks

*The Inside Story of Lindsey and Stevie's
Pre-Fleetwood Mac Duo*

Keith Olsen (producer): I grew up in Minnesota and played in a band called the Music Machine. We had one hit and a lot of stinkers. So I learned the tools of the trade, started doing independent production and formed my own company. In 1972 an agent asked me to go to San Jose to check out a band called Fritz. They only got me because they'd asked every A, B and C-list producer in town, and they'd all said no. I figured I'd get a free trip for the weekend. Little did I know I'd be picked up by the band in their van and asked to help unload the gear.

Lindsey Buckingham: Fritz were doing okay in Northern California. But that was it. The one thing that came out of that was some interest in Stevie and me – so that set off a light bulb.

Keith Olsen: Fritz's music was pop-rock for the early '70s. But the bass player, Lindsey Buckingham, could really sing, and the female singer, Stephanie [Nicks], had a unique voice. But it was great when they sang together. So I persuaded those two to cut a demo with me at Sound City Studios in LA. I told Lindsey and Stevie they sounded great, and I wanted to work with them but not the rest of the band. That wasn't what Lindsey wanted to hear. So I told them we were at an impasse.

Lindsey Buckingham: I never had an agenda to make it in the business. It was one of those things that was brought to us.

Stevie Nicks: I think there was always something between me and Lindsey, but nobody in that band wanted me as their girlfriend because I was just too ambitious. These guys didn't take me seriously at all. I was just a girl singer, and they hated the fact that I got a lot of credit.

Keith Olsen: Lindsey then proceeded to get mononucleosis and was bedridden for three months. He was so debilitated all he could do was lie there watching daytime TV. This was the '70s when even America only had seven TV channels, and three of them were full of nothing. I recall him telling me he couldn't lift his arm and play bass, so he'd lie there with an acoustic guitar, open his fingers, and try playing. I think that's where Lindsey's 'sound' came from – lying in bed for three months and only being able to play acoustic.

Lindsey Buckingham: I kept going to the doctor's because something was wrong and they didn't know what it was. One day I had this mystery illness and then one day I didn't. But weirdly, it wasn't a bad thing for re-booting one's musical vocabulary.

Stevie Nicks: They said to us, 'Go back to San Francisco and record some songs.' We went back, and Lindsey's dad gave us a room in his coffee plant near the Cow Palace. We'd drive up there at seven at night and leave at three in the morning, and that's how we ended up with the ten songs on the record, and that's how we fell in love.

Keith Olsen: They'd written these songs, 'Frozen Love', 'Races are Run' and 'Crystal'. Lindsey demoed them on the four-track, played them for me, and asked what I thought. After picking my jaw off the floor, I said, 'We can run with this.' So Lindsey and Stevie moved to LA, and into my place for a time. I signed them to my production company, and then they shared an apartment with my second engineer Richard Dashut, but we couldn't get them a record deal.

Stevie Nicks: When we moved there it was lonely. I didn't have any girlfriends, I had to be a waitress and a cleaning lady in order to support us because Lindsey didn't want to play four sets a night at Chuck's Steakhouse, where we could have made $500 a week. To him that was selling out. He wanted to play original music, so we went along with that.

Keith Olsen: Stevie had so little, I offered her $35 – which was all I could afford – to clean my house. She'd show up in the morning with a scarf around her head, looking like [the American comic actor] Carol Burnett, who used to play a cleaner on a TV show. Stevie did an excellent job.

Stevie Nicks: We were broke. One day, I came home with my big Hoover vacuum cleaner, my Ajax, my toilet brush, my cleaning shoes on, and Lindsey has managed to have some idiot send him eleven ounces of opiated hash, and he and his friends are in a circle on the floor.

Keith Olsen: I eventually got us enough money to make an album. We made *Buckingham Nicks* as cheaply as possible, stretching and scrimping so the three of us could make $5,000 each.

Stevie Nicks: I'm actually quite prudish. So when they suggested they shoot Lindsey and me nude for the cover, I could not have been more terrified. Lindsey was like, 'Oh, come on – this is art. Don't be a child!' I thought, 'Who are you? Don't you know me?' I did it because I felt like a rat in a trap.

Lindsey Buckingham: Our record company had no idea what to do with us. They wanted us to play steakhouses.

Stevie Nicks: Lindsey refused to play steakhouses where we could have made some actual money because he didn't want to compromise his *art*.

Keith Olsen: The album came out in September 1973 and didn't take off. It was on Anthem, an imprint of Polydor, who had no faith in anything and didn't spend any money on promotion. Buckingham Nicks went on tour and lost money.

Stevie Nicks: We couldn't even find our album in the record shops, let alone hear it on the radio. Then we were dropped by Polydor after about three months and Lindsey and I were devastated. He went back to writing his angst-laden songs and I went back to being a waitress.

Keith Olsen: In December 1974, Mick Fleetwood was looking for a studio and came to Sound City. To demonstrate the studio, I played him some James Gang and Emitt Rhodes and 'Frozen Love' and 'Django' from the *Buckingham Nicks* record.

Lindsey Buckingham: We were working on songs for a second Buckingham Nicks record and I remember seeing this giant of a man with a beard in the next studio. I didn't know who he was.

Keith Olsen: Mick asked if I wanted to produce the next Fleetwood Mac record. I was a fan, so I jumped at the chance, and he told me we'd be starting on February 1.

Mick Fleetwood: Then I got the bad news that our guitarist Bob Welch was leaving. None of us saw that coming. But a lightbulb had gone off in my head. I remembered the couple I'd seen at Sound City. So I rang up Keith.

Keith Olsen: It was New Year's Eve, and he called me from the airport – 'Keith, I have good and bad news. The bad news is [guitarist] Bob Welch has left, so we won't be starting the new record on February 1. The good news is, you know that thing you played me with the two kids? Do you think the guy would like to join Fleetwood Mac?' I told him Lindsey and Stevie came as a duo – they are inseparable. So Mick said, 'Okay. Can you ask them if they would both like to join Fleetwood Mac?' Stevie and Lindsey were having people over to their apartment on Fairfax [Avenue]. I took my date over there and told them we needed to talk. As an independent producer, you only get three albums a year, so you set aside your time. If Fleetwood Mac's next album was cancelled, a third of my income would be gone. I needed this too.

Lindsey Buckingham: I was hesitant because although the Buckingham Nicks record had not really sold, we were working on material for the second album and things started happening. We'd done some dates opening for Poco in Alabama and Tuscaloosa, and the record was getting played on the radio.

Keith Olsen: I sat down on the ottoman in Stevie and Lindsey's bedroom and, for the next four hours, tried to convince them to join Fleetwood Mac. Lindsey told me he couldn't possibly follow in the footsteps of the great Peter Green. But I kept telling him this was a great opportunity. My date was about to leave with somebody else when Lindsey finally agreed.

Stevie Nicks: I said to Lindsey, 'We're destitute! We are joining Fleetwood Mac.'

Keith Olsen: Lindsey said, 'Okay, we'll try it for four weeks, and see what happens.'

Lindsey Buckingham: It was bizarre because someone in Birmingham, Alabama, called and asked if Buckingham Nicks

162

would headline a show there. So we went to Birmingham and discovered we'd sold out an auditorium. It just blew our minds because we couldn't get a gig at a club in LA. And here we were, with six thousand people, going nuts. Buckingham Nicks played three dates out there, and then announced we were joining Fleetwood Mac and everybody went, 'You're doing *whaaaat?!*'

Stevie Nicks

'Does Everybody Know Who I Am?
I'm a Rock Star'

'Stevie was always more ambitious than I was.'

Lindsey Buckingham

'The first time I heard her sing, I thought, "Oh shit, this is great."'

John McVie

'Stevie never stops. I'm worried she's turning into Édith Piaf.'

Mick Fleetwood

'All Stevie's songs are like babies to her, even though some of them are rubbish.'

Christine McVie

Stevie Nicks' Greatest Fleetwood Mac Moments

'Rhiannon'
'Crystal'
'Landslide'
'Dreams'
'I Don't Want to Know'
'Gold Dust Woman'

'Silver Springs'
'Sara'
'Storms'
'Beautiful Child'
'Gypsy'
'Seven Wonders'
'Illume (9-11)'
'Without You'

The inaugural Night of a Thousand Stevies fan event took place in 1992 at Jackie 60, a club in the meatpacking district of Manhattan. The venue was filled with Stevie Nicks lookalikes, as drag performers and audience members in lace shawls, platinum wigs and suede heels, paid homage to their queen with 'Stand Back', 'Edge of Seventeen' and other hits. A year later, they did it all over again.

Today, Night of a Thousand Stevies is a bi-annual fancy-dress ball held in New York and New Orleans. According to its co-founder Chi Chi Valenti, the celebration attracts every demographic from seventeen to seventy-year-olds, like 'a Noah's Arc of Stevie love'.

It's also a sharp reminder that Stevie Nicks is bigger than Fleetwood Mac. At the time of writing, her latest tour was scheduled to continue past her seventy-sixth birthday, including a summer 2024 headline show at London's Hyde Park. Then again, Stevie Nicks has been on the road forever.

In one childhood anecdote, her grandfather, struggling country singer 'AJ' Nicks, dressed five-year-old Stevie in a cowgirl outfit and took her with him all over Arizona's saloon and gin-house circuit. The double act stopped when Stevie's parents, Jess and Barbara, intervened. In another version of the story, 'AJ' and Stevie never went beyond singing duets to the family at home.

Stevie later named *The Little Mermaid* and *Beauty and the Beast* as two of her favourite fairy tales. 'I'm like your romantic fiction writer,' she explained. 'I flower things. I toss a gardenia in here and a rose in there.'

This much is true. Stephanie Lynn Nicks was born in Phoenix, Arizona, on 26 May 1948, and thinks being a Gemini empowered her as a songwriter, due to her 'two opposing personalities'. The nickname 'Stevie' came from her inability to pronounce 'Stephanie' as a toddler.

Stevie's father, former chief naval warrant officer Jess Nicks, was a senior manager for Lucky Lager and deodorant soap manufacturer, Armour-Dial. The family followed him from city to city, from Albuquerque to El Paso to Salt Lake City and beyond, as he rose through the corporate ranks to become vice president of the Greyhound bus company.

The singer and her younger brother, Christopher, had unsettled childhoods. 'When we transferred from El Paso to Salt Lake City I was pretty bummed,' Stevie recalled. 'We'd been in Texas for five years and I'd settled in. I remember my mom saying, "You better learn how to make friends fast. Open up a bit – you're too much in your own world." I was singing all the time to the radio, to the Ronettes, the Beach Boys, the Shangri-Las, anybody and everybody.'

'Stevie's dad was willing to uproot his family over and over,' said Lindsey, decades later. 'I think that affected her on some level. It taught her how to make a splash.'

Apparently, Stevie trailered an early version of her '70s-era stage outfit, aged ten. 'I did a tap dance to Buddy Holly's "Everyday" with my friend Colleen,' she recalled. 'Black top hat, black hat, a black vest and skirt, a white blouse, black tights and black tap shoes with little heels. That was my "Rhiannon" outfit in the fourth grade. I had the look even then.'

After moving to Arcadia, California, Stevie learned to play the guitar and joined a school folk group. She also wrote her first song, 'I've Loved and I've Lost', a country tearjerker about her boyfriend who left her for her friend after just one date.

She'd get over the rejection soon enough, when Jess uprooted his family again, this time to San Mateo, California. Seventeen-year-old Stevie's first meeting with Lindsey Buckingham lasted all of three minutes. She'd just enrolled at his *alma mater*, Menlo-Atherton High

School, and they both attended an after-school music club. 'It wasn't any big deal,' she said. 'He was singing "California Dreamin'" and I joined in.'

By the summer of 1968, both Lindsey and Stevie were attending San Jose State University. She was studying speech therapy and planning to become a teacher, when they ended up in the same local band, apprentice acid-rockers Fritz.

'I knew that I was "Stevie Nicks" after about three weeks of being in Fritz,' she claimed. 'I would stroll through San Jose State with my guitar case, thinking, *Does everybody know who I am? I'm a rock star.* I felt it and I believed it.'

Stevie learned her stagecraft by supporting Hendrix, Santana, Moby Grape and Creedence Clearwater Revival. When Fritz played the Stanford Frost Theatre, she saw the headline act Janis Joplin – 'all red-and-purple feathers in her hair and silky bell-bottoms' – tear into the second-on-the-bill act for running over time: 'She screamed, "Get off my fucking stage right now or I'll kill you!" She was this magnificent little person with this huge attitude.'

In another possible fairy tale, Jimi Hendrix shyly dedicated 'Angel' to Stevie after spotting her side-stage at the Santa Clara County Fairground. She was impressed by his white-fringed jacket and head scarf: 'So from Jimi, I got flamboyance and humility, and from Janis, I learned that to make it as a female musician in a man's world is going to be tough. I decided to be somewhere between Janis and Jimi.'

However, Fritz operated what she called a 'hands-off Stevie policy', forbidding any of them from asking her out. 'So it had a long time to fester with Lindsey,' she said. 'He had a girlfriend for five years and I had been with someone since 1966. We were both in serious relationships.'

Then Lindsey and Stevie split from Fritz in 1971. Producer Keith Olsen saw their potential as a folky, boy-girl duo, and invited them to LA. The couple also fell in love. Those who saw them at the Troubadour and other clubs were struck by the pair's sense of purpose; by Lindsey's intensity and Stevie's unwavering gaze.

Really, Stevie gazed unwaveringly because she was too vain to wear her glasses.

The duo might have exuded confidence, but they couldn't get a record deal. 'It was a terrible time,' reflected Stevie. 'It was like, "We don't belong here, *nobody* understands us."'

Keith Olsen understood, but Stevie tested his patience. One weekend, Olsen went to New York for work and left her the keys to his Corvette Stingray. Stevie parked the vehicle on the steep hill outside his house but forgot to apply the handbrake. She went to bed, as the Corvette rolled backwards over the edge of the cliff and landed in the building below. Incredibly, nobody was hurt.

Stevie indulged Lindsey's art and then some. He didn't want Buckingham Nicks to compromise and become a top-forty covers band, even if it paid the bills. So, Stevie worked at the Copper Penny coffee house on Sunset and La Brea, and Lindsey stayed at home composing songs. Then she came home and wrote what became 'Rhiannon', 'Gold Dust Woman' and 'Landslide'.

Stevie claimed the failure of 1973's *Buckingham Nicks* album had one upside. She'd reluctantly taken her blouse off for the cover picture, then hidden the sleeve from her family for weeks: 'I said, "Daddy, I didn't feel like I had a choice – I'm so sorry." He said, "Okay, move on. But you always have a choice." I learned a big lesson.'

Barbara Nicks offered more advice. 'You will never stand in a room full of men and feel like you can't keep up with them,' she told her daughter. 'And you will never depend upon a man to support you.'

Stevie's songs about heartache and magic were always tempered by a strong commercial nous. Stevie pushed Lindsey into joining Fleetwood Mac for the money too. Mick Fleetwood was driving a Cadillac, while the couple's Toyota was running on fumes. Yet she carried on waitressing even while making the '*White Album*': 'I was thinking, "What if this doesn't work?" I just wanted to make sure that when we joined Fleetwood Mac, we didn't burn our bridges.'

It worked better than either of them could have imagined. 'Before Lindsey and I joined Fleetwood Mac, we had to steal ourselves not to go into stores,' recalled Nicks. 'Six months later we were earning $400 a week each and I was totally famous. We used to pin $100 bills up on the walls of our apartment just for fun.' Now, when Fleetwood Mac came to London, Stevie swept through Antiquarius on the King's Road, buying up as much vintage lace as she could afford, and probably more.

However, success spelt the end of Stevie and Lindsey as a couple. 'When you break up with someone, you don't want to see him,' she said. 'You especially don't want to see him the next morning, all day, all night and all day after . . . I think there's a part of Lindsey that thinks if we hadn't joined Fleetwood Mac, Buckingham Nicks would have had some success and we'd have got married and had kids. Maybe, but it wasn't to be.'

Instead, she and Christine McVie become like blood sisters and swore never to let 'the boys' tell them what to do. It was the '70s, when a headline act's manager once shouted, 'Get those broads off the stage!' at them. Christine had proved herself and more with Fleetwood Mac. But Stevie was five years younger and aware that Mick Fleetwood had taken her as part of a package deal with Buckingham.

'I fell madly in love with all of them even though I knew they didn't really need me,' she said in 1976. 'Christine very willingly gave me the stage, which I thought was very cool, for a woman to say, "Oh, I've worked for ten years on the road, killed myself, and here she is our new frontwoman." There's not another band in the world that has two lead women singers, and two lead women writers. That was my world mission.'

Stevie's version of Fleetwood Mac was a long way from the blues, but she identified with what she called 'the haunted castles' in their early songs. 'Not witchery, not the occult, not turning to toads or anything like that, just a freedom to be mystical,' she explained.

This captured their audience's imagination too. It was the era of the Stones, the Who and Led Zeppelin. Stevie singing about a Welsh witch and spinning around in a blur of hair and chiffon was the closest Fleetwood Mac had to a showboating Jagger, Daltrey or Plant.

'I don't sing,' she half-joked. 'I scream and crash the tambourine on my leg and dance around a lot.' But within a year of her joining, young women wearing variations on the fourth-grade 'Rhiannon' outfit started appearing in the audience.

It was harder in the studio, though. Stevie didn't play an instrument as proficiently as the others. 'So I used to sit there and read, crochet or draw,' she recalled. 'And I would make my little suggestions, like a wingman.'

She also composed so many songs, of frankly variable quality, that it became an in-joke. Christine would glide through the studio, spot Stevie plinking away on the Fender Rhodes and declare, 'Oh my *God*, she'd writing another one!' Stevie drove Lindsey half mad mixing up her tenses in the lyrics or ignoring conventional metre. But out of this came 'Dreams', 'Silver Springs', 'Sara', 'Gypsy'.

In the end, Stevie had so many songs that she made a solo record. Stevie formed Modern Records with former Bearsville Records president Paul Fishkin and ex-Led Zeppelin PR Danny Goldberg and released 1981's *Bella Donna*. It became a US number-one hit, which wasn't what anyone in Fleetwood Mac expected.

'Stevie's always been a little hard for me to take seriously,' confessed Buckingham at the time. 'But there's something emotional that gets through, and her voice is so recognisable. I've been listening to Stevie sing for years and when you're that close to it it's easy to overlook certain aspects of anything.'

'The band weren't that impressed,' suggested Stevie. 'I'd told them, "I swear to God I'm not leaving ever." But when I signed my solo deal, I started this whirlwind thing of being able to flit between two worlds, and on it went.'

The mangled tenses and quavering register didn't matter here. Audiences warmed to solo Stevie. *Rock* magazine in the US cringingly anointed her 'Sexiest Woman in Rock', but her image was never overtly sexual.

'I kind of draped it all in chiffon and soft lights and suede boots,' she joked. 'Personally, I think being mysterious works better, and it lasts longer, because, no matter how cute you are or how sexy you are, in fifteen years, that won't be the most important part of your music. I knew that in my twenties.'

Stevie was like an Emily Brontë heroine for the MTV generation, all spun candyfloss hair, lace wedding dress and witchy cape. Her greatest songs usually sounded like she was singing them while fleeing a Gothic castle. Stevie was thirty-two when 'Edge of Seventeen' became a hit, but she tapped into the adolescent mindset, where everything was life and death and nothing in between.

She was funny too, whether she meant to be or not. The ridiculous video for her solo hit, 'If Anyone Falls in Love', had Stevie and her backing singers riding a fairground waltzer and Mick Fleetwood walking her up the aisle in a monk's cowl. 'I have an English sense of humour,' she once said. 'Because I am used to being around English people.'

However, according to Christine, it took time for Stevie and Lindsey to acclimatise to the humour: 'There is a darkness to it, which the Americans never quite got. But they twigged in the end.'

The insecurity lingered, too. Stevie trailed around after her 'Stop Draggin' My Heart Around' duet partner, Tom Petty, like a doting superfan, and told everyone she was in awe of her boyfriend Don Henley's songwriting. She needed validation from musicians outside of Fleetwood Mac, especially ones that weren't Lindsey Buckingham.

'When you work with somebody who is that much in control and who has always been that much in control, you forget that you're even capable of doing something yourself,' she said.

Things became serious when her second solo album, 1983's *The Wild Heart*, followed *Bella Donna* into the US top five. 'I'm the baby of Fleetwood Mac,' she said at the time. 'A very old baby, but it's hard for them to watch me do anything because everybody in Fleetwood Mac, including me, is possessive and jealous.'

The money poured in, and after watching ex-boyfriend Don Henley ordering Learjets like they were taxis, Stevie knew how to spend it. She acquired a hillside apartment with ocean views in the Pacific Palisades and a huge house in Phoenix. One morning, she phoned her business manager and asked them to buy her the rose-coloured Porsche she'd seen in the Tom Cruise movie, *Risky Business*. Not one like it, but the same one.

However, while Stevie's career flourished, her private life floundered. She and Mick Fleetwood found some semblance of normality after their affair. But relationships with Don Henley and her producers Jimmy Iovine and Rupert Hine proved impossible to sustain. The music and the band always came first.

Then, in January 1983, Stevie shocked her family and bandmates by marrying her best friend's widower. Speech therapist Robin Snyder Anderson had died of leukaemia, three days after giving birth to a son, Matthew. 'I just went insane and so did her husband Kim,' said Stevie. 'We were the only two who could understand the depth of the grief. I was determined to take care of their baby.'

Christine claimed she knew the relationship wouldn't survive and refused to buy the couple a wedding present. The marriage lasted just three months before both parties realised their mistake. But it was Nicks' subsequent relationship with ex-Eagles guitarist Joe Walsh that left a deeper impression.

When the couple started seeing each other in 1983, Walsh was still mourning the death of his daughter in a car accident, and obliterating himself with cocaine. Stevie's lifestyle was similarly excessive, and Walsh ended the relationship, convinced they were killing themselves and each other. Walsh cut her dead, and Stevie still describes him 'as the love of my life'.

Buckingham Nicks' former mentor and 'White Album' producer, Keith Olsen, oversaw Stevie's third LP, 1986's *Rock a Little*, but the rot was setting in. Stevie was taking so much cocaine she couldn't sing in tune, and she winced when she saw the final edit of her next video, 'I Can't Wait': 'I thought, "Could you have laid off the pot, the coke and the tequila?" I wanted to climb into the video and stab myself.'

That year, Stevie checked into the Betty Ford Center, where she saw country star Tammy Wynette drifting around the corridors in the grip of a painkiller addiction. It was a glimpse into her future, and Stevie was barely there for the making of Fleetwood Mac's next album, *Tango in the Night*.

It was the Lindsey and Christine show instead, and 'Seven Wonders' aside, Stevie's songs weren't hits. On the eve of their next world tour, Buckingham announced that he was leaving and Nicks chased him around Christine's house in a blind rage.

Fleetwood Mac could still play arenas without Buckingham, but not without Nicks. However, there were times when she looked like she was sleepwalking through the set. Stevie had recently befriended Ann and Nancy Wilson from the Canadian hard rock group Heart. She called them 'fellow outsiders', as the Wilson sisters had experienced the same macho bullshit that she had. Heart had been on the road since the early '70s when one promoter described them as 'Led Zeppelin with tits'.

'Stevie Nicks became our best friend,' recalled Nancy. 'She came to one of our shows and became part of our entourage.' The Wilsons once spent a night at Stevie's house in Phoenix, drinking Courvoisier, snorting coke, and trying on her clothes. 'The closets were full of millions of shawls and coloured tights wedged into teeny drawers.'

But they couldn't keep up with the host. The sisters watched as Stevie came down by swallowing a powerful sedative, which sent her spiralling into the land of nod.

A psychiatrist, whom Stevie later referred to only as 'Doctor Fuckhead', had prescribed her the sedative Klonopin to combat anxiety and sleeplessness. 'It was like a horse tranquiliser,' she said. 'I just stayed in my house, watched TV and drew. It calmed me down, but all my crazy Stevie Nicksness just fell away.'

Stevie's Klonopin addiction lasted eight years and had devastating consequences. She quit Fleetwood Mac, undertook a four-month world tour of which she has no memory, and recorded 'Sometimes it's a Bitch', a bombastic duet with Jon Bon Jovi, whom she told interviewers had a wonderful-looking bottom. 'Stevie was away with the fairies for a while,' said Christine. 'They definitely moved in.'

One evening in December 1993, while hosting a baby shower for a friend, Stevie passed out and narrowly missed landing on an open fire. She was now taking up to eight doses of Klonopin a day: 'And if I went without it, I'd start to shake.'

In January 1994, Stevie checked into a rehab facility in Venice Beach and went cold turkey. She claimed her hair turned grey in the process but she felt reborn after the forty-seven-day detox. She also realised how creatively spent she'd been when she listened to her latest album, *Street Angel*. 'I knew it was terrible,' she admitted. 'But I had to go and do interviews and it was all I could do not to say, "I hate this record."'

While she'd beaten her addiction, she faced new challenges on the road. 'Something Mick Jagger doesn't have to worry about is touring when you're in the middle of menopause,' she revealed. 'When you're sweating from the top of your scalp to your toes.' Stevie went on a health kick: she adopted the Atkins diet, curbed her sixty-a-day cigarette habit and had her leaking silicone breast implants removed.

Creatively, Fleetwood Mac's 1997 reunion came at the ideal time. Emotionally, it meant confronting her past love affair, but with two major differences. Stevie was sober and Buckingham was about to have the first of three children with his new wife, Kristen Messner.

In interviews, Stevie put a heady romantic spin on their story. 'He is my love. My first love and my love for all time. But we can't ever be together,' she told *Mojo* magazine. 'The way he is with his children just knocks me out. I look at him now and just go, "Oh, *Stevie*, you made a mistake."'

Nicks never followed Buckingham down that path, though. Like Christine McVie, she chose not to have children. 'There's just no way that I could have had a child then, working as hard as we worked constantly. And there were a lot of drugs.'

Later, after breaking her Klonopin addiction, she wondered if life could have been different: 'I look back and think, "*What could I have done during that time?*" I *could* have gotten married or had a baby or adopted one.'

Stevie's solo albums now arrived less frequently but she survived the passage of time and the passing of trends by just being Stevie Nicks. Her songs were still dreamily romantic and absurdly melodramatic, and she still wore the lace shawls and the platform heels. She was also a source of fabulous stories, and happy to 'toss a gardenia or a rose in' to make them even more fabulous.

Stevie told journalists that she carried her grandmother 'Crazy' Alice's ashes with her at all times; insisted her mother's ghost once chastised her for drinking Gatorade; revealed that she kept her collection of stage feathers and shawls in a temperature-controlled storage unit; complained that Botox 'made her look like Satan's angry daughter'; and claimed a mystic told her she'd been a world-famous concert pianist *and* an ancient Egyptian princess in two of her past lives.

Those '70s kids who'd grown up with Fleetwood Mac and were now making music treated her like a queen. Hole vocalist Courtney Love interviewed her for *Spin* in 1997 and was so effusive that even Stevie was taken back.

'You had such great hair, you still do, and back then rock divas didn't have high-end colourists,' gushed Courtney, while sipping coffee out of Stevie's Betty Ford-branded mug. Courtney asked her why she didn't sing more 'big sexy love ballads for men'. Stevie told her she didn't even write about sex in her diary. Courtney suggested if Stevie's diaries were ever printed, 'empires would fall' and asked if Don Henley was sexy. 'Very sexy,' confirmed Stevie.

Modern-day artists including Adele, Haim, Harry Styles, Dave Grohl, the Chicks, Miley Cyrus and Lana Del Rey have queued up to work with Nicks or just kiss the hem of her garment. Stevie and the equally ethereal-sounding Del Rey were a fine match on the 2017 duet, 'Beautiful People Beautiful Problems'. 'Because we're witchy sisters,' claimed the elder sibling.

Meanwhile, the never-ending Buckingham Nicks saga has played out at almost every Fleetwood Mac show since the '90s. During a 2013 date in Las Vegas, Stevie began weeping during hers and Lindsey's duet, 'Say Goodbye'. The audience gasped when they saw the first tear roll down her cheek, and Buckingham looked like he might join her. 'We write these songs and we struggle with them, we cry and we throw them out to you, then you throw them back to us,' she explained.

As touching as it was, it wasn't enough to save them, and the ex-couple's differences derailed Fleetwood Mac for good. Even Christine McVie's death in 2022 couldn't put Buckingham Nicks back together again.

Meanwhile, Night of a Thousand Stevies continues each year with the promise of a visit from the star herself. 'One of these days,' Stevie teased, 'and I'm gonna dress up like me and nobody will know it's me. Then I will saunter up on stage, take off my mask and break into "Edge of Seventeen".'

Then again, she might not. 'I like being a mystery,' she once said. 'There are parts of me that nobody knows about and that nobody will ever know about. Being mysterious is very attractive, and that's where my little world has always been.'

'Landslide'

Heartache and Dangerous Weather Conditions

In the summer of 1974, a penniless Lindsey Buckingham took a job playing guitar in Don Everly's backing group. His and Stevie's album, *Buckingham Nicks*, had tanked and they needed the cash.

Don Everly's keyboard player, fledgling singer-songwriter Warren Zevon, offered Stevie the use of his family's ski lodge in Aspen, Colorado, while they were on tour. Stevie leapt at the chance to get away from Los Angeles, packed up her Toyota and her pet poodle, Ginny, and made the thirteen-hour drive.

Holed up in the lodge, she started writing 'Landslide'. The failure of *Buckingham Nicks* had impacted on the couple's private life, and she expressed mixed emotions in the song. Lines such as 'I saw my reflection in the snow-covered hills' were inspired by her surroundings, but also became a metaphor for the state of her relationship. Should she continue pursuing her music and her demanding boyfriend? Or go back to live with her parents in Phoenix, and re-enrol in college?

Out on the road, Don Everly's new material was greeted with indifference. His supper-club audience wanted to hear the Everly Brothers' hits. Don pulled the tour, and Buckingham arrived at the ski lodge six weeks earlier than planned and in a foul mood. The couple had a screaming row, and he threatened to leave.

'So I told him, "Fine! Take the car and the dog!"' recalled Stevie. So, Lindsey took the Toyota and Ginny and drove home without her.

Stevie's father, Jess Nicks, was the vice president of the Greyhound bus company, and his daughter had a complimentary pass. But when Stevie arrived at the bus station the next day, she discovered that Greyhound had gone on strike. Her parents reluctantly sent her a plane ticket instead.

Stevie had written 'Landslide' for a second Buckingham Nicks LP. Instead, she and Lindsey joined Fleetwood Mac, who recorded it for 1975's self-titled '*White Album*'. By then, the couple's relationship was unravelling, and the lyrics seemed even more poignant.

On Fleetwood Mac's subsequent reunion tours, 'Landslide' became a showcase for the Buckingham Nicks duo. Lindsey stared into the middle distance, fingers gliding over the guitar strings, as his ex-partner rewound the clock to summer 1974, the snow-covered hills, the Toyota, the poodle and the empty Greyhound bus station. As the couple passed through their fifties and into their late sixties, lyrics such as 'Can I handle the seasons of my life?' and 'I'm getting older' resonated even more.

In the intervening years, Fleetwood Mac had gained currency with a younger generation, who'd heard their music as kids. In 1994, grunge-rockers Smashing Pumpkins acknowledged the love with a cover of 'Landslide'. But the song always belonged to its composer.

In March 2023, Stevie performed 'Landslide' during a solo show at Inglewood's SoFi Stadium as a tribute to the late Christine McVie and broke down in tears. Almost fifty years on, the song had acquired another sadder meaning.

'Crystal'

Fleetwood Mac's Most Powerful Song
(According to Mick Fleetwood)

'I saw a girl rehearsing a song in the next room,' recalled Mick Fleetwood. 'I even remember what she was wearing – a long, sort of Indian-y cotton skirt and a little blouse – really pretty.'

This was Fleetwood's first memory of Stevie Nicks. It was 1974 and he was on a spur-of-the-moment visit to Sound City studios in Van Nuys. Fleetwood was looking for somewhere to make a new record and Buckingham and Nicks were working on a second album.

Producer Keith Olsen played Fleetwood some of their previous songs to demonstrate the studio sound. But as Fleetwood has been telling interviewers for almost half a century, it was the songs that grabbed him. '"Crystal" was one of maybe three I heard that day,' he said in 2018. 'That song had so much connective power to our story and so much power in terms of what happened next.'

So much so, that Fleetwood Mac recruited the duo and recorded a version for the following year's '*White Album*'. 'Crystal' was a Stevie composition that used water and mountains as metaphors for an enduring romance. Its first dazzling vocal harmony at 0:50 seconds summated what the pair brought to Fleetwood Mac just as well as any individual song.

Buckingham sang lead on the original 'Crystal' and on Fleetwood Mac's cover. But Stevie recorded a version for the soundtrack to 1998's witchy fantasy, *Practical Magic*, starring Sandra Bullock. It wasn't as good as the original, but it was her song, after all.

In reality, Mick Fleetwood only wanted Lindsey, but these days he credits 'Crystal' as the song that swung it for him.

Why question this version of the story, then? After all, 'Crystal's opening line, 'Do you ever trust your first initial feeling?', could have been written for the serendipitous, superstitious Mick. 'It's a signpost in this band's story,' he says.

The 'White Album'

How to Pluck Victory from the Jaws of Defeat

Fleetwood Mac's future would have been very different had Mick Fleetwood not gone food shopping at the Canyon Country Store in Laurel Canyon one afternoon in December 1974. 'This little rustic hippie supermarket was near our house,' Fleetwood recalled forty years later. 'David Crosby and Mama Cass hung out there, and Jim Morrison used to have a place behind it.'

Fleetwood was carrying a bag of groceries to his car when he ran into someone that he knew from Sound City studio in the San Fernando Valley. In his first memoir, *Fleetwood: My Life and Adventures with Fleetwood Mac*, Mick claimed the man's name was 'Thomas Christian'. In his second memoir, *Then Play On*, he said he 'couldn't for the life of me remember'.

Fleetwood told him that the band was looking for somewhere to record the follow-up to their last LP, *Heroes are Hard to Find*, so the mystery man suggested Sound City. Fleetwood threw his groceries into the back of the car and followed him into the valley.

Sound City was a converted former warehouse close to the Budweiser factory in Van Nuys. Neil Young recorded some of his *After the Gold Rush* album there and was pictured on the inside sleeve, stretched out on the studio couch in his patchwork jeans.

Sound City's in-house producer Keith Olsen gave Fleetwood the grand tour and the hard sell. 'Keith put on two tracks by a duo

181

he'd recorded called Buckingham Nicks,' Fleetwood recalled. 'It was to demonstrate the sound of the studio. But the music made an impact. By coincidence, the two of them were in the studio next door.'

Fleetwood liked Sound City's ambience and immediately hired Olsen to co-produce Fleetwood Mac's next album. Then Bob Welch left the band. 'I already knew he wasn't super-happy,' admitted Fleetwood. 'He had concerns with his marriage, but I also think he was heartbroken about the amount of work we'd done for so little reward.'

The group were devastated, but Fleetwood had another brainwave. 'When Keith played me those Buckingham Nicks songs, the music resonated with me. But it wasn't until Bob quit that I realised how much it resonated. I'd heard something in Lindsey's playing that reminded me of Peter Green. Straight away, I said, "Who are those people? I need to find those people".'

Fleetwood called Olsen on New Year's Eve 1974 asking for the guitarist's number. Olsen impressed on him that Buckingham and Nicks came as a couple. So, at Fleetwood's urging, he convinced the duo to abandon their second album and consider joining an ailing Fleetwood Mac.

Nicks has always loved telling interviewers that 'Mick only wanted Lindsey.' 'The guitar was the first thing I noticed when I heard them,' he confessed. 'But they came together, and I accepted that.'

'I scraped together every dime I could find, went to Tower Records and bought all the Fleetwood Mac records,' said Nicks. 'And I listened to them. Lindsey did not. He listened to the songs that had been hits in England. I told Lindsey that we could add a lot to this band. And Lindsey said, "Well, I think this next Buckingham Nicks record will be great. I don't want to stop our vision . . ."'

'I wouldn't say I had to be persuaded to consider joining Fleetwood Mac,' insisted Buckingham. 'But there was some . . . ambivalence.'

Fleetwood played the *Buckingham Nicks* record to his bandmates: 'They liked what they heard, but Christine had to meet Stevie first because there would have been nothing worse than two women in a band cat-fighting. So we invited them to dinner.'

Buckingham and Nicks could barely afford next month's rent when they met Fleetwood Mac for the first time at El Carmen, a Mexican restaurant on LA's West 3rd Street. 'Listen, Lindsey, we're starving to death here,' said Nicks, 'If we don't like them, we can always leave.'

'Then these two old white Cadillacs with big tail fins pulled up. I immediately thought, well, they're doing better than we are. Mick was dressed beautifully with a fob watch in his vest pocket, John was so handsome, and I adored Christine. As soon as she spoke to me, I said to Lindsey, "We need to join this band."'

Everybody got tipsy on margaritas, and Christine gave the new recruits her seal of approval. The rejuvenated Fleetwood Mac began work on their tenth album in February 1975. 'As soon as we started rehearsing, we found this tremendous chemistry,' said Buckingham. The union of Buckingham, Nicks and Christine's rich harmonies on her new song, 'Say You Love Me', impressed even hard-nosed John McVie.

'Oh, it was magic,' he said. 'When we heard Stevie, Lindsey and Chris singing a cappella, it was like, "Oh shit, this is great."'

However, Buckingham also pointed out that they were 'five people who, on paper, wouldn't necessarily have been in a band together.' Never was a truer word spoken. 'I think John saw me and Stevie coming into the band and thought, "Oh my God, they're turning us into the Eagles,"' he said.

During one recording session, John McVie watched Stevie dancing in her ballet slippers and shawl and turned to Keith Olsen. 'We used to be a blues band,' he grunted. Olsen grinned and said, 'But John, this is a much shorter road to the bank.'

Buckingham admired Peter Green but was bemused by Fleetwood Mac's zigzagging fortunes. Mick Fleetwood was clearly the boss, but Buckingham saw a chance to become their musical leader.

Nicks, meanwhile, wanted a home for her songs and the security of a working band. She'd spent two years waiting on tables and cleaning houses while Buckingham stayed at home smoking dope and being creative.

Stevie and Lindsey's personal relationship had only begun when they'd left their previous group and was now in trouble. But joining Fleetwood Mac forced them to put their differences aside. 'Because things were going way too well to consider a break-up,' she admitted.

The couple brought ready-made songs with them, too. 'Monday Morning', 'Landslide', 'Rhiannon' and a cover of country rockers the Curtis Brothers' 'Blue Letter' had all been earmarked for a second Buckingham Nicks album. Fleetwood Mac would also re-record 'Crystal' from the duo's debut LP.

It was a steep learning curve. Christine watched with admiration and concern as her handsome, opinionated new bandmate tried to assume control. She explored her feelings with a coded message to him on the first single, 'Over My Head'. 'You can take me to paradise,' she sang, 'And then again you can be cold as ice.'

Stevie always claimed that Christine was the only band member that Lindsey would listen to. Together, the pair fashioned the bluesy 'World Turning', which reworked 'The World Keeps on Turning' from Fleetwood Mac's debut.

'I remember getting very upset when I realised he and Christine had written "World Turning",' admitted Stevie. 'I had been with Lindsey all these years, and we had never written a song together.'

McVie's songwriting had flourished with Bob Welch, but Buckingham and Nicks 'made my songs sound the way they should.' 'Sugar Daddy' could have dropped off *Heroes are Hard to Find*, but 'Say You Love Me' was the blueprint for all those Christine McVie hits driven by what she called 'that left-hand boogie bass thing' (see 'Don't Stop', 'You Make Loving Fun', 'Love in Store', 'Everywhere').

Stevie's songs were similarly assured. 'Landslide' was thoughtful and sad, with lyrics older than its writer's twenty-six years. Nicks had composed it a year before when Buckingham was touring in

Don Everly's band. But it was 'Rhiannon' that would become her statement song.

Listening to Fleetwood Mac's previous albums, Stevie spotted a common thread: mysticism. She traced a line from 'Oh Well' to 'Woman of 1000 Years' to 'Future Games' and now on to her own 'Rhiannon', about the Welsh witch in author Mary Bartlet Leader's *Triad: A Novel of the Supernatural*.

Buckingham closed the album with the ominous-sounding 'I'm So Afraid', which signposted the sadness to come. The group's two romantic relationships were already unravelling, as examined in excoriating detail on 1977's *Rumours*. In the meantime, this was the sound of the band enjoying a fleeting honeymoon period.

Fleetwood Mac was released in July 1975. The title suggested a new beginning, and its plain sleeve background inspired the nickname the '*White Album*'. To Nicks' disappointment, though, only Fleetwood and John McVie appeared on the front cover.

Buckingham Nicks offered the existing band a shot of youth, energy and songwriting chops. But they needed the band's swinging rhythm section and earthy keyboard player to ground them. 'And it was all a happy fucking accident,' marvelled Fleetwood.

To begin with, though, radio support was slow. '"Oh, it's just another Fleetwood Mac album," was the popular consensus at radio,' said Fleetwood. So they went on the road, touring the college circuit in two rented station wagons, selling their wares from town to town the way they'd been for the past seven years. They sneaked new songs into the set, but Buckingham and Nicks also bit the bullet and understudied their predecessors on 'Oh Well', 'Station Man' and 'Hypnotized'.

The redux Fleetwood Mac were a motley crew comprising what Mick Fleetwood later called 'deeply ingrained Anglo-American archetypes'. Fleetwood suggested that he was the 'public-school aristocrat', John McVie 'the English cloth-cap working-class type', Christine 'the English rose', Stevie the 'California girl' and Lindsey 'the Byronic rock star'.

The tour was another learning curve, especially for Stevie: learning to sleep in the back of a van on top of the amps, learning to sleep at all after the cocaine needed to keep them functioning, and learning to find her place as the American lead singer in a re-booted British blues band.

Then Warners released 'Over My Head' as a single. It was the push that *Fleetwood Mac* needed, and it delivered their first US top-twenty hit, followed by two more, 'Rhiannon' and 'Say You Love Me'.

By the end of 1975, the album had sold a million. For Buckingham Nicks, this was validation – and a payday – beyond their wildest dreams. 'It was like coming out of a cave,' said Nicks. 'Like coming into the light. For the first four weeks in Fleetwood Mac, we got paid $200 apiece. Then, for the second four weeks, $800 a week *each*. It was like we were fucking rich.'

Fleetwood Mac's success meant more than a payday for its founder members. 'Only me and John knew what it felt like,' insisted Fleetwood. 'Because we had been there when the band were huge in England. For the rest of the gang, it was a case of, "Oh my God! What is this?" For John and me, it was more emotional. After living through the Peter Green era, we realised something special was happening again.'

Today, the Canyon Country Store still stands at 2018 Laurel Canyon Boulevard, dispensing coffee and condiments to hungry locals and tourists eager to walk in Jim Morrison's footsteps. But the mysterious 'Thomas Christian', or whatever his name was, was never seen or heard of again.

'That guy is responsible for Fleetwood Mac as most people know it,' said Fleetwood. 'He should be bragging about it to this day. Maybe he is because, honestly, I've never heard from him since.'

'Rhiannon'

Season of the Witch

'Rhiannon is like your fairy-princess godmother, who lives in a magical kingdom,' claimed Stevie Nicks superfan Courtney Love. It's also the acorn from which all of Nicks' witchy power ballads grew. No 'Rhiannon', no 'Gold Dust Woman', 'Sara' or 'Sisters of the Moon'.

Like her predecessor, Bob Welch, Nicks was drawn to the mystical. But while Welch riffed on flying saucers and the Bermuda Triangle, Nicks named 'Rhiannon' after a celestial spirit in author Mary Leader's *Triad: A New Novel of the Supernatural*, which its publishers claimed was for 'the millions of readers who enjoyed *The Exorcist*'.

'Rhiannon' was mooted for a second Buckingham Nicks album but recorded for 1975's *Fleetwood Mac* at LA's Sound City Studios. Whoever she was, Rhiannon sounded otherworldly and irresistible. 'Rhiannon rings like a bell through the night/And wouldn't you like to love her,' Nicks purred over Mick Fleetwood's pattering drums and a spine-chilling backing choir.

Finishing the song nearly broke Fleetwood, though. 'Mick just couldn't get the feel,' explained co-producer Keith Olsen. 'He is Mister Rubber Man, so it should have been easy, but he'd tighten up and get frustrated with himself.'

The band worked on the song for two days, burning through hundreds of dollars' worth of tape, until the second night, when

Fleetwood threw his sticks in the air and announced he was done. 'So I went back to the first reel,' said Olsen, 'made enough copies, cut it into pieces and spliced it together eleven times until we had an almost perfect drum take. If you listen closely, you can hear "little scars". The cymbal gets clipped in the outro.'

The scars didn't show, and 'Rhiannon' gave Fleetwood Mac a US top-ten hit and nudged the '*White Album*' towards its first 1 million sales. Three years later, Nicks discovered Rhiannon's true origins. Mary Leader had borrowed the name from a goddess in the medieval Welsh tales, *The Mabinogion*.

Nicks now started introducing 'Rhiannon' as 'a song about an old Welsh witch'. On stage, it acquired a darker hue, with Nicks transforming into the mythical being and becoming a blur of twirling chiffon and silken hair, to the delight of arena audiences.

Lindsey Buckingham found it hard to watch. 'Once we were playing bigger places, I think Stevie felt the need to get some costumes and really *project*,' he said. 'On paper, a song about a Welsh witch is not my thing, but it was elevating the show and giving the band an identity. It's not to my taste, but that becomes irrelevant.'

The song's composer has never had any misgivings and still performs it in her solo act. 'There's something to that song that touches people,' said Nicks. 'I don't know who Rhiannon is, but she's not of this world.'

Richard Dashut

The Sixth Member of Fleetwood Mac's Tale

The first time Richard Dashut toured with Fleetwood Mac in May 1975, the road crew brutalised him. He was Lindsey Buckingham's best friend and a debonair hippie prince who'd arrived from nowhere to mix their live sound.

Tour manager John Courage was aggrieved, as the job had previously been his. As punishment, he bundled Dashut into a station wagon with the crew's biggest party animals. The drive from California to the tour's opening night in El Paso, Texas, saw the new boy undergo a savage initiation involving rails of cocaine and numerous joints. Dashut was orbiting Pluto by the time they arrived but still managed to do his job. He'd passed the test.

Buckingham was once asked what Richard Dashut did for Fleetwood Mac, and replied, 'I'm not really sure, but I wouldn't want to do it without him.' Mick Fleetwood was more direct and called him 'the sixth member of Fleetwood Mac'. Dashut's co-production and engineering credits on *Rumours*, *Tusk*, *Mirage* and *Tango in the Night* suggest he was doing something right.

Richard Dashut started his musical career as a caretaker at Hollywood's Crystal Sound Studios in 1973. When he wasn't mopping floors, he was watching Stevie Wonder make his *Talking Book* album. Nothing if not resourceful, he graduated to a maintenance job at Sound City, in Van Nuys, where he persuaded in-house producer Keith Olsen to let him loose on the mixing desk.

Dashut was promoted to assistant engineer and met Buckingham when he and Stevie Nicks arrived in the summer of 1974 to make their duo album. Theirs was an instant friendship: the boys shared a joint in the carpark and fifteen minutes later decided to get an apartment with Stevie in North Hollywood.

It was a baptism of fire for the young engineer. Dashut quickly learned to negotiate an assault course of tape machines, cables and guitars whenever Buckingham stayed up late working on his songs, but he also offered Stevie a sympathetic ear after one of the couple's frequent bust-ups.

When the duo joined Fleetwood Mac, Dashut was disappointed not to work on the '*White Album*'. But he was given the job of live sound engineer and bag man instead. Having survived his initial hazing ritual, Richard joined Lindsey and the band's luggage in one car, while Courage chauffeured the rest of the group in another.

When they arrived at a hotel, though, Buckingham invariably swanned off to his room leaving his best friend to unload his bags. The flip side was that Dashut also enjoyed privileges denied to other crew members and often shared a limo with the band.

In February 1976, Fleetwood Mac offered Dashut the producer's chair for *Rumours*. The group had started working with the Record Plant studio's house engineer but sacked him after just four days. 'I was there basically keeping Lindsey company,' said Dashut. 'Then Mick takes me into the parking lot and says, "Guess what? You're doing it."'

Dashut thought he was being overpromoted but took the job on the proviso that he could share it with his friend and fellow engineer, Ken Caillat. Unlike Caillat, Dashut didn't see himself as a technician. He'd always wanted to be a filmmaker and compared his role in the studio to directing Fleetwood Mac.

'Lindsey was tough to work with, and a lot of people were afraid of him,' he explained. 'The be-all and end-all for Lindsey was to make a great record. But he has so many radical ideas, I tried to keep him a little more commercially minded.'

Caillat managed to keep some distance from what Mick Fleetwood called 'the emotional holocaust'. But it was harder for Dashut. He and Buckingham were bosom buddies and he was unavoidably seen as 'Lindsey's guy'. But he still indulged the others, diffusing the tension with his stoned humour and acting as a buffer between Buckingham and the outside world. 'I always saw myself as like the clownfish that could swim with the sea anemone and not get stung,' he said, a quote surely worthy of *This Is Spinal Tap*.

Caillat and Dashut shared the Producer of the Year award for *Rumours* at the 1978 Grammys. Three years earlier, Dashut had, literally, been cleaning studio toilets. But the more successful Fleetwood Mac became, the more they closed ranks, around themselves and those they trusted. 'And Lindsey didn't trust many people,' said Dashut.

Both producers were part of the inner circle but pushed to their limits accommodating Buckingham's wayward ideas on *Tusk*. Dashut burned out and quit during the subsequent tour. There was a cruel streak to Fleetwood Mac, though. His parting gift from the band was a gold Rolex, buried inside an enormous cake.

'To give Dashut his watch, he had to crawl through a gauntlet of crew members, who taunted him with cruel ditties,' recalled Fleetwood. 'Then he had to grovel before Fleetwood Mac, and we gave him his watch after a cake fight.'

Yet Dashut still came back for more. He worked on band members' solo albums, before co-producing and co-writing songs on 1982's *Mirage*, including 'Book of Love', about his relationship with *Playboy* centrefold and *Dynasty* actor, Pamela Sue Martin.

Caillat quit Fleetwood Mac straight after *Mirage*, believing that Dashut would do the same. But Dashut co-produced the fraught sessions for 1987's *Tango in the Night*. Then Fleetwood Mac quit him and everybody else.

During the hiatus, Dashut helped make Buckingham's third solo album, 1992's *Out of the Cradle*, and suggested that his old friend's later solo records missed 'the friendliness' that he brought to the music. He wasn't wrong. After co-producing four platinum-selling albums, Dashut wasn't asked back when the classic Fleetwood Mac re-formed in the late '90s.

By 2012, he was living in Las Vegas and ran into Stevie Nicks when she came to town for a solo show. 'Where have you been for the past thirty years?' she asked him. Dashut told her he'd been trying to live down his Fleetwood Mac experience. The pair ended up in tears while consoling each other.

Dashut and his old friend swapped text messages after Lindsey Buckingham's emergency heart operation in 2019 before the lines of communication shut down again. Ill health had affected Richard's life too, and he was now using a wheelchair.

When the Buckingham-less Fleetwood Mac played Las Vegas, they sent a car for him, but only Mick Fleetwood came out of his dressing room to talk. The two fell back into the same routine, trading the same punchlines and telling old war stories.

However, Dashut worried that the others still regarded him as Lindsey's guy. 'I seem to be Fleetwood Mac toxic right now,' he wrote on his website. 'Kind of in a no-man's zone of frozen friendships and love. The truth of the matter is, they are all my good friends, either from the past, the now or the present. I still love and respect them, and always will.' Reading it, you couldn't help wishing one of them, anyone, would pick up the phone and make the call.

Part Four

'I socked him on the jaw as hard as I could'

Over 40 million record sales; three broken relationships and the most ruinously expensive follow-up album of all time.

Rumours

A Doomed Romance in Six Acts

Act I

How it began

Lindsey Buckingham occasionally hears a song from *Rumours* on his car radio. 'I sometimes listen,' he said. 'But my knee-jerk reaction is to turn it off or change the station. Why? Because it dredges up the subtext around the song, and that's not always pleasant.'

There are many numbers attached to Fleetwood Mac's eleventh album. *Rumours* is the twelfth biggest-selling album of all time (gazumped by *Thriller*, *Back in Black* and *The Bodyguard* soundtrack, among others), but its 40 million-plus sales haven't healed Buckingham's wounds.

'There is still work to be done,' he said in 2013. 'Although that's the very thing that makes the album attractive – us following our destiny while everybody's heart was breaking.'

Fleetwood Mac's '*White Album*' was still selling when the group started the follow-up in early 1976. Mick Fleetwood rented a house for them all in the Miami suburb of Homestead. They shunted the furniture out of the living room and turned it into a rehearsal space, though tensions between the couples meant that the conversation was stilted. 'What key is this in?' was the best John McVie could manage with Christine.

Later, with several songs underway, they checked into the Record Plant studio north of San Francisco at Sausalito Bay. From the outside, it looked like a cross between a surf shack and a hobbit's house. Inside, it was all shag carpeted walls, stained glass and secret boudoirs.

The band enlisted their studio associates Richard Dashut and Ken Caillat to become their co-producers. Fleetwood handed them both a Chinese I-Ching coin for luck. They'd need it.

Fleetwood Mac were now a multi-million-selling act. But the more successful they became, the more their personal relationships splintered. On the surface, 1977's *Rumours* embodies the silver coke-spoon, jet-set rock 'n' roll that the Sex Pistols and their peers sought to destroy. Dig deeper, though, and it's all black emotions, stir-craziness and psychic trauma. Almost every song contained a thinly coded message to somebody else in the group or one of their familiars. And almost everybody was sleeping with everybody else – or just about to.

Act II

'Like Jekyll & Hyde'

Starring Christine McVie, John McVie, Curry Grant, Sandra Elsdon, Mick Fleetwood, Jenny Boyd and 'The Lunar Tuner'.

Christine McVie knew her marriage was over when her husband came at her with a turkey knife. 'It was in New York,' she told *Mojo* magazine. 'John was raging drunk at the time, like Jekyll & Hyde. He won't mind me saying that because he's not like that anymore.' John McVie's drink problem had been chipping away at their relationship for years. In 1973, though, Christine had an affair with Fleetwood Mac's engineer Martin Birch. The McVies reconciled before splitting up during the *'White Album'* tour two years later.

'Chris saw me at my worst one time too many,' John admitted. 'It was awful. You're told by someone you adore and love that they don't want you in their life.'

John left the couple's Malibu home and moved a portable TV and his collection of penguin figurines onto a 41-foot ketch moored at Marina del Rey. Meanwhile, Christine started wearing her wedding ring on the other hand and wrote 'Don't Stop'. 'Don't stop thinking about tomorrow,' she implored her estranged husband, 'Don't stop, it'll soon be here.'

John, baseball cap yanked down over bloodshot eyes, mutely played bass. In the meantime, Christine had begun a relationship with Fleetwood Mac's lighting engineer, Curry Grant, and nobody bought her feeble explanation that her bouncy, sunny future hit 'You Make Loving Fun' was 'about my dog'.

In keeping with the incestuous nature of band life, John McVie was now seeing Peter Green's ex-girlfriend, Sandra Elsdon. Even though Christine had welcomed Sandra into the dysfunctional family, John was unhappy about Grant visiting his estranged wife at the studio.

One afternoon, Ken Caillat heard a commotion coming from the studio. 'I looked up and saw Sandra throw a glass of champagne in John's face,' he said. 'Then Stevie and Lindsey started arguing over the microphone. Then Mick walked in with tears in his eyes as he'd just gotten off the phone with his wife, Jenny, who wanted a divorce . . . I started to think it was contagious.'

Jenny once dropped by the studio, where John McVie made a sarcastic remark to her. 'So I wheeled round and socked him on the jaw as hard as I could,' she said. 'John put his arms around me after and thanked me. He knew he deserved it.'

Christine said she composed the ballad, 'Oh Daddy', for Fleetwood and his wife. Jenny had mixed feelings: 'Every time I heard it, I got a knot inside. He is their daddy, and I wished he was ours.'

Fleetwood continued to rally the troops while his marriage went to shit. 'For some reason, Mick was obsessed with working thirty-five days straight without a break – twelve, fourteen hours a day for a month and a half,' recalled Caillat. 'He said, "We're not getting enough done," as he wanted to get home.'

The Record Plant's cocoon-like ambience encouraged such madness. Daylight never intruded on the space, making it difficult to gauge the time. A bag containing several ounces of cocaine was left on the mixing desk if anyone flagged, and Buckingham and Dashut chain-rolled spliffs.

'On *Rumours*, I don't think I went more than thirty-six hours straight without sleep,' said Buckingham. 'Though I can't speak for the rest of the band, and certainly not Mick. Sometimes, those boys stayed up for three or four days at a time.'

One night, Fleetwood lashed two bass drums together in his search for the perfect beat; on another, a precious take was chewed up by a volatile tape machine, nicknamed 'Jaws'. Caillat first heard Christine's beautiful 'Songbird' after smoking an opium-tipped cigarette. Even through the narcotic haze, it sounded like a love song/ rallying cry for her damaged bandmates.

Caillat also wondered if he was going insane when Christine kept complaining that the studio piano was out of tune. The Record Plant's piano-tuning engineer insisted it wasn't, but Christine was convinced.

'We went through nine pianos and seven piano tuners and ended up with one guy we called the "Lunar Tuner,"' recalled John. 'The Lunar Tuner' was a blind pianist whose acute hearing confirmed that the instrument was out of tune.

All the album's piano tracks were scrapped. But only after Christine had played them a new composition, 'Keep Me There'. The band toyed with the tune before putting it aside, unaware they had the bones of *Rumours*' signature song.

Act III

'Fuck You! Asshole!'

Starring Lindsey Buckingham, Stevie Nicks, Christina Conte, Carol Ann Harris and 'Kowloon's'.

One night at the Record Plant, Buckingham and Nicks were recording backing vocals for 'You Make Loving Fun' when they both exploded. Nobody remembers why. 'Fuck you! Asshole!' yelled

Nicks, while Buckingham told her he was moving out of their apartment as soon as *Rumours* was finished. Then, the moment the tape started running again, they returned to singing in perfect harmony.

Stevie had just ended their relationship, but the band still came before everything else. Stevie was becoming the star of the show, but Lindsey made her songs sound better. Her increasing role as Fleetwood Mac's frontwoman irked Buckingham, while she was frustrated by her dependence on him as a musical foil.

Fleetwood had rented a house for them all near the Record Plant. Christine and Stevie lasted a night before finding apartments in a nearby condominium. 'Meanwhile, the boys were all in the Sausalito house raving with girls and booze and everything,' recalled Christine.

Buckingham couldn't help thinking that Christine's newfound independence had influenced Stevie. So, the estranged couple began swapping messages on *Rumours*. Buckingham only recorded his vocals for 'Second Hand News' at the last minute to not alert Stevie to lines such as 'I ain't gonna miss you when you go'.

Buckingham's emotions spilt out across the accusatory 'Never Going Back Again' (created after 'four beers, six joints and two sets of guitar strings', according to Caillat) and the spiteful 'Go Your Own Way', where his ex-lover sang backing vocals through gritted teeth after being told 'Shacking' up is all you wanna do'.

Stevie's friend and voice therapist, Robin Snyder, arrived with a tray of hash cookies one night. Everyone, even Buckingham, downed tools. 'And we all sat there for hours, staring at each other,' said Nicks.

Sometimes, when they needed a break, Buckingham and his coterie repaired to Kowloon's, a Chinese restaurant in Sausalito. Here, they necked potent cocktails and deliberately spilt drinks over each other. After several visits, they started bringing waterproof clothing; Stevie even arrived in an ankle-length plastic mackintosh one afternoon. The staff didn't mind as the rock stars always left a big tip.

Like John McVie, Buckingham had tumbled from one relationship into another. He'd started seeing Christina Conte, a waitress whose voluminous curly hair matched his own. The couple didn't survive the album, though. Ken Caillat claimed Buckingham became physical with Christina during an argument. 'I felt sick, as if the magic had been destroyed,' he wrote in his memoir, *Making Rumours*.

Caillat also experienced Buckingham's anger first-hand. At Lindsey's request, he'd wiped a solo on 'Go Your Own Way'. Buckingham forgot and later asked to hear it. After being told it was gone, he charged into the control room and clamped his hands around Caillat's neck. 'A musician works himself into a fever,' explained the producer, sounding remarkably forgiving. 'It wasn't about that [the solo]. It was the tip of something bigger.'

Soon after, Buckingham began a relationship with studio manager Carol Ann Harris, who was one of the first outsiders to hear *Rumours*, and summed up Fleetwood Mac's lifestyle: 'We were an incestuous, intense, self-sufficient group, crowding around and protecting the five band members at its hub.'

The environment at the Record Plant had become too much: estranged couples were screaming at each other or not speaking at all; days blurred into nights, and Richard Dashut had begun sleeping under the mixing desk, claiming, 'It was the safest place to be.'

One particular incident convinced Mick Fleetwood that it was time to leave. 'One night, I turned up and saw John McVie on his own, trying to master a bass part,' he said. 'This very well-grounded Scotsman was on his hands and knees praying with a bottle of brandy in front of him. And John was so *not* that sort of guy. I knew then that we had to get out of there.'

Act IV

'Do we still have a band, Mick?'

Starring Stevie Nicks, Lindsey Buckingham, Don Henley and the Record Plant coffee pot.

Stevie Nicks didn't play guitar, bass or drums and wasn't caught up in her bandmates' battle over an out-of-tune piano. Instead, she brought her cassette demos to the Record Plant and left them for Lindsey next to the coffee pot: 'With a note saying, "Here is a new song. You can produce it, but don't change it."'

While Stevie sang backing vocals on Lindsey's songs about her, he sprinkled fairy dust on the ones she'd written about him. But while he raged at the dying of the light in 'Never Going Back Again' and 'Go Your Own Way', his ex-partner sounded infuriatingly Zen.

Rumours' US number one hit, 'Dreams', addressed their broken romance without resentment or bitterness. Nicks scribbled down the lyrics and worked out the melody while hiding in Sly Stone's private recording space at the Record Plant. 'Listen carefully to the sound of your loneliness/Like a heartbeat drives you mad,' she sang, while the song's subject later supplied harmonies and a wonderfully measured guitar solo.

The pair even shared lead vocals on Stevie's 'I Don't Want to Know', an upbeat country number, which seemed to suggest, 'I wish you well . . . even though I hate you'.

'They were writing these songs about and to each other, and then singing them on the same mic,' recalled Mick Fleetwood. 'I don't know how they did it. Warners were terrified. I had executives phoning up and asking, "Do we still have a band, Mick?" And I said, "Yes, because we will not stop what we are doing for anything – even if we have to crucify ourselves."'

'I Don't Want to Know' remains one of *Rumours'* greatest non-hits but was included at the expense of another song. Stevie pushed hard for her brooding ballad 'Silver Springs', but the others deemed it too downbeat for the final album. She arrived at the studio one day to be told the band had completed 'I Don't Want to Know' in her absence. Instead, Stevie closed *Rumours* with 'Gold Dust Woman', an incantatory song, partly about the drugs threatening to subsume some of the band.

By now, Stevie's private life had taken another turn. In the summer of 1976, partway through *Rumours*, Fleetwood Mac played live, including a date opening for the Eagles. The band's singing drummer, Don Henley, had been wooing Stevie Nicks by phone for

Dreams

some time. To complicate their lives further, Stevie and Don would become West Coast rock's new premier power couple.

Act V

'It was the perfect fantasy'

Starring Stevie Nicks, Mick Fleetwood and 'the monsters'.

Rumours was due for release in September 1976 but wasn't finished in time. After the Record Plant, the band spent months overdubbing. 'We booked every studio in LA,' recalled Nicks. 'Spending even more money, being self-indulgent, spoiled and excessive.'

They'd amassed 3,000 hours of recordings, and the master tape was wearing perilously thin. Another tour was postponed as Caillat, Dashut and Buckingham toiled away in a tiny studio beside a porn cinema on Hollywood Boulevard. During one painstaking sixteen-hour session, the overdubs were transferred from the deteriorating master to another first-generation master containing the basic tracks. 'If we hadn't done that, we would have lost everything,' said Caillat.

Perversely, one of the first songs recorded for *Rumours* and then abandoned brought them all together at the end. Christine McVie's 'Keep Me There' (also known as 'Butter Cookie') had been kicking around since the first week at the Record Plant. It was a so-so piano vamp until 2:47 minutes, when John McVie plucked a ten-note bass riff, which Ken Caillat described as, 'Uh-oh, the monsters are coming.'

The song was taken apart and reassembled, beginning with its climactic outro and working backwards. Christine's opening verses were replaced by parts of an unused Stevie Nicks song, cued up with a guitar intro repurposed from Buckingham Nicks' 'Lola (My Love)'. During one final, concerted push, 'Keep Me There' was transformed into 'The Chain', the only song here credited to all five band members.

Meanwhile, Fleetwood announced that he wanted the picture on the LP cover to look 'Shakespearean'. Stevie appeared looking like

202

a sort of hippie ballerina, and Mick, a ponytailed matador with his trademark wooden balls dangling between his legs.

However, photographer Herbie Worthington's images on the reverse were more revealing. Partway through a group pose, John McVie broke ranks to hug Lindsey Buckingham. 'At this point, nobody was getting along,' explained Worthington. 'Lindsey looks a bit put out because this wasn't staged. John just spontaneously hugged him.' This action prompted Christine and Stevie to cuddle up, while Mick pulled faces on the sidelines.

Rumours finally arrived in February 1977. John McVie insisted on the British spelling rather than '*Rumors*'. It received advance orders of 800,000, the highest in Warner Bros' history, topped the charts in the US, Canada, Australia and the UK, and won a Grammy for Best Album of 1977.

Just as *Rumours* took off, Fleetwood Mac appeared on the cover of *Rolling Stone*. Photographer Annie Leibovitz shot them lying together on an unmade bed. This time, the two ex-couples refused to get close, so Lindsey and Christine and Mick and Stevie snuggled up while John lay on the edge of the mattress reading a magazine.

For one of these non-couples, the image was a premonition. In November 1977, Mick and Stevie began an affair. 'We were each other's perfect playmates,' wrote Fleetwood years later. 'That's not all it was, but that's what we needed and what we needed to be. It was the perfect fantasy.'

Act VI

How it ends

Fleetwood Mac fired Curry Grant, but he and Christine stayed together as a couple until she met Beach Boy Dennis Wilson. Buckingham lived with Carol Ann Harris until 1984, with their relationship inspiring his second solo album, *Go Insane*, and several songs on *Tango in the Night*.

Stevie Nicks' romance with Don Henley struggled to accommodate their conflicting schedules. But her subsequent affair with

Mick Fleetwood illustrated Carol Ann Harris' second description of Mac life: 'We were part religious cult, part sex surrogates, part battle partners or sworn enemies, but always drifting as one.'

Today, Stevie Nicks occasionally hears a song from *Rumours* by accident. 'If it's on the radio, I stop and listen and think, "Oh, I would just love to be in that band." If I'm walking down the street and it's playing somewhere in a store, I realise I am hearing Mick's drumming or John's bass. I can feel it in the ground, and it always makes me smile.'

As of April 2024, *Rumours* had spent an astonishing 1,042 weeks in the UK album chart, and was still a top-twenty best-selling vinyl LP. Not that any of this softened the blow for Lindsey Buckingham. When told that he usually changed the radio station if 'Dreams' or 'Go Your Own Way' came on, Stevie laughed. 'Oh *Lindsey*,' she sighed. 'What's the *matter* with you?'

'Second Hand News'

Lindsey Buckingham loves the Bee Gees

So bitter were Lindsey Buckingham and Stevie Nicks about the break-up of their relationship that, while making *Rumours*, Lindsey started hiding lyrics in case she objected to what he was singing about.

'Second Hand News', the opening song on *Rumours*, spent months as an instrumental nicknamed 'Strummer' because Buckingham wouldn't put any vocals on it. When he finally relented, the song's early takes had him mumbling incoherently, as heard on 2016's deluxe edition.

As Lindsey Buckingham lyrics go, this one was pretty tame. 'I know there's nothing to say/Someone has taken my place,' he sang. Who? Presumably, Stevie's new beau, Don Henley? The anger increased with lines such as 'I've been tossed around enough.' But this was a love song compared to 'Go Your Own Way'.

The real trouble started when Buckingham told Mick Fleetwood and John McVie that he wanted them to play like the Bee Gees' rhythm section on their recent hit, 'Jive Talkin''. In contrast, Fleetwood sounded like an Irish folk drummer, and McVie played a trademark bluesy walking bassline.

Buckingham kept charging out of the isolation booth where he was playing acoustic guitar to correct them. The problem was getting them to recreate the rhythm that he heard in his head. At some point in the sessions, McVie flung the contents of a glass of vodka in Buckingham's face, and Fleetwood took him aside like a football manager counselling a headstrong young striker: 'You need to be more of a team player, Linds,' he implored.

They got there in the end. McVie went on holiday, and Buckingham replaced his bassline with a simpler one of his own. Listen closely, though, and you can still hear him beating out the 'Jive Talkin'' rhythm on a faux-leather studio chair in the split-second gaps between Fleetwood's fills. Right to the end, he *still* couldn't surrender control.

'Dreams'

How a Song Conceived in Sly Stone's Bed Went Viral in the Twenty-First Century

Even in the chaotic world of '70s rock, the customer was always right. So much so that the owners of Record Plant Studios allowed funk-rock royalty Sly Stone to convert one of their disused offices into a bespoke recording space. Stone's private room, nicknamed 'The Pit', functioned as a studio, a drug den and an occasional boudoir.

Its *pièce de résistance* was a raised doubled bed, concealed by velvet drapes shaped like a pair of buttery lips. The floor, walls and ceiling were carpeted with synthetic fur ('a revolting burgundy shag,' recalled Fleetwood), which surrounded a 10-foot-deep bunker containing a console, Sly's nitrous oxide tank, electric piano and often members of his retinue, hacking out lines of cocaine.

One day during the making of *Rumours*, Stevie Nicks slipped away from the others at Studio B. A storm raged outside as she wandered around, 'looking for somewhere I could curl up with my lyrics and my Fender Rhodes, my cassette tape recorder'. A studio employee saw her roaming the corridor and produced the key to Stone's room with instructions not to tell anyone.

Nicks felt like Alice disappearing down the rabbit hole as the door closed behind her. She climbed through the velvet drapes and lay back on the bed. Safe in the womb, she opened her notebook,

207

finished composing her riposte to Lindsey Buckingham's 'Go Your Own Way' and illustrated the lyrics with drawings of hearts and flowers. 'I found a drum pattern, switched on my cassette player and wrote "Dreams" in about ten minutes,' she said.

Where 'Go Your Own Way' was accusatory, 'Dreams' was as soft and sumptuous as Sly's bed. 'Lindsey is saying, "Go ahead and date other men and live your crappy life,"' she explained, and Stevie is 'singing about the rain, washing you clean. We're coming at it from different angles, but we were really saying the same thing.'

Stevie reappeared in Studio B and played 'Dreams' to the rest of the group, who nicknamed it 'Spinners', as it reminded them of the soul group the Spinners' hit, 'I'll Be Around'.

'When Stevie first played it for me, I thought, "This is really boring,"' admitted Christine. 'Dreams' contained just two chords, F to G, all the way through. 'But the Lindsey genius came into play, and he fashioned three sections out of identical chords, making each sound different.'

However hard she tried, though, Nicks couldn't match her original vocal. She tried a shot of brandy, a bump of cocaine and a few tokes on a joint to get her voice to that special place. Nothing worked, and Ken Caillat eventually grafted her original vocal onto the new arrangement.

The finished song's atmospheric feel came from a last-minute drum loop. Engineers and band members stood around the studio delicately feeding a 20-foot-long spool of tape through the recorder. From such Heath Robinson-style origins came a US number-one hit.

'Dreams' became one of Fleetwood Mac's signature songs. Then, in 2020, during the global pandemic, it experienced an unexpected revival. On 25 September, Nathan Apodaca, a potato warehouse worker from Idaho Falls, was driving to work when his car battery died. Apodaca, who posted on TikTok as 420DoggFace208, abandoned his vehicle and filmed himself skateboarding up the freeway's offramp while drinking Ocean Spray cranberry and raspberry juice and miming to 'Dreams'. 'I'd scrolled through my phone for something to listen to, and luckily I had "Dreams" in my top ten,' he explained. 'It was the best one to vibe to.'

By the end of the year, the video had amassed more than 51 million views and netted its creator thousands of dollars in donations, and a new Nissan Frontier, courtesy of Ocean Spray.

'Dreams' uplifting lyric resonated during lockdown, and copycat videos appeared across all social media. Soon enough, Mick Fleetwood had joined what was being called 'The Dreams Challenge', appearing on TikTok roller-skating around his Maui estate, glugging Ocean Spray and mouthing the lyric, 'It's only right that you should play the way you feel it. . .'

Even Lindsey Buckingham had a turn but claimed one of his daughters had duped him into drinking Ocean Spray while innocently riding his horse. Not wanting to miss out, Stevie appeared on TikTok, lacing up a pair of roller-skates next to a grand piano, while 'Dreams' played in the background.

Both the song and its parent album, *Rumours*, were soon back in the US charts. 'It's been such a wonderful surprise to see TikTok bring some joy in challenging times and encourage creativity among so many young people,' declared Fleetwood. Nathan Apodaca was living in an RV when he made the clip. Since then, he's bought a $320,000 home. '"Dreams",' he said, 'changed my life.'

'Don't Stop'

Christine McVie's 'Dear John' Letter

Christine McVie once told *Rolling Stone*'s cub reporter Cameron Crowe that she wrote 'pretty basic love songs'. 'I don't really write about myself,' she told him, 'which puts me in a safe little cocoon.'

Christine was being disingenuous. At the time, she'd just written 'Don't Stop' (provisionally titled 'Yesterday's Gone') in which she urged her estranged husband, John, to get on with his life.

Recorded for *Rumours*, Christine's song was a hit single in waiting and would become a staple of their live show into the next century. But to begin with, it didn't thrill them. 'It lacked bounce,' recalled Ken Caillat.

Caillat's solution was to hire an old-fashioned tack piano, like the ones heard rattling away in vintage Charlie Chaplin and Laurel and Hardy films. The bouncing tack piano combined with a cranked-up backing track and Christine and Lindsey Buckingham's shared vocals breathed new life into the song. Meanwhile, Mick Fleetwood lurched around the studio wearing a grotesque rubber mask and making the vocalists crack up between takes.

The lyrics helped too. 'Don't Stop' was about embracing a new day. Its positive message inspired US presidential candidate Bill Clinton to adopt it as his campaign song, Elton John to record a cloying electro-pop version for 1998's *Legacy: A Tribute to Fleetwood Mac's Rumours* and supermarket giant Asda to license it for a

Christmas TV advertisement. Christine also suggested 'it would make a great song for an insurance company'. But none have come forward so far.

The song's subject, John McVie, played dumb for decades. 'I never put it together,' he claimed in 2015. 'I've been playing "Don't Stop" for years, and it wasn't until someone told me, "Chris wrote that about you." Oh, really? I never twigged.'

In fact, it was so much about John McVie that his then-girlfriend, Sandra Elsdon, sang backing vocals on the chorus. 'I told him all along it was written about him,' said an exasperated Christine, years later. 'Countless times, completely, totally, singly about *him*.'

'Go Your Own Way'

The Mac's 1976 Triple-Platinum Hit in their Own Words

Lindsey Buckingham: I put this song together when we were taking a break in Florida. We rented a house to start rehearsing before *Rumours*. It was an immediate song in terms of the response it got from the band.

Mick Fleetwood: By the time we set about writing *Rumours*, we'd all fallen to pieces. After seven years, John and Christine called it quits, Lindsey and Stevie's four-year relationship was over, and my marriage to Jenny was on its way to divorce. The band rented a house in Florida to work on new songs, but it was hardly a vacation. Apart from the obvious unstated tension, I remember the house having a bad vibe as if it was haunted.

Ken Caillat: 'Go Your Own Way' was something [Lindsey] had been tinkering with. Lindsey played a hard-strummed acoustic guitar and sang loudly. They cranked the volume up on the big control room monitors. The fidelity was pretty bad. I was a little surprised at the intensity of his vocal, almost angry, and I wondered what Lindsey was driving at. At this point, I thought it was kind of a stinker. But I couldn't wait to hear what would happen when everyone played on it.

Buckingham: I'd been listening to the Rolling Stones' 'Street Fighting Man' and Charlie Watts does this kind of offbeat rhythm. Mick came up with his own version. Mick has an exquisite sense of rhythm, but he has no idea what he's doing technically.

Fleetwood: 'Go Your Own Way's rhythm was a tom-tom structure that Lindsey demoed by hitting Kleenex boxes or something to indicate what was going on. I never quite got to grips with what he wanted, so the end result was a muted interpretation. It's completely back to front and I've seen really brilliant drummers totally stumped by it.

Stevie Nicks: 'Dreams' and 'Go Your Own Way' are what I call the 'twin songs'. They're the same song written by two different people about the same relationship. Lindsey took a more punk-rock approach. But that was his way of getting through it. I still don't like 'shacking up is all you wanna do', but unfortunately that's how he felt about me, and I have to live with that.

Buckingham: I guess Stevie would rather have seen that song politicised. But what are you going to do? There is so much truth going on in all of those songs that there is no way you change them.

Nicks: I still don't like it. But I have never said to anybody, 'Don't write what you feel.' I write what I feel.

Buckingham: We released 'Go Your Own Way' as a single when we were still mastering the album. I was driving along Hollywood Freeway to Capitol Records, listening to [radio station] KMET, and the legendary DJ in LA at this time was B. Mitchel Reed. I heard the song on my car radio, and it sounded great. The song finished, B. Mitchel paused and went, 'That was the new Fleetwood Mac . . . Nah, I don't know about that one.' Being the cocky young guy I was I got to Capitol, where we were mastering, and got B. Mitchel's number. I asked him, 'What did you not like about it?'

He said, 'I couldn't find the beat.' The thing is, I'd put this disorientating guitar part on the song at the eleventh hour. And, you know what, I sort of know what he means.

Fleetwood: 'Go Your Own Way' was released just before Christmas 1976. It became an instant radio hit, going straight to the top ten.

'Songbird'

Say a Little Prayer

Christine McVie's psychic mother, Beatrice Perfect, claimed to have a Native American spirit guide named Silver Shadow, who enabled her to paint pictures. 'But she couldn't paint at any other time,' said Christine, who wondered if she'd ever inherit her mother's gift.

By the time Fleetwood Mac made *Rumours*, she presumed not. Then she wrote 'Songbird'. 'I don't know where that song originated from. It was as if I'd been channelled. I've never experienced anything like it before or since.'

It happened when Christine was alone in the condominium that she rented with Stevie and couldn't sleep. 'Because I'd had a couple of toots of cocaine and half a bottle of champagne,' she recalled. 'I went to bed, but then I got this song in my head, and it wouldn't go away.'

It wasn't just a verse or a melody. Christine sat at the piano in her room and played 'Songbird' straight through. And then again. 'This was at three o'clock in the morning, and I couldn't sleep in case I forgot it. So I had to write the words down and play it all night until I could get into the studio the next day. The whole song came out in an hour. I wish all songs were that easy. It was like a gift from the angels.'

215

Ken Caillat remembers hearing it while in a heightened state and was so transfixed he broke protocol by sitting next to Christine on the piano stool to listen. 'Not a good move,' he recalled.

Caillat thought 'Songbird' needed an auditorium's acoustics rather than a sterile studio sound. He knew just the place, having recently recorded Joni Mitchell at the University of California's Zellerbach Hall.

Fleetwood Mac took over the Zellerbach on the night of 3 March 1976. Caillat arranged for the venue's Steinway grand to be decorated with a bouquet of spot-lit red roses, and had microphones placed around the hall with military precision.

Christine began to play the piano, but the tempo went awry. Playing to a 'click track' in her headphones further threw her off. Instead, Lindsey Buckingham became a human metronome, strumming an acoustic guitar through Christine's headphones to keep the tempo steady.

Problem number two: Christine couldn't sing and play simultaneously, as the piano mics would pick up her voice. Instead, she sang 'Songbird' in her head while playing the piano and then performed her vocal with the piano take playing back through her headphones. Once Christine left the hall, Caillat and his team created the final vocal take by recording her voice booming from the auditorium speakers.

'Songbird' was weighted with meaning in the context of Christine's tortuous love life. 'It's a personal song,' she said in 1977, 'and I don't like hearing it too much.'

However, out on tour, 'Songbird' became the final song of the night, performed alone by Christine while her ex-husband sobbed quietly in the wings. 'I cried every time I heard it,' he confessed.

Fleetwood Mac never released 'Songbird' as a single, but jazz singer Eva Cassidy and country star Willie Nelson had minor hits with it in 1998 and 2006, respectively.

Nevertheless, the song followed its composer around for the rest of her life. Despite the lyric, 'I love you, I love you, I love you, like never before . . .' Christine insisted it wasn't a love song. 'It's universal,' she said. 'It's about you and nobody else and about you and everybody else. A lot of people play it at their weddings or bar mitzvahs or their dog's funeral.'

After Christine left the band in 1998 and bought a big house in the Kent countryside, she stopped playing the piano. 'Because every time I sat down at it, I wanted to make "Songbird" again,' she admitted, 'and I was disappointed I couldn't.' Christine was still waiting for her version of Silver Shadow to return.

'The Chain'

'Dum . . . dur-dur-dur-dur-dur-dur-dur-dur . . . Dum'

In 1978, not long after it arrived as track one, side two of *Rumours*, 'The Chain' became the theme music to the BBC's Formula One motor racing coverage. For nearly twenty years, its foreboding bassline and outro triggered a mental connection with fast cars whizzing around a race track.

Then, in 1996, the BBC lost Formula One to rivals ITV. 'The Chain' was replaced with a specially commissioned instrumental by '90s Brit funk poster boy Jamiroquai. That theme lasted two years before the station tried several different songs, including Bachman–Turner Overdrive's '70s drivetime classic, 'You Ain't Seen Nothin' Yet'.

However, 'The Chain' was so ingrained in the public consciousness it was still being used in any TV or radio programme with a motor racing connection. In 2009, the BBC regained the rights to Formula One and brought 'The Chain' back where it belonged.

It's not just the song's climactic finale, though, the whole piece screams drama. As cohesive as it sounds now, 'The Chain' was patched together in the studio from several different sources including an unused Stevie Nicks song.

'Lindsey said, "You know that song that you wrote about 'If you don't love me now, you will never love me again' – can we have that?"' recalled Stevie. 'He said, "Because we have this amazing solo at the end of it when John comes in . . . but we don't really have a song. Would you consider letting us have that song that I know you have because I've known you a long time and I've heard it?"'

'The Chain's inherent drama is partly why director James Gunn used it in his 2017 sci-fi blockbuster, *Guardians of the Galaxy Vol. 2*. The song first appears in the film when its tight-knit gang of superheroes began to unravel. The parallels with Fleetwood Mac creating the song while relationships shattered were obvious. 'It's about the bonds of love breaking or potentially not breaking,' explained Gunn. 'The first time we hear it, it's about the chain seeming to break.' The song reappears when the gang reunite to defeat a common enemy, proving the chain is still strong. Or, as Mick Fleetwood said, 'The realisation that the music we were making together was more powerful than any of us.'

Gunn sent clips of the scenes to all five band members who agreed to license 'The Chain' for an unknown but presumably astronomical sum of money. Fleetwood Mac never released 'The Chain' as a single, but it's as famous as any of their hits. Whether it's soundtracking death-defying motorsport, an emotional meltdown, or Marvel superheroes saving the universe, it has something for everyone. Especially Stevie Nicks. 'It's really my song,' she said. 'We split the royalties five ways, but the fact is, I wrote most of those words and that melody.'

'You Make Loving Fun'

Meet 'the Sexy Lighting Guy'

The man who made loving fun in this 1977 US top-ten hit was Christine McVie's partner at the time, lighting engineer Curry Grant. According to one of Fleetwood Mac's entourage, he was 'handsome and debonair, with enough playboy charm to make George Clooney jealous.' But his real name wasn't Curry.

Growing up in Houston, Texas, everybody called Charles Curry Grant by his middle name because it made him sound like the handsome, debonair actor Cary Grant. The name stuck when Grant dropped out of business college to help the lighting director on a Humble Pie tour.

It was Grant's entrée into the music business, and in the spring of 1974, Fleetwood Mac hired his company, Lone Star Lighting, for an upcoming tour. Grant took the job but discovered he was working for the fake Fleetwood Mac, assembled by their manager when Mick Fleetwood was away trying to fix his marriage.

Nevertheless, Grant was re-hired when the real Mac returned later that year. He stuck around as the personnel changed and witnessed the first baby steps of the Buckingham Nicks line-up. After which, he began a clandestine relationship with a newly single Christine McVie. 'Only three people knew,' said Grant, 'and one of them was Stevie Nicks.'

Stevie ferried the couple around in the backseat of her car so that John McVie wouldn't see them together. 'Wherever John was, Curry couldn't be,' said Christine. 'There were some very delicate moments.'

Christine wrote *Rumours'* big hit 'You Make Loving Fun' and told everyone it was about her dog 'to avoid flare-ups with John'. The secret soon came out, and Christine's estranged husband seethed with jealousy. The band eventually fired Grant, partly at John's behest. But Curry and Christine lived together for a couple of years before she began dating Dennis Wilson.

After Fleetwood Mac, Grant became a feted lighting director for Hall & Oates, Crosby Stills and Nash and solo Stevie Nicks, and is currently vice president of Concert Touring at the PRG group, a giant in entertainment and live events.

Still, the rumours about Curry Grant and Fleetwood Mac refuse to die: how Christine wrote the ballad 'Oh Daddy' about him (and not Mick Fleetwood, as she later claimed); how he also had a fling with Stevie Nicks, and how the rest of the crew refused to travel with him because of his affairs.

Grant denied ever being spurned by his workmates but remains tight-lipped about everything else. In 2022, the US podcaster Candice Fairorth asked him the million-dollar question, 'Were you the sexy lighting guy canoodling with the two ladies in the band?'

'We were all very close,' Grant replied, suppressing a laugh. 'It was definitely a family. We were all real cute. It was a great time with lovable people.' After which, he quickly moved the conversation on to something else.

'Gold Dust Woman'

More Cowbell!

'It was a typical Stevie song,' said Ken Caillat, remembering the first time he heard 'Gold Dust Woman'. 'It had a couple of piano chords, clanging back and forth, and her distinctly nasal vocal.'

It was hardly a ringing endorsement, but 'Gold Dust Woman' became the last song on *Rumours* and a runic anthem to rival 'Rhiannon'. But it took Fleetwood Mac almost a year to get it right.

'Rock on gold dust woman,' sang Stevie. 'Take your silver spoon, dig your grave.' Nicks has offered several clues to the song's origins. These include the addicts drifting around her old hometown of Phoenix; the groupies pursuing her male bandmates; her destructive relationship with Lindsey Buckingham, and, inevitably, cocaine.

One evening, at the Record Plant, the band managed eight takes of the song while wired on their respective drugs. 'We were looking for transcension,' said Fleetwood, describing the moment everybody hit a simultaneous musical and narcotic peak.

During one transcendent moment, Fleetwood swapped his hi-hat cymbal for a cowbell, which ticked, like a speeding clock, throughout the song. 'Gold Dust Woman' predated Blue Öyster Cult's '(Don't Fear) The Reaper', the subject of comic Will Ferrell's famous *Saturday Night Live* sketch, 'More Cowbell!'

One night, Nicks and Buckingham were recorded howling like coyotes on the song's fadeout. On another, Fleetwood clambered up a ladder, wearing goggles and a rain mac, and smashed panes of glass with a hammer while the tape ran.

'The song grew more evil as we built it,' said Caillat. 'We weren't looking for musicality. We were looking for accents, mood.'

But it was Stevie's voice that cut through all the noise. She recorded her vocals, huddled in the corner, wrapped in a shawl, sipping Courvoisier and surrounded by her lucky charms: packets of throat lozenges, boxes of tissues and Vicks nasal inhalers.

'We were in a wicked little circle,' Stevie admitted. 'Brandy, cigarettes, pot and coke. You'd do some coke and get nervous, so you'd smoke some pot, then you'd get too stoned and do some more coke, then you'd get nervous and have some brandy . . .'

Stevie took 'Gold Dust Woman' with her when she went solo and opened the show with it on her 1985 solo tour. By then, everybody listening presumed 'gold dust' meant cocaine and the song was about her, especially when she checked into the Betty Ford Center soon after.

Courtney Love's group Hole had just recorded a thrashing, alt-rock version of the song and she wanted to know what it was all about. 'You know what,' said a now sober Stevie. 'I don't really know.' Only that it offered a glimpse of life inside her wicked little circle.

'Silver Springs'

How a Fleetwood Mac Song Inspired a TV Show

In spring 2023, the musical drama *Daisy Jones & the Six* premiered on Amazon Prime. Based on author Taylor Jenkins Reid's best-selling novel, it told the story of a '70s rock 'n' roll group imploding at the height of their success.

In the story, the Six's star-crossed lovers, 'Daisy' and 'Billy' (played by Riley Keough and Sam Claflin), vent their feelings about each other with passive-aggressive lyrics and reproachful live performances. So far, so Stevie Nicks and Lindsey Buckingham, then . . .

In 1997, Fleetwood Mac released *The Dance*, a film and album of their reunion show at Burbank's Warner Bros studio. Taylor Jenkins Reid watched the film as a teenager and was fascinated by their performance of 'Silver Springs'.

Stevie wrote the song about Buckingham after seeing a freeway sign for 'Silver Springs, Maryland'. 'I thought it sounded like a pretty fabulous place. "You could be my silver springs . . ." is a symbolic thing of what you *could* have been to me.'

Stevie was furious when the song was excised from *Rumours*. The others deemed it too slow for the final running order and replaced it with 'I Don't Want to Know'. 'They didn't even ask me,' she complained. 'I was told in the parking lot after it was done.'

'Silver Springs' found a home on the B-side of 1976's 'Go Your Own Way', but wasn't performed live for twenty years. It starts as a pretty country-rock ballad before Nicks drives a metaphorical stake through Buckingham's heart with the line, 'You'll never get away from the sound of the woman that loves you . . .'

'What it's basically saying to Lindsey is, "I'm so angry with you. You will listen to me on the radio for the rest of your life, and it will bug you,"' explained Stevie. 'And "I *hope* it bugs you."'

Stevie demanded that they play 'Silver Springs' on *The Dance*. About four minutes into the song, she started singing, 'I'll follow you down, and the sound of my voice will haunt you' directly at Lindsey. Then he faced her and voiced her anguished lyrics about him. It was either an excellent bit of method acting or two ex-lovers re-opening old wounds and watching the blood flow. Or a bit of both.

'You're never going to take back the fact that there are two ex-couples on that stage,' explained Stevie, 'and you're never going to take back the fact that many of those songs were written about each other. No matter how cool anybody is, when you get up and sing them to each other, we can't ever look at each other as if we hadn't been totally involved.'

Daisy Jones & the Six's 'Regret Me' was their 'Silver Springs'. In the show, 'Daisy' started singing at 'Billy', forcing him to sing back. Sam Claflin later revealed that before auditioning for the role, a friend sent him the 'Silver Springs' clip from *The Dance* and a simple instruction: 'Just channel this, mate.'

In August 2023, Stevie Nicks revealed that she'd watched the show. 'It brought back memories that made me feel like a ghost watching my own story,' she tweeted. 'It was very emotional. I just wish Christine could have seen it. She would have loved it.'

Ken Caillat

The Therapist's Tale

As a student in Santa Clara, California, in the early '70s, Ken Caillat briefly considered a career in psychiatry. But every therapist he asked for advice told him the same thing: listening to people's problems day in, day out, would affect and even destroy his own life. Caillat abandoned the idea. Then he met Fleetwood Mac.

Kenneth Caillat was a twenty-nine-year-old engineer when the band came into his life in 1976. 'I never intended to be an engineer or producer,' he explained. 'I wanted to be a singer-songwriter.'

After graduating from business school, Caillat took a job at ex-jazz musician Wally Heider's studio in Los Angeles. It was only meant to be a temporary position, but Heider spotted his potential. By the time that Caillat realised nobody wanted him as an artist, he'd learned to mix and had credits on Crosby, Stills & Nash, Wings and Joni Mitchell albums.

In January 1976, Caillat was asked to help mix a Fleetwood Mac show for an upcoming radio broadcast. He undertook a crash course by listening to their current hit, the '*White Album*'. But their first meeting didn't go well. When Stevie Nicks wafted into the studio, Caillat greeted her as 'Lindsey'. 'I didn't know that their pictures were reversed on the album cover,' he pleaded later.

Everybody in Fleetwood Mac was impressed by Caillat's mixing skills. But he was so quiet some of them wondered when he was going to learn to talk. 'I was a little quiet,' he concurred. 'But I was pretty determined and confident in my abilities.'

Within days, Caillat had joined Richard Dashut to start work on *Rumours*. Caillat had discipline, a good memory and made notes after every take. A few days in, the band began asking what he thought of each take and how they could be made better. Now Caillat started talking: 'They wanted me to learn how to be a producer. They taught me how to produce.'

Then Mick Fleetwood offered Dashut and Caillat a co-production credit and royalty points on *Rumours*, changing their lives forever. But it came at a price. 'I thought I was just making a regular album,' explained Caillat. 'Then whenever one couple started fighting, the other couple would start. I kept my head down and tried to be logical – "Hey, you two go outside, Lindsey come and work while they're fighting, Mick come and play percussion, let's keep the ball rolling . . ." It was a challenge.'

Caillat insisted that some stories, such as the one about a Mount Everest of cocaine on the mixing desk, were exaggerated. 'The coke thing pisses me off. They did use cocaine. But it was the beginning of it on *Rumours*. It got crazy later on. Everybody got delirious on *Tusk*. That was decadence at its worst.'

Caillat co-produced *Tusk*, with accompanying royalty points, but struggled to accommodate Lindsey Buckingham's vision. 'Some of the guitars and distortion were so bad, it made me nauseous,' he admitted.

On the day of Caillat's wedding, Mick Fleetwood rang him at the hotel with some bad news. *Tusk*'s early sales figures had come in and weren't good. 'We're screwed,' Caillat told his bride-to-be shortly before the ceremony. It was a special day: the one on which he realised the band had officially taken over his life.

Caillat co-produced the follow-up, *Mirage*, but declined to work on *Tango in the Night*. 'I didn't think I could go through it again, butting heads with Lindsey,' he said. As 'the guy who made *Rumours*' his stock had risen, and he went on to work with Lionel Richie and Michael Jackson, among many others.

But he could never fully escape. Caillat returned to the dysfunctional family in 2004 to co-produce Christine McVie's *In the Meantime*, and later wrote two books, *Making Rumours* and *Get Tusked*, about working with the band.

'It's not their story,' he pointed out. 'It's my story, of what I went through being a fly on the wall.' Like a psychiatrist and their patient, Fleetwood Mac were still under his skin.

The Eagles

Know thy Enemy

Day in, day out, every time they switched on the radio or walked through a shopping mall they heard it: Glenn Frey crooning, 'Well, I'm a-standing on a-corner in Winslow, Arizona . . .'

It was the late summer of 1972, Lindsey Buckingham and Stevie Nicks had just moved to Los Angeles, and the Eagles' 'Take It Easy' was everywhere. Then came the follow-up hits, 'Witchy Woman' and 'Peaceful Easy Feeling'. Soon there was no escape.

Before the Eagles, Glenn Frey and his bandmate, Don Henley, had played in Linda Ronstadt's backing band, and been part of the hip crowd populating Sunset Boulevard's post-hippie hangout, the Troubadour. Now they were the double-denim kings of Californian country rock.

Buckingham and Nicks were next in line for the Troubadour crown, surely? But not until they joined Fleetwood Mac and had a hit with the '*White Album*'. Which was when Don Henley began pursuing Stevie. The couple talked on the phone and met for the first time when Fleetwood Mac opened for the Eagles at Greensboro Coliseum, North Carolina.

The headliners were basking in the glow of yet another hit, 'The Best of My Love'. Word arrived via their road crews that Henley was excited about finally meeting Stevie. Mick Fleetwood and John McVie pounced on this information and had a bouquet of red roses delivered to Nicks with a card that read, 'To Stevie, the best of my love, tonight? Love Don'. Nicks was outraged by Henley's presumption until she saw her rhythm section giggling hysterically, and realised she'd been had.

Stevie and Don became an item anyway, and their relationship lasted for around a year and a half. But it took a while for Nicks to feel equal. 'The Eagles were such good songwriters, I was blown away,' she admitted. 'I was very famous, but it didn't make me less awestruck with these men than anybody else.'

Fleetwood and McVie's earlier prank wasn't wide of the mark either. Henley was big on grand gestures. When both groups were staying in Miami, Nicks came down to breakfast to find a limousine driver delivering Henley's gifts to the dining room, where Lindsey Buckingham was eating. Buckingham glowered as the table filled up with baskets of flowers and fresh fruit and even a brand-new stereo and several LPs. 'I was going, "Please, please . . . This is not going to go down well,"' Stevie recalled. However, Buckingham respected his rivals' single-mindedness. 'One thing I admire about the Eagles is they always seem to know what they want,' he said. 'They always seem to know why they want it. They always seem to want it at the same time.'

There were obvious comparisons between Buckingham and Henley, too. Don was another studious singer-songwriter wedded to his craft, with a 'fro to rival Buckingham's. 'Don Henley is good for [Stevie],' Lindsey told *Crawdaddy* magazine. 'I really thought it was going to bum me out, but it actually made me happy.' Nobody believed him, and it couldn't have been easy when Henley's grand gestures became even grander. He once sent a private Learjet to fly Nicks to Atlanta where the Eagles were having a day off. Stevie wasn't the only one receiving what the roadies called 'the love 'em and Lear 'em treatment'. But apparently, her plane was in a delightful shade of cranberry red. 'Oh, it was wonderful,' she swooned. 'It was one of the most romantic things that ever happened in my whole life.'

These gestures also gave Stevie a taste for spending her own money: 'Once you learn to live like that there's no going back. Like,

"Gimme a Learjet, I need to go to LA, I don't care if it costs fifteen thousand dollars, I need to go now!'"

Come the summer of 1977, the Eagles' *Hotel California* and Fleetwood Mac's *Rumours* had become America's soundtrack. If it wasn't Don crooning about 'a dark desert highway', it was Stevie purring about how 'thunder only happens when it's raining'. If one of them wasn't at number one in the LP charts, it was the other.

A year later, the two groups were vying for the top prize at the American Music Awards. *Rumours* won Favourite Pop/Rock Album over *Hotel California*, and Fleetwood Mac beat the Eagles to Favourite Pop/Rock Band. Buckingham had washed down a quaalude with a shot of Jack Daniel's before the ceremony. Despite his wobbly demeanour, he was thrilled to have beaten the Eagles.

Stevie and Don's relationship had now cooled off. A few months earlier, Nicks discovered she was pregnant with Henley's child. This wasn't part of the plan: their lives were a merry-go-round of recording sessions and live shows, and Stevie quietly arranged for a termination.

Two decades later, during which time Stevie had never spoken publicly about the pregnancy, Henley told all to *GQ* magazine, saying Nicks believed she was having a girl and wanted to call her Sara, hence the Fleetwood Mac song of the same name.

After splitting with Don, Stevie began seeing his friend, the Eagles' co-writer, J. D. Souther. She and Henley later reconciled in the studio to sing their hit duet, 'Leather and Lace', and Stevie hired the Eagles' hard-nosed handler, Irving Azoff, to become her manager.

Fleetwood Mac followed *Rumours* with the experimental *Tusk*, while the Eagles followed *Hotel California* with *The Long Run* (which sounded like *Hotel California*, just not as good). The Eagles broke up soon after, and Stevie began a relationship with their ex-guitarist Joe Walsh, a notorious party animal whose appetite for cocaine rivalled even hers.

The romance started when Walsh was the opening act on Stevie's 1983 solo tour. But their demanding careers and recreational habits made it hard to maintain a relationship. Stevie claimed to be head-over-heels in love with Joe, and composed the ballad, 'Has Anyone Ever Written Anything For You?' for him. Walsh didn't reciprocate.

The tipping point came in 1986, when he visited Nicks in the studio, proceeded to get high and refused to engage in any meaningful conversation. Stevie presumed Joe was staying for a few days until he told her he was leaving the next day and expected her to come with him. She refused and went to leave the studio, when Walsh called out, 'If you walk out that door, you cease to exist.' She kept walking, and Walsh's parting words were used in the lyrics to Fleetwood Mac's 'Welcome to the Room . . . Sara'.

'Joe and I broke up because of the coke,' she divulged. 'He told my friend, "I'm leaving Stevie, because I'm afraid that one of us is going to die and the other one won't be able to save the other person. The only way to save both of us is for me to leave."'

'Joe was the one I would have married,' said Stevie in 2008, 'and that I would probably have changed my life for.'

By then, Fleetwood Mac and the Eagles had both re-formed. Despite stating that 'hell would freeze over' before they got back together, the Eagles' Hell Freezes Over reunion tour lasted two years. Fleetwood Mac's The Dance tour in 1997 lasted three months.

For Lindsey Buckingham, though, the victory was all theirs. 'Once we get out the road we'll take a few hits,' he said at the time. 'But in the same way, people can sense that Don Henley and Glenn Frey maybe aren't that crazy about being up on stage with each other, they can sense that we are really digging it. You won't get this emotional resonance from the Eagles.' Buckingham was right: you wouldn't.

Rod Stewart

Some Guys Have All the Luck

Rod Stewart was a notorious rascal. Especially in the '70s, when he was touring the US with his group, the Faces. It was the height of what Stewart called 'my knob period'. Like today's street artists tagging railway bridges, Rod left a trail of hand-drawn penises on hotel walls and airline seats worldwide.

The Faces' graffiti and their other habit of vandalising Holiday Inns led to a lifetime ban from the hotel chain. 'But there's always a way around these things,' said Stewart, whose manager duly booked the Faces into the same hotels under the name 'Fleetwood Mac' instead.

Fleetwood Mac and Rod Stewart had started in the business around the same time. In 1967, Rod was one of two lead singers in Peter Green and Mick Fleetwood's R&B group, Shotgun Express. 'It was my first experience working with a prima donna,' recalled Fleetwood. 'Rod was a star, and he behaved like one.' This extended to the singer refusing to unload the band's van in case it messed up his trademark cockatoo hairstyle.

Green was seeing Stewart's co-vocalist, Beryl Marsden, and the band imploded when she ended their relationship. But Green and Stewart took part in a recording session together in November that year. Ex-Bluesbreakers drummer Aynsley Dunbar was assembling a new group and enlisted Rod to sing, with Green playing guitar and Cream's Jack Bruce on bass. Three songs were recorded under the name Crazy Blue, but only one, 'Stone Crazy', has survived. Rod Stewart's voice sounded sublime, and producer Mike Vernon thinks it's one of Green's greatest sessions.

However, the band members' other commitments meant the secret supergroup never progressed, and Stewart joined the Jeff Beck Group instead. The session was forgotten until Vernon included 'Stone Crazy' on 1973's *History of British Blues (Volume One)*. By then, the Faces were falling apart, and Fleetwood Mac had discovered their Holiday Inn scam.

The band would have their sweet revenge, though. In August 1977, Stewart rolled up backstage for Fleetwood Mac's sold-out date at the LA Forum. Nobody on the crew challenged him because he was Rod Stewart. Then Lindsey Buckingham discovered the singer hovering around his partner, Carol Ann Harris. After much scowling, Buckingham asked for Rod to be removed from the backstage area and Carol to sit at the side of the stage where he could see her.

Stewart went home alone. Meanwhile, his new album, *Footloose & Fancy Free*, reached number two but failed to knock *Rumours* off the top of the US charts. Fleetwood Mac were now even, and Rod's knob period had entered its long, slow decline.

Eric Clapton

'God' versus Fleetwood Mac

Eric Clapton and Fleetwood Mac were in and out of each other's lives for decades. It began when Peter Green took Eric's job – twice. In March 1965, blues aficionado Clapton left the Yardbirds, complaining that their music had become too commercial. He joined the more purist John Mayall's Bluesbreakers for a few months before quitting them too.

Clapton was a guitar prodigy tipped for superstardom. But he'd decided to join some friends in a new group called the Glands, who were planning a road trip to Australia, with gigs *en route*. Mayall agreed to keep Clapton's job open but hired nineteen-year-old Peter Green in the meantime.

Green made his Bluesbreakers debut at the Britannia Rowing Club, Nottingham, in August 1965. He won over most of the 'Where's Eric?' hecklers, but only lasted a week. By then, Clapton had made it as far as Athens before bailing on his friends and asking for his old job back.

'I got the impression that [Peter] was a real Turk,' said Clapton. 'A strong, confident person who knew exactly where he was going. He was a phenomenal player with a great tone. But he was not happy to see me as it meant a sudden end to what had been a good gig.'

In July 1966, Clapton left the Bluesbreakers again; this time to form the trio Cream. Green took his place again, before also quitting to form Fleetwood Mac. It didn't end there. Cream were also on the bill when Fleetwood Mac made their debut at the Windsor Jazz and Blues Festival in August 1967.

In the meantime, the slogan 'Clapton is God' had appeared on a wall in Islington, north London. It was a bold statement to live up to. Cream lasted two turbulent years, after which Clapton muddled his way towards a solo career while pickling himself for a time in heroin and alcohol. 'There seemed to be a post-psychedelic drunkenness which swept over everybody in the entertainment business,' he recalled.

Eric also embarked on an affair with model Pattie Boyd, who was inconveniently married to George Harrison at the time. Pattie's sister, Jenny, was wed to Mick Fleetwood, and the siblings spent most of the '70s dealing with their feckless partners.

Clapton was a frequent visitor to Mick and Jenny's houses in England and Los Angeles; usually pursuing Pattie, for whom he wrote the hits 'Layla' and 'Wonderful Tonight' and eventually married in 1979.

On stage, Clapton was never a showman, though. He sometimes killed the mood at Bluesbreakers gigs by spending too long tuning his guitar, and his manager later drew up his setlists to give the shows some pace. But Clapton's blues purism never fully deserted him.

Eric hadn't seen Fleetwood Mac for years, before joining the Boyd sisters for a show at London's Wembley Arena in 1980. The band's hedonism and showmanship were at their peak. 'Eric and Peter were like two musical peas from the same blues pod,' wrote Jenny in her memoir, *Jennifer Juniper*. 'But Mick, John and Chris had become an American supergroup with a snazzy, slick West Coast show.'

Clapton was still 'God' to a younger generation of guitar players. But the feeling wasn't reciprocated. 'He's a good guitarist,' said Eric, pointing at Lindsey Buckingham. 'But he's too tight, too locked inside himself to be great.'

Clapton had been drinking, and his mood darkened as the show progressed. When Stevie Nicks began whirling around the stage, channelling her inner sorceress, Clapton mumbled that she was 'a witch' and flounced off to the bar, where he remained for the rest of the night.

Backstage, Mick Fleetwood threw up, nearly fell into a hypoglycaemic coma and burst into tears before the encore. Everybody had come a long way from the Windsor National Jazz and Blues Festival.

Rumours about Fleetwood Mac

True or False?

Did Fleetwood Mac thank their cocaine dealer on the sleeve of Rumours*?*

Mick Fleetwood admitted that in 'my state of dementia', he'd considered including a credit for their dealer, but he'd disappeared before *Rumours* was released: 'Unfortunately, he got snuffed, executed.'

Did Stevie Nicks insist on staying in pink hotel suites only during the Tusk *tour?*

'No, I wasn't that bad! But I always wanted a fabulous room,' she said. However, when the band's accountants asked where most of the profits from the *Tusk* tour had gone, Mick Fleetwood asked them, 'If they knew how much it cost to find a hotel chain that allowed you to paint their suites pink?'

Did Stevie and Christine insist on having grand pianos in their hotel suites during the Tusk *tour?*

Yes. 'We used to get grand pianos craned into our bedrooms,' admitted Christine, who also claimed that while Nicks always had a piano in her suite, 'she couldn't play it. So she'd have me come down and play it for her.'

The Many Lives of Fleetwood Mac

Did every member of Fleetwood Mac have a black-belt karate bodyguard?

Not quite. Fleetwood Mac employed two Australian bodyguard/ martial arts experts, Bob Jones and Richard Norton. Jones was later photographed performing karate with Stevie Nicks in his 1983 self-defence book, *Hands Off!* 'On the day of the shoot, Stevie appeared, her hair done to resemble the mane of a lion,' he wrote. 'Stevie wore her familiar thick-soled, thick-heeled, knee-high brown suede kid leather boots ... The seductiveness of her partially exposed cleavage was the next thing any red-blooded male would have his attention drawn to.'

Did Mick Fleetwood remove all the studio clocks to make the band work longer hours on Rumours?

'No,' insisted Ken Caillat. 'But it was so dark in there you never knew if it was day or night anyway.'

Did Stevie Nicks employ an aide to blow cocaine up her backside?

New Order's ex-bassist Peter Hook heard this urban myth from Geordie Hormel, the owner of Village Recorder studios, in 1985. 'It was him who told us about Stevie Nicks having a girl who blew coke up her arse because her nose was so fucked,' claimed Hook.

'I heard that rumour too,' Stevie told *Q* magazine in 2001. 'But of course, that never ever happened. That is an absurd statement. It's not true.' However, Nicks does have a puncture in her septum due to her past cocaine use. 'Maybe that nasty rumour came from people knowing I had such a big hole in my nose.'

Did Mick Fleetwood attend a fancy-dress party dressed as Jesus?

Yes, Stevie Nicks' Halloween party in October 1988. Besides wearing a loin cloth and a crown of thorns, Fleetwood rode in on a donkey.

Did Fleetwood Mac once steal a cat?

Yes. Fleetwood's future wife, Sara Recor, stole the house cat from the Albuquerque Tingley Coliseum in November 1979. The male members of the band didn't want the animal on their private plane, but Recor, Nicks and Christine McVie insisted.

Did the band once request a medieval marquee as part of their backstage rider?

Yes. Fleetwood Mac's 1980 Australian tour included outdoor stadium dates, where promoters had to supply a medieval-style tent for the backstage enclosure. The contract also stipulated a selection of English-branded cigarettes and two ounces of pharmaceutical cocaine.

Did Fleetwood Mac snort the equivalent of seven miles of cocaine in their heyday?

Possibly. In June 2019, Mick Fleetwood told the *Sun* newspaper that he once calculated the approximate amount of cocaine the band had consumed between them during the '70s and '80s. 'And then some goofball got out a calculator and came up with that seven miles figure. But I want to speak appropriately about this. Because the romance of those war stories can adulate something which is not a good idea.'

Tusk, the Album

Songs from the African Burial Ground

For a time, Mick Fleetwood claimed that the group's twelfth studio album, *Tusk*, was named after his slang expression for an erect penis. Perhaps he was restating his masculinity now that Stevie and Christine had helped the former boys' club sell so many records?

'*Tusk* had nothing to do with Mick's penis,' insisted Ken Caillat. 'I used to get so annoyed when those guys talked about it – "What are you? Six years old?"'

Confusion reigns. Cover artist Peter Beard said the LP was named after the elephant tusks in its inner-sleeve collage. Stevie Nicks says it was named after the two fake tusks mounted on either side of the studio console. Nicks also says they called the board 'Tusk' and credited it with supernatural powers. 'Tusk was very native, very African,' she said. 'Mick thinks he is a Watusi warrior . . . and he is. Everything on *Tusk* is warrior-esque.'

Released on 12 October 1979, *Tusk* was a bold departure after *Rumours* and sold a fraction of its predecessor. Warners complained and nicknamed it 'Lindsey's folly'. Almost fifty years later, though, history has been kind to *Tusk*. This curious-sounding double album also helped Fleetwood Mac survive into the 1980s.

By the time they made the record, everybody's lives had become even more tangled and incestuous. Christine McVie was in a relationship with Dennis Wilson, and her ex-husband John had

241

married Fleetwood Mac's secretary, Julie Rubens. Meanwhile, Stevie Nicks and Mick Fleetwood were having an affair, which continued until the early *Tusk* sessions, when Fleetwood fell for Nicks' best friend, Sara Recor, and she began seeing the group's engineer Hernán Rojas.

Before anybody played a note, Fleetwood and Lindsey Buckingham had a 'What the fuck are we going to do now?' crisis meeting at Mick's Bel Air mansion. Buckingham told him he wouldn't make '*Rumours Part Two*' and would record his songs at home and bring them to the band for overdubs. Fleetwood gave in to his demands because he was worried Buckingham would leave. However, this power shift affected the mood within the group.

It was the summer of 1978, and Buckingham was smitten with punk and new wave. *Rumours* had been a huge commercial hit, but critics were talking about Talking Heads' *77* and the Sex Pistols' *Never Mind the Bollocks* instead. Buckingham wanted to experiment and turned one of the reverb-heavy bathrooms in his LA residence into a studio. He used a twenty-four-track recorder to tape his vocals on the tiled floor and played the 'drums' on a Kleenex box beside the toilet.

He wanted to subvert the norm. 'Because I hate turning on the radio and being able to guess what an entire song will sound like in the first five seconds,' he said. 'It sickens me.'

This was fighting talk. Fleetwood primed the rest of the group about Buckingham's intentions before a listening session at Santa Monica's Village Recorder studio. Mindful of what he was about to unleash, Lindsey suggested Stevie and Christine play their demos first. But nobody had a chance to play anything after Fleetwood received a shocking phone call.

The drummer's new Ferrari had been on the back of a flatbed trailer on the way to his house when a truck broadsided it on Beverly Hills and sliced the uninsured vehicle in half. The listening party was abandoned in favour of a conciliatory all-night cocaine binge.

It set the tone. Village Recorder at 1616 Butler Avenue, West Los Angeles, had history. This former Masonic temple was owned by food tycoon Geordie Hormel (whose claim to fame was inventing the 'corndog') and also housed the Beatles' guru Maharishi Mahesh Yogi's transcendental meditation centre.

Hormel understood rock stars' recreational habits. Village Recorder's mirror-lined hallway was designed to disorientate any visiting cops from the nearby precinct, and Hormel had a false wall in his office behind where he could hide in the event of a raid.

Fleetwood Mac recorded *Tusk* in their own custom-built Studio D, which later included isolation booths tiled to recreate the lavatorial ambience of Buckingham's bathroom. Fleetwood wanted them to partner with Hormel and buy Studio D outright, but his bandmates refused. Instead, they ended up paying the same amount for the space in monthly rent and filled it with their special taste in esoterica.

'Shrunken heads and leis and Polaroids and velvet pillows,' recalled Nicks, 'and saris and sitars and all kinds of wild and crazy instruments and the tusks on the console, like living in an African burial ground.'

With songs arriving from three sources, Fleetwood informed Warners that *Tusk* would be a twenty-song double album: 'They thought I was insane as the industry was in recession, and it would have to retail at twice the price. But we went ahead and did it anyway.'

Over the next thirteen months, the band burned through between $1 and $1.4 million, some of which went on platters of lobster and crates of Dom Pérignon. Only the booze was consumed, as no one could stomach solid food after a nose full of Bolivia's finest. 'They could have made an entire album with the money we spent on champagne in one night,' said Christine. 'It was absurd.'

A battle of musical wills raged too: Stevie's ghostly ballads and Christine's pristine pop versus Buckingham's primal therapy sessions. John McVie later described *Tusk* as 'the work of three solo artists'.

Christine's pillow-soft 'Over and Over' and 'Think About Me' wouldn't scare the fanbase, while her song 'Brown Eyes' is one of *Tusk*'s greatest non-hits.

Stevie's compositions began with the haunted-sounding 'Sara', supposedly inspired by Sara Recor and the name Nicks wanted to give her unborn child with Don Henley. However, aside from the country-tinged 'Angel', Nicks' other contributions, 'Storms', 'Sisters of the Moon' and 'Beautiful Child', were gorgeous but glum, as if all those endless nights and doomed romances had caught up with her.

Buckingham's initial response to 'Storms' was especially lukewarm, but he still contributed soaring backing vocals. Whatever personal issues he had, Buckingham did his best work on some of Nicks' and McVie's songs here, deserving his 'special thanks to . . .' mention in *Tusk*'s production credits.

However, Buckingham's compositions were the ones that would define *Tusk* and suggested a solo album smuggled inside a Fleetwood Mac record. The segue between McVie's 'Over and Over' and Buckingham's 'The Ledge' illustrated the stylistic leap and was like being woken up by a one-man band walloping a bass drum and blowing a kazoo at the foot of the bed. Lindsey described this new approach as 'rockabilly on acid'.

Such was his grip on *Tusk* that none of the others even played on 'The Ledge'. Elsewhere, Fleetwood replicated the composer's tissue-box percussion on 'What Makes You Think You're the One' by recording his at night on two boombox cassette recorders. 'It made this really trashy, explosive sound,' said Buckingham, admiringly.

Fleetwood followed his boy genius's demands, but John McVie bristled when Buckingham told him how to play a bassline. 'I think there were times when John was railing against something good for the band but not for his ego,' said Buckingham.

Caillat and his co-producer Richard Dashut also learned to accept Buckingham's counter-intuitive demands. 'He would physically make me distort the guitar to sound like fingernails scraping across a chalkboard,' recalled Caillat.

'Sometimes I could go too far, doing things more gratuitously than needed to be done,' conceded Buckingham. *Tusk* soundtracked a fraught time in his life. He was experiencing seizures and was diagnosed with mild epilepsy. One night, he cut off his long, curly locks with a pair of nail scissors and was greeted by gasps of shock the following day. 'Lindsey,' boomed Christine. 'What have you done to your beautiful hair?'

Caillat also recalled Buckingham taking the same scissors to his perfect Levi's and wearing eyeliner: 'Every time he walked by a mirror, he'd check himself out and suck in his cheeks.'

The change of image was a symbolic gesture. 'Really, I wanted to be in the Clash,' he admitted. But it suited the music. The lyrics to 'Not That Funny' and 'What Makes You Think You're the One' were as accusatory as 'Go Your Own Way' but passed on the guitar-hero solos and radio-friendly choruses.

Buckingham also sounded like a frightened young man, and showed a vulnerable side on 'Save Me a Place', 'That's All for Everyone' and 'I Know I'm Not Wrong'. The sound of these songs, rather than their content, subverted the norm. Frantic rhythms and primitive-sounding guitars had replaced *Rumours'* crushed-velvet, silver coke-spoon vibes.

All parties found the middle ground on *Tusk*'s title track, which evoked Stevie's 'Watusi warrior', but with a woozy brass arrangement anchoring the shamanic vocals and non-linear verses. When Warners refused to pay for the University of Southern California Trojan Marching Band to play on the track, Fleetwood stuck the bill on his overloaded credit card. In doing so, he helped make 'Tusk' a UK and US top-ten hit.

One evening at Village Recorder, Fleetwood toppled over and lay like a felled tree among the empty champagne bottles. He was diagnosed with hypoglycaemia, exacerbated by too many drugs and not enough vitamins. But he was also struggling with his father's death, the end of his marriage, his affair with Sara Recor and the pressure of being the band's drummer and manager.

Tusk eventually ground to a halt in the late summer of 1979. The tapes were then taken to the audio-digital company Soundstream's HQ in Salt Lake City for a final mix and to achieve the perfect gap between songs. The band had decided the optimum time between tracks should be 6.67 seconds, but Soundstream's scientists revealed that their facility only dealt in whole seconds. They had to call in their boss, Dr Thomas Stockham (who'd helped analyse the doctored Watergate tapes), to fix the problem.

Later, back in LA, each band member was given a recording of the final sequenced album. Christine called Caillat and told him that the fade on 'Never Forget' needed longer than its designed 6.67 seconds. Ken was in a Learjet heading back to Salt Lake City within the hour.

A few weeks before *Tusk*'s arrival, the Eagles released *The Long Run*, their safe-as-houses follow-up to *Hotel California*. Buckingham was delighted that Fleetwood Mac had broken the musical mould and their rivals hadn't. But it would be a pyrrhic victory.

Buckingham defended *Tusk*'s ruinously expensive costs by reminding the press that *Rumours* had taken just as long but was recorded in a cheaper studio. 'It's all been taken out of context,' he protested. Every dollar counted, though. Being a double album, *Tusk* would have to sell 500,000 to break even.

The LP reached number one in the UK and even received praise in the punk-conscious *New Musical Express*. 'If you reckon you're too hip for *Tusk*, then you're just too hip,' suggested *NME*'s Nick Kent.

But *Tusk* stalled at number four in the US. 'We all expected it to sell more,' admitted Buckingham. 'Maybe not like *Rumours*, certainly' – which had sold 13 million by 1980 – 'but a couple of million more wouldn't have hurt.'

At the time, Buckingham was accused of self-sabotage: 'Mick said to me, "We went too far, you blew it."' Publicly, though, Fleetwood blamed Warners for allowing *Tusk* to be broadcast in full on the US radio network Westwood One. 'Everyone listening taped it on their cassette players,' he complained, 'and didn't bother buying the record.'

As of 2018, though, *Tusk* had sold a respectable 6.6 million, and Mick was calling it his second favourite Mac album after *Then Play On*. Time has been a great healer. Buckingham finessed *Tusk*'s wilful experimentation into 1987's *Tango in the Night*. The traits that baffled Warners and the fanbase in 1979 have attracted listeners this century. The New Pornographers, St. Vincent, Tame Impala and Bonnie 'Prince' Billy were among the hipper, younger things covering *Tusk*'s songs on 2012's *Just Tell Me That You Want Me: A Tribute to Fleetwood Mac*.

Nowadays, *Tusk* gets compared to the Beatles' '*White Album*' and the Stones' *Exile on Main Street*, the acclaimed but less user-friendly follow-ups to *Sgt. Pepper's Lonely Hearts Club Band* and *Sticky Fingers*.

Tusk's bloody-mindedness is part of its enduring appeal and another possible origin for the title. 'The term "Get tusked" means "Go fuck yourself",' explained Ken Caillat, determined to bury the 'Mick's penis' rumours once and for all. 'This was the attitude Fleetwood Mac had adopted under the onslaught of its new-found fame and fortune. They reacted in the most outrageous way possible – *Tusk*!'

'Tusk', the Single

The Jungle Book Revisited

In June 1979, John McVie had a near-death experience when a whale almost sank his sailing boat, Challenger, on a voyage to Tahiti. On the day of this nautical mishap, Fleetwood Mac were making a video for their new single, 'Tusk', and using a cardboard cut-out of the absent bassist. Coincidentally, 'Tusk's tribal drums and chanting vocals suggested an old sea shanty, and it's one of Fleetwood Mac's greatest, oddest songs and their unlikeliest hit.

Composer Lindsey Buckingham had been fooling around with the song's riff forever. 'We used to jam it at soundchecks,' recalled Fleetwood. 'When we started on the album [in 1978], we worked on it, but everybody lost interest, and it went in the dustbin.'

That summer, Fleetwood joined his mother and sister on vacation in the French fishing village of Barfleur. His father, Mike, had recently died, and it was a rare opportunity for the surviving family to be together.

A boozy Fleetwood remembered tottering off the plane straight into a stretch limo with a well-stocked drinks cabinet for the final leg of the journey: 'And by the time I arrived, I was pretty well gone.'

He awoke the following day to the din of a brass band marching past his window. Fleetwood nodded off before being disturbed by the band marching back minutes later. His visit had coincided with Barfleur's annual Mardi Gras-style celebration for a local saint.

Fleetwood threw on some clothes, grabbed the previous night's half-finished bottle of vino and followed the band as they made further laps of the village, joined by more of its townsfolk.

Months later, Fleetwood remembered this communal celebration while recording at LA's Village Recorder. 'Tusk' had started to take shape: Buckingham's guitar riff was retrieved and turned into a loop, enabled by the band and its familiars feeding a length of tape into the recorder.

The riff was merged with Fleetwood's drum pattern, into which he'd thrown everything – including Sunday lunch. Besides wooden drums, floor toms and tissue boxes, Fleetwood beat out the song's martial rhythm on a leg of lamb. 'It's one of the greatest drum tracks I've ever heard,' said Buckingham, years later. 'It's up there with "Instant Karma".'

But Fleetwood was convinced the song needed more. 'I wanted to capture the energy, the sense of community created by that band in Barfleur,' he said. Enter the University of Southern California's (USC) Trojan Marching Band. Fleetwood Mac's fixer Judy Wong had a contact at the university and arranged a meeting with the USC Trojan Band's director, Dr Arthur C. Bartner. Fleetwood Mac invited Bartner to their studio, where Buckingham played him the riff. 'You know, "Buh-buh-buh-Buh-buhbuh . . ."' recalled Bartner, who composed a score with trumpets, trombones, saxophones, flutes and piccolos.

Fleetwood decided to pay for the band, the cost of hiring Los Angeles' Dodger Stadium and a camera crew to film the performance himself.

On 4 June 1979, Dr Bartner, the USC's 112-strong marching band, Fleetwood Mac, a mobile recording unit and a film crew descended on the Dodger Stadium. 'The marching band was Mick's idea, and it was a stroke of genius,' said Buckingham. 'But the challenge was getting them on the existing track, in sync with the other instruments.'

The problem was the band could only play if they were marching. 'And we couldn't follow them around the field with microphones,' said Ken Caillat. Just when it looked like they'd have to postpone, Caillat discovered the band could play if they marched on the spot. Special microphones were placed around them to capture the music but not 112 pairs of feet stamping on the grass.

The subsequent video contained several wonderful cameos. There was Dr Bartner conducting from a stepladder; Mick Fleetwood, headphones clamped to his ears, gyrating to the rhythm; Christine McVie wafting around, cradling a glass of wine; Buckingham trying on one of the Trojans' plumed helmets; and Stevie Nicks performing some cheerleader baton twirls while strutting across the pitch. John McVie was off sailing that day and was replaced by the aforementioned cardboard cut-out.

At 2:58 minutes, the Trojan Marching Band re-appeared, blasting out the riff and sashaying into the stadium in their cardinal red and gold uniforms. Fleetwood Mac watched from the bleachers, where Stevie jumped to her feet and Buckingham told her to sit down, like a parent reprimanding a naughty toddler.

Inevitably, as it was recorded on the hoof and in a baseball stadium, there was leakage between tracks on the final single. Those blessed with a dog's hearing might be able to identify the words 'How are the tenors, Tony?' among the blur of voices. 'Real savage, like,' drawls another.

The USC Marching Band's brass arrangement compounded 'Tusk's ear-worm hook and gave its whispered vocals and primal howls a radio-friendly sheen.

Some listeners of a particular vintage may be reminded of 'Colonel Hathi's March (The Elephant Song)' from *The Jungle Book*. Though it's unlikely Buckingham had Disney's hit animation in mind when he wrote it. It's also difficult to imagine 'Tusk' being as big a hit without those swaggering horns.

'Tusk' was released in October 1979 and went up against ABBA's 'Gimme! Gimme! Gimme!' and the Jam's 'The Eton Rifles' in the UK and trailed behind Michael Jackson's 'Don't Stop 'Til You Get Enough' in the US. It sounded unlike anything else in either chart but reached numbers six and eight, respectively.

More than forty years later, the song remains a huge part of USC life. 'Tusk's riff is the first sound that students hear when entering campus through the college's north-eastern gate, and the song's history is still being taught to new students.

'But what does it all *mean*?' wondered those watching Fleetwood Mac perform 'Tusk', as Buckingham roared into his mic and lurched around the stage like the hunchback of Notre Dame. 'It's Tusk, the elephant,' explained Stevie. 'That whole African-drum-tusk-in-the-air, happy, religious, ritualistic thing, with Mick as the African chief.'

'It is,' said Fleetwood, finally, 'a glorious noise.'

'Sara'

A Song About Life, Death and Fleetwood Mac

Two to three hits of marijuana, a mouthful of hot lemon tea, a few sips of Courvoisier – and Stevie Nicks was good to go. This was Nicks' magic formula for recording her vocal on 'Sara', one of Fleetwood Mac's greatest non-hits.

The question, 'Who was Sara?' has followed Nicks around since the song appeared on *Tusk*. Her answer has revealed more over time. 'I remember the night I wrote it,' she said. 'I sat up with a very good friend of mine whose name is Sara. She likes to think it's completely about her, but it's really not.'

'Sara' was Sara Recor, wife of Loggins and Messina's manager, Jim Recor, whom Nicks met in 1976. Sara and Nicks' close friendship was upended when Sara fell for Mick Fleetwood while he was already having an affair with Nicks.

Stevie and Mick's romance had begun on tour, fired by road fever and loneliness. Neither planned to be together for ever, but the *ménage à trois* cast a shadow over the early *Tusk* sessions. 'That just turned into a nightmare,' said Nicks. 'Sara moved in with Mick overnight, and I got a call from her husband telling me the news. Neither of them bothered to tell me.' But was Sara or Mick 'the poet in my heart' in the song? Nicks wasn't saying.

Stevie's first 'Sara' demo was sixteen minutes long. 'It was about myself, Sara, Mick and what all of us in Fleetwood Mac were going through at the time,' she said. 'It was a saga, with many verses people haven't heard.'

But the finished song was filled with references to all kinds of life-and-death stuff. Apparently, the 'Great Dark Wing' was about Mick, and many, including her ex-boyfriend, the Eagles' Don Henley, presumed the line 'When you build your house, call me home' referred to a house Henley was building with his vast royalties from *Hotel California*.

'He wishes!' scoffed Nicks when she heard this. 'If Don wants to think the "house" was one of the ninety houses he built and never lived in . . .'

However, Henley was one of the first to hear 'Sara', as he and Nicks became a couple around the time of *Rumours*.

'Sara' was reworked for *Tusk* at Village Recorder studio with plenty of dope, brandy and lemon tea to hand. The band wrestled it down to six minutes and thirty seconds and stripped in Buckingham and Christine McVie's ethereal backing vocals and Christine's rattling tack piano. Fleetwood created a mesmeric shuffle, using a brush instead of a stick in his left hand, giving the song its cyclical feel.

Released as the second single from *Tusk*, 'Sara' made it as far as number seven in the US but failed to reach the UK top thirty. 'You have your happy favourites and your miserable favourites,' said Nicks. '"Sara" is one of my favourites.' But she didn't say if it was happy or sad.

Perhaps 'Sara' was both. It was also a song almost without a conventional beginning, middle and end, as if the listener was eavesdropping on parts of an extended conversation. This theory was born out by another Nicks song, 'Welcome to the Room . . . Sara', on 1987's *Tango in the Night*.

By then, Fleetwood was preparing to marry Sara Recor, and Nicks had used the pseudonym 'Sara Anderson' when checking into the Betty Ford Center. 'This is a dream, right,' she sang. 'Did I come here on my own?' This certainly wasn't one of the happy favourites.

Meanwhile, the song's legacy has lasted longer than Sara Recor's seven-year marriage to Mick Fleetwood. '"Sara" is the kind of song you can fall in love with,' said its composer. 'Because I fell in love with it.'

'Not That Funny'

The Push-ups Song

In 1979, the scale and expense of Fleetwood Mac's *Tusk* caused palpitations among their record company staff. So, imagine how Warners' senior management felt when the band announced the clattering, lo-fi 'Not That Funny' as the double album's third single?

'Not That Funny' was one of several pieces worked up during the *Rumours* tour. Lindsey Buckingham created eight-track demos in his hotel suites: recording in the bathrooms and playing the 'drums' on mattresses, pillows and tissue boxes. Although Ken Caillat called it 'One of Lindsey's punk rock songs,' it's the execution rather than the song that challenged the norm.

Buckingham later played everything on 'Not That Funny' at Village Recorder's Studio D, overdubbing tom-toms, snares, detuned bass and guitars and augmenting its jagged rhythm with the cello setting on a primitive polyphonic keyboard. It sounded like a drunken mariachi band trying to impersonate the Clash.

To do justice to the angry lyrics – 'No one to turn you on/All your hope is gone' – Buckingham sang while doing push-ups on the floor. 'He made us tape a microphone to a tile floor,' recalled Caillat, 'and he was doing a push-up over the microphone, singing, "Not . . . that . . . funny . . . is . . . it!" and screaming "You bitch" and "You son of a bitch" into the backing vocals.'

255

The irony of Fleetwood Mac using a high-end studio to create something that sounded like it was recorded in a toilet wasn't lost on anyone. Undeterred, Buckingham presided over a nine-minute jam of 'Not That Funny' on Fleetwood Mac's next tour. However, the single failed to chart in either the UK or the US: 'And I was told in no uncertain terms, "Lindsey, we are not doing that again."'

'Brown Eyes'

Peter Green's Slight Return

'Brown Eyes', written by Christine McVie, is tucked away on side three of *Tusk*; a beautiful song, but too sad and slight to have been considered as a single. Instead, it posed a set of questions ('What do you want to do? . . . What do you want me to say?') over a ghostly piano figure, later sampled by producer DJ Shadow on his 1994 single, 'Lost and Found'.

It's sparse too, almost ambient, as if the rhythm section isn't fully present. Conflicting stories surround 'Brown Eyes'. According to Ken Caillat, Mick Fleetwood was 'too screwed up to play', and Richard Dashut took over instead.

The group also received an unexpected visitor when Peter Green showed up at the studio. Green played ghostly sounding guitar, only some of which was used on the song's fade-out. An alternative version featuring more of his playing was included in 2015's *Tusk* deluxe edition.

Green's cameo was all part of Mick Fleetwood's cunning plan to get his old friend working again. In 1979, Green was living in Los Angeles, and Fleetwood persuaded Warner Bros to offer him a half-a-million-dollar contract. Green pondered the paperwork for a few minutes but refused to sign, believing it was a deal with the devil. 'At which point I said, "I'm done with you, Peter,"' complained Fleetwood. 'Brown Eyes' would be the last Fleetwood Mac song on which Peter Green ever played.

257

'Beautiful Child'

The (Not So) Secret Love Affair

'A grown-up adrift in rock 'n' roll's crazy kindergarten,' was how Beatles biographer Philip Norman described the group's publicist, Derek Taylor. By 1977, the Fab Four were over and Taylor was living in Los Angeles with his wife, Joan, and their six children, and employed as vice president of creative services at Fleetwood Mac's record company, Warner Bros.

Taylor was noted for his dapper dress sense, bottomless well of Beatle anecdotes, dry British wit and flair for understatement. When a journalist asked him why Fleetwood Mac's *Rumours* had been such a big hit, he suggested because 'it was a very, very good two-sided pop record'.

Following her split from Lindsey Buckingham, Stevie Nicks embarked on what she later described as 'another one of my doomed romances . . . with an English man who was older than me'. This was forty-five-year-old Derek Taylor, and their fleeting affair was recounted in 'Beautiful Child' on 1979's *Tusk*.

When Eagle Don Henley disclosed that Nicks had become pregnant by him, some presumed 'Beautiful Child' referred to their unborn baby. But the lyrics suggested a woman reassuring an older man that she wanted to pursue their relationship, despite the age gap. The line, 'You fell in love when I was only ten,' referred to Taylor marrying Joan in 1958.

Stevie later recalled sitting at Taylor's feet while he read her poetry, told stories about John Lennon and called her 'a beautiful child'. The affair ended during an emotional night at the Beverly Hills Hotel. 'We stopped because it was going to hurt a lot of people,' she said. 'The song is a straight re-telling of the last night of that relationship.'

Even without knowing the back story, Stevie's melancholy ballad suggested something heartfelt. But it was brought to life by the vocals (created in an echo chamber at LA's Village Recorder studios), which made the group's three vocalists sound like they were singing side by side in the same church choir.

In 1980, Derek Taylor resigned from Warners and returned to England. He'd dodged a bullet. *Tusk* was a ruinously expensive album and led to tough questions in the Warners boardroom. Tougher still, when track two, side four, was about one of the senior staff.

Back in the UK, Taylor wrote books, produced records and held the surviving Beatles' hands when they launched their *Anthology* project in the mid-'90s. Derek and Joan were still together when he died of cancer in September 1997.

'Beautiful Child' was added to the setlist for Fleetwood Mac's next world tour. Stevie introduced it most nights as 'a really special song' and 'one of those songs that got lost.' But she waited until 2013 before revealing who it was about. For Ken Caillat, it outshone everything else on *Tusk*. 'It was,' he said, 'the most gorgeous song on the album.'

Scooter

Stevie Nicks' Least Favourite Dog

The cover of *Tusk* shows a dog biting the cuff of an unseen man's jeans. The trousers belonged to Ken Caillat, and the assailant was his brown-and-white beagle mix, Scooter.

Caillat and Scooter went everywhere together, and the dog attended recording sessions for both *Rumours* and *Tusk*. Not everybody was a fan, though. The band first met Scooter at LA's Record Plant studios while making *Rumours* in 1976. Stevie Nicks and Christine McVie arrived with their respective pooches, Duster and Ginny, immediately attracting Scooter's unwanted attention.

Neither the dogs nor their owners were impressed, and, over time, Scooter embodied Fleetwood Mac's ongoing battle of the sexes. 'Stevie and Christine never liked Scooter,' said Caillat. 'But all of the guys in the band liked him.'

Then Scooter sneaked onto the cover of 1979's *Tusk* album, causing a further rift. After Scooter passed away in 1983, Stevie jokingly told Caillat she'd placed a hex on him some years earlier. 'Stevie said, "Your dog had that album cover,"' recalled Caillat. '"And it should have been mine."'

'The Elephant Man'

When a Rock-Star Wildlife Photographer Met Fleetwood Mac

'He's a genius, but he's a fruitcake,' said Iman about Peter Beard, the artist/photographer who took the Somali supermodel and future Mrs David Bowie's first pictures. A year later, in 1976, Iman made her debut appearance in the fashion bible *Vogue*. Instead of mentioning that he'd met Iman when she was studying political science at the University of Nairobi, Beard told the world he'd discovered her tending goats in the Somalian bush.

'Half Tarzan, half Byron' was another description of the artist behind the inside sleeve of Fleetwood Mac's *Tusk*. Peter Beard threw himself at life ever since being born into a monied New York family in 1938. He first visited Africa after graduating from Yale and taking a job in Kenya's Tsavo National Park. Beard's first book, 1965's *The End of the Game*, documented the plight of the African elephant and later shared a title with Peter Green's first solo album.

Beard's passion for environmental and wildlife issues was ahead of the curve, if at odds with his lifestyle. 'He accelerated through the decades like a freight train,' wrote his biographer, Graham Boynton, 'hunting wild animals, making art, taking photographs, celebrity friend-hopping and effortlessly seducing some of the world's most beautiful women'.

Beard's three wives included fashion model Cheryl Tiegs; he partied with Francis Bacon and Mick Jagger; and listed marijuana, ecstasy and cocaine as his favourite drugs. 'Genius fruitcake' also made Beard the ideal collaborator for Fleetwood Mac.

In 1979, the band's art director, Larry Vigon, wanted to shake up their image for *Tusk*. Vigon commissioned three photographers for the project. Norman Seeff shot the group posing in dry ice, and fine art photographer Jayme Odgers created a surreal photo-composition of an upside-down room (which Fleetwood Mac purportedly loathed).

Meanwhile Vigon commissioned Peter Beard after seeing one of his journals, filled with Polaroids, torn-out newspaper headlines, dead insects, dried leaves, feathers, rocks, bones and all kinds of ephemera documenting his travels and adventures.

Beard spent a week photographing Fleetwood Mac in their natural habitat (LA's Village Recorder studio), where he apparently upset Stevie Nicks by calling her a 'lard arse'. His two LP collages then layered Polaroids of the group's members alongside images of dogs, human ears, naked women, babies, bones, handwritten song titles, elephants and tusks, *lots* of tusks.

One night, Richard Dashut came home to find his house guest Beard had cut his hand with a razor and was dripping plasma over the collage. Beard casually told him not to worry, and that he often signed his work in blood. Another night, Dashut returned to find one of Beard's friends, an unnamed 'James Bond Girl', lying in his bed waiting, apparently as a 'thank you' present for letting him lodge at the property.

Like the music inside, *Tusk*'s artwork divided opinion. Stevie Nicks was cross about not being pictured on the cover, and an appalled fan mailed Larry Vigon an envelope containing the sleeve torn into tiny pieces.

In November 1979, Beard staged an elephant benefit at Manhattan's infamous Studio 54 nightclub. Fleetwood Mac were among the guests, and the event raised thousands of dollars. But it was his last dealings with the band.

Beard continued to accelerate through life, but his relationship with his beloved animals wasn't without its pitfalls. In 1996, a cow elephant in Tanzania charged at him, goring his thigh and smashing his pelvis in five places. Beard defied his doctors and survived the attack. But from here on, his personal life became even more chaotic.

Beard eventually suffered a stroke, leading to dementia. In March 2020, during the early days of the global pandemic, he went missing from his home in New York. His body was discovered a month later in the woods at Camp Hero State Park. Against all odds, though, the 'genius fruitcake' had made it to eighty-two years old.

The Harmonica Killer

Fleetwood Mac's Homemade Horror Movie

Mick Fleetwood made his big screen debut playing 'Mic', a veteran freedom fighter in the 1987 thriller, *The Running Man*. Fleetwood's white wig and beard looked like they might blow away any second, as he delivered his first line – 'Mister Richards, I'm surprised you were so easily caught' – to Arnold Schwarzenegger's 'Captain Ben Richards'.

More token-Brit roles followed in the TV series *Wise Guys* and *Star Trek: The Next Generation*, and the comedy-drama, *Snide and Prejudice*, where Fleetwood played a mental-health patient convinced he was Pablo Picasso. Less well-known was his early role in 1980's *The Harmonica Killer*, until an enterprising Fleetwood Mac insider uploaded ten minutes of it onto YouTube.

The Harmonica Killer was a horror movie skit filmed at Santa Monica's Village Recorder during the making of *Tusk*. It was based around a tortuous in-joke, about a murderer who announces his arrival with a dissonant blast of harmonica, and suggests studio fever and cocaine madness had spread throughout the camp. Apparently, Lindsey Buckingham and his guitar tech Ray Lindsey shot the footage with a camcorder on the staircase outside Studio D and inside the Maharishi Mahesh Yogi's temple on the floor above. The lo-fi production values gave it a sort of pre-*Blair Witch Project* flavour. But it was downhill from there.

Richard Dashut was shown lecturing about transcendental meditation behind a pulpit in the Maharishi's temple, before being attacked by a harmonica-blowing Mick Fleetwood. In one scene, Fleetwood chops off Dashut's rubber hand, and somebody, possibly Buckingham, can be heard laughing off-camera.

'I was a truly bad actor,' confessed Dashut. 'But we went at it without even a hint of a script.' In contrast, Fleetwood played 'deranged' very well. His eyes were on stalks, his hair matted, and he looked like he'd been up for days – which he probably had.

The Harmonica Killer was lost until 2013 when the clip mysteriously appeared online. In the meantime, the killer's deadly instrument could be heard to much better effect on 'I Know I'm Not Wrong', Lindsey Buckingham's favourite song on *Tusk*.

Fleetwood Mac Live

Merry Christmas, 1980

As soon as John Courage opened the door to his hotel suite he knew
something was awry. The tour manager gazed through a haze of
feathers, and saw that his room was filled with bales of straw and
fifty chickens, squawking, fluttering and defecating over every
surface. One had even laid an egg on top of the TV set.

Mick Fleetwood had arranged the chicken prank as a birthday
gift. But when Courage spotted the group's drug buddy, Dennis Wilson, drunk in the bath and holding two lit cigarettes, he
sprang into action. Courage tossed the dry straw into the corridor and shooed as many of the birds as he could into a nearby
lift. A minute later, the chickens were promenading through
the lobby of San Francisco's St James Hotel, trailing feathers
and shit.

The cost of cleaning the suite was added to Fleetwood Mac's
escalating bill. It was December 1979, three months into the
Tusk tour, but with another five more to go. However, the album
was selling far less than *Rumours* and Warners needed to plug the
hole. 'What about a double live LP?' someone at the company
suggested.

Only Fleetwood agreed. Buckingham, especially, was wary of
Fleetwood Mac following similar double-live sets from Kiss, Lynyrd
Skynyrd and Peter Frampton. But needs must, and the prosaically

266

titled *Live* was patched together from shows all around the world, including Tokyo, Paris and Wembley, and rushed out in time for Christmas 1980.

Despite the rest of the band's antipathy, *Live* gave Fleetwood Mac's audience a greatest hits set with added applause and three new songs. Alongside the evergreen 'Say You Love Me' and 'Don't Stop', were Stevie's 'Fireflies', Christine's 'One More Night' and a harmony-heavy cover of the Beach Boys' 'Farmer's Daughter', recorded after-hours at the Santa Monica Auditorium.

Live also documented Fleetwood Mac in the throes of a huge identity crisis. Buckingham's stage look fell into two categories, as captured on the inside sleeve. There was 'Zoolander Lindsey' in his eyeliner and Armani suit and 'Amish Lindsey' wearing a work shirt and a straw hat. The music was similarly schizophrenic.

'We haven't played anything from *Tusk* yet, so we're going to try something out for you,' announces Christine after four songs. The audience gets off lightly with 'Over and Over' and 'Sara'. Less so, an 8:59 version of 'Not That Funny' in which Buckingham whispers, screams, yodels and solos with such ferocity he must have drawn blood.

There were times though when the after-hours fun and romantic tension impacted on the performances. John McVie was struck down with food poisoning partway through a date in New Orleans, and Fleetwood frequently collapsed in the dressing room with dangerously low blood sugar.

Also, while Stevie and Lindsey delivered one of *Live*'s highlights, Buckingham Nicks' sweet country-rocker, 'Don't Let Me Down Again', their musical empathy couldn't prevent an ugly incident in Auckland, New Zealand. That night, a whisky-drunk Buckingham pulled his jacket over his head to mimic Stevie's trademark shawl and kicked out at her. After the show, Christine slapped him around the face, screaming, 'Don't ever do something like that to this band again!'

'I wouldn't doubt that I mimicked Stevie on stage,' he admitted in 2013. 'And kicked her? . . . That could have happened too.'

Dreams

The *Tusk* tour ended in September 1980 with two sold-out dates at the Hollywood Bowl. After which band manager Mick sheepishly revealed they'd squandered most of the tour profits on luxury hotel suites, limousines, drugs, champagne, Led Zeppelin's private plane (cost: $2,500 a day) and chickens.

There was more expense to come when Christine and Stevie refused to sanction the album's inside-cover portraits, taken after one of the shows. The women insisted they were photographed again, with proper hair and make-up in a professional studio.

Live sold modestly. After which, the band fired Mick Fleetwood as their manager, and Lindsey and Stevie both rushed off to make solo albums. Welcome to the '80s.

Part Five

'I knew I was going to die and
I didn't want to die'

Creative warfare, solo superstardom, mind-boggling excess and a roll call of understudies: How Fleetwood Mac navigated two challenging new decades.

Mirage

Rumours *Partie Deux*

'We pulled into the drive and saw Stevie Nicks peering out of the ancient leaded glass window, looking like Queen Guinevere in the misty early light . . .' Mick Fleetwood's memories of making *Mirage* at France's Château D'Hérouville suggests *The Count of Monte Cristo* meets *This Is Spinal Tap*.

Returning to the Château after an all-night soirée, Fleetwood passed a stable: 'So I got this big grey mare, took a long pull from my ever-present silver flask of good Cognac, and rode right up the stone steps of the main entrance.' After which Stevie swept down the staircase, jumped on the horse, 'and cantered off through the greening orchards, her long cape billowing behind her.'

Fleetwood recounted these scenes in his first memoir, *Fleetwood*. It was April 1981, and the band had decamped to France. 'It was Mick's idea,' said Christine, 'to get back into that bubble, as we did in Sausalito with *Rumours* – see what would come out of a confined space.' But Fleetwood also needed to work abroad for tax reasons.

The Château D'Hérouville was an eighteenth-century pile near Auvers-sur-Oise and the former residence of composer Frederic Chopin. Elton John and Pink Floyd had made records here (*Honky Château* and *Obscured by Clouds*, respectively), and porn movies, including *The Kinky Ladies of Bourbon Street*, had been filmed in its ornate surroundings.

271

One of the master bedrooms was reputedly haunted by the ghosts of Chopin and his mistress, Amantine Dupin de Francueil (the birth name of French novelist George Sand). When David Bowie recorded some of his *Low* album at the Château, he sensed bad vibes and refused to stay in the room. His co-producer Brian Eno took the suite instead and claimed to have been woken up one night by a pair of ghostly hands shaking him by the shoulders. Christine and co-producer Ken Caillat sat up one night waiting for the ghost, with a bottle of Courvoisier for company, but didn't encounter another spirit.

Staying under one roof was meant to get everyone out of their comfort zones by sharing bathrooms and eating meals together. 'For a while, it was quaint,' said Lindsey, 'and then it quickly got not to be.'

The five were rarely together, as each one recorded their parts separately. They also found any excuse to down tools and have fun. John McEnroe and Vitas Gerulaitis stopped by one week on their way to compete in a German tennis tournament, prompting several chemically enhanced games of ping-pong. But most of the time, Buckingham and Nicks complained about having nothing to do.

'Lindsey and Stevie became the biggest babies I've ever seen,' recalled Caillat. 'It was like, "I don't have any TV, I'm so *bored*."' Caillat hired video machines for them all and had films of baseball games couriered over from the States. But it still wasn't enough.

After a couple of months, everybody flew back to the US, where work resumed at Sausalito's Record Plant. After *Tusk*'s disappointing sales figures, Warner Bros wanted another *Rumours*. 'I got a lot of support from the band during *Tusk*,' said Buckingham, 'but the attitude changed when it became apparent it wasn't going to sell 15 million.'

Mirage took fourteen months to make and was fitted in around extra-curricular activities. Fleetwood was promoting his first solo LP, *The Visitor*, and Buckingham and Nicks both released their own albums. Lindsey's *Law and Order* didn't make the *Billboard* top thirty, but Stevie's *Bella Donna* reached number one, helped by

'Stop Draggin' My Heart Around', her US top-ten duet with grizzly southern rocker Tom Petty.

Jealousy was rife within the camp and Buckingham nicknamed the song 'Stop Draggin' My Career Around'. Meanwhile, Stevie gave him a signed copy of *Bella Donna*, which he left propped against the studio wall until she eventually crossed out the dedication and gifted it to somebody else.

The group's bad habits also resumed with a vengeance. 'In the studio, we had a ritual, in which the engineers and band members all started humming a tune which would serve as a siren's call for cocaine,' said Fleetwood.

During *Mirage*, it was Vangelis' synthesiser theme to *Chariots of Fire*, the hit movie about two Olympic runners. Right on cue, Fleetwood would begin 'running' towards his bandmates in exaggeratedly slow motion, before dispensing the goods.

Mirage was meant to be out in time for Christmas 1981 but didn't appear until June 1982. Veteran Hollywood photographer George Hurrell had already photographed Buckingham in the style of a matinée idol for *Law and Order*. His *Mirage* cover shot continued the theme and showed Lindsey about to tango with a swooning Stevie, while Christine leant over his shoulder.

At the time, Lindsey described *Mirage* as a 'reconciliation of opposites'. In 2012, he called it 'a drag'. But, while a compromise, *Mirage* is better than received wisdom suggests. It's just that only two of Buckingham's songs, 'Empire State' and 'Eyes of the World', referenced his more adventurous work on *Tusk*.

Instead, the UK top-ten hit 'Oh Diane' was nouveau '50s pop; 'Can't Go Back' yoked Buckingham's frantic vocal to a nursery-rhyme tune, and he impersonated his bandmates' voices so well on 'Book of Love', Christine and Stevie wondered if they'd sung on it after all.

'There's nothing weird on *Mirage*,' explained Christine. 'There's no hidden hobgoblins. It's straightforward, simple rock 'n' roll songs.'

McVie kept it simple on the so-so ballad 'Wish You Were Here' and 'Only Over You', written for her troublesome boyfriend,

Dennis Wilson. Meanwhile, 'Love in Store' and 'Hold Me' (the album's biggest hit, co-written with singer-songwriter Robbie Patton) were shimmering soft-rock with the same rhythm as 'Don't Stop', and suggested a concerted attempt to woo back listeners disturbed by *Tusk*.

Nicks managed three songs on the finished record. 'That's Alright' displayed what Caillat called 'the ironic country tinge' and the doomy 'Straight Back' shared the same DNA as her recent solo hit 'Edge of Seventeen'. Had there been a video, it would have shown Stevie cantering through the greening orchards on a long grey mare.

Nicks hit paydirt with 'Gypsy', though. 'So I'm back to the velvet underground,' she purred, over the prettiest of melodies and Buckingham's deft guitar flourishes. 'Gypsy' became *Mirage*'s second biggest hit aided by a ruinously expensive video.

Other songs were recorded but shelved. Among them was Nicks' bitter-sounding 'Smile at You', which was later reworked for 2003's *Say You Will*, and an old country song, 'Cool Water', sung by John McVie and used as the B-side of 'Gypsy'.

Christine told interviewers that *Mirage* was a much happier-sounding album than *Rumours*. Its sales figures certainly made Warners happy: it reached number five in the UK and knocked soft-rock supergroup Asia's debut off the top spot in the States. Nothing could top *Rumours*, but *Mirage* went platinum twice over in the US.

Then Nicks pulled the rug from under them. She told the rest of the group she'd only commit to a short tour. 'The success of Stevie's solo career did much to boost our sales,' admitted Fleetwood. 'But her career was in full swing and she didn't want to commit to a marathon Fleetwood Mac tour.'

Stevie's best friend, voice therapist Robin Snyder Anderson, was also dying, and her own health was suffering. Nicks' cocaine use had escalated and she'd been diagnosed with bronchial asthma. Up on stage, she shrouded herself in a white shawl, like an Egyptian mummy, and exchanged black looks with Buckingham.

In September, the band pocketed $800,000 to headline the final night of the inaugural US Festival in San Bernardino. But the *Mirage* tour ended abruptly a month later. The LP dropped off the charts, and *American Fool* by their opening act, heartland rocker John Cougar, took its place at number one.

'It was nice while it lasted,' said a frustrated Fleetwood, 'but *Mirage* died as soon as we came off the road.' The drummer watched as their superstar lead singer disappeared into the mist like Chopin's ghost.

'Hold Me'

How to Make a Fleetwood Mac Video in 1982

Ingredients

1 desert location
5 band members (four of whom aren't talking to each other)
2 pairs of khaki shorts
2 pith helmets
1 piano and several guitars (to be buried in the sand)
1 psychiatrist's couch
1 white horse
1 painter's easel
Various René Magritte artworks
Several shards of mirrored glass
Mix for three days and then stand well back

US music television network, MTV, launched on 1 August 1981, and was soon being beamed into homes nationwide twenty-four hours a day. 'I was living in the Pacific Palisades,' recalled Stevie, 'and would sit on the edge of the bed, watching video after video, just stupefied.'

A year later, the video for Fleetwood Mac's new single, 'Hold Me', was on MTV heavy rotation alongside the Human League's 'Don't You Want Me' and Toto's 'Africa'.

The Many Lives of Fleetwood Mac

'Hold Me' was a bittersweet song, sung by Christine McVie and Lindsey Buckingham, and splattered with oddball percussion effects and sonorous backing vocals. How, though, to illustrate it on film? Fleetwood Mac surrendered control to video director Steve Barron and producer Simon Fields, who'd just made the acclaimed promo for Michael Jackson's 'Billie Jean'.

The pair took the group to a stretch of California's Mojave Desert, which they augmented with half-buried pianos, guitars and mirrored glass, and knowing nods to the Belgian surrealist painter René Magritte. The black-suited figure seen in the dunes borrowed from Magritte's 'The Art of Conversation', the bowler hat and carriage clock from his paintings, 'The Son of Man' and 'Time Transfixed'.

The narrative was confused at best, utter nonsense at worst. But it was the '80s, and such things didn't matter. Mick and John played archaeologists, exhuming the musical relics; Buckingham attempted to paint Nicks reclining on a psychiatrist's chaise longue, and Christine watched them through a telescope before leading a white horse over the sand.

Buckingham and Nicks seemed the most comfortable in front of the lens, and Lindsey's attempt to capture the elusive Stevie on canvas suggested a metaphor for their difficult relationship. Meanwhile, Fleetwood and McVie, in their pith helmets and khaki shorts, looked like they'd wandered in off the set of '70s TV comedy *It Ain't Half Hot Mum*.

Poor Christine, though, was required to act. 'Baby, don't you hand me a line,' she mimed while crumpling a love letter and attempting to portray 'angry and spurned'. In real life, she'd just given her boyfriend, Dennis Wilson, his marching orders.

Nobody was having a good time, and Fields later described the shoot as a 'fucking nightmare'. Band politics, various substances and the Mojave's 110-degree heat all took their toll. Christine spent ten hours in the make-up trailer and only emerged, eyes ringed black, when it was too dark to film; John McVie drank himself silly and tried to punch Fields, and Stevie couldn't walk across the dunes in her five-inch platform heels.

277

'Four of them – I can't recall which four – couldn't be in the same room for long,' said Barron. Which is why all five never appeared in the video simultaneously. It didn't matter. MTV propelled 'Hold Me' into the US top five, and Barron and Fields went on to create the video for Dire Straits' 1985 hit 'Money For Nothing'. That song's telling line, 'I want my MTV', was now a mission statement for all, even Fleetwood Mac.

'Gypsy'

The Most Expensive Pop Video in the World

In September 1982, MTV broadcast the world premiere of Fleetwood Mac's 'Gypsy'. Never ones to do anything by halves, the video was directed by hip film-maker Russell Mulcahy and cost $750,000, making it the most expensive promo of its time.

MTV's youthful audience wanted gripping narratives and fancy locations. For 'Thriller', Michael Jackson transmogrified from high-school student to werewolf, and Mulcahy had just shot Duran Duran posing in the Caribbean for 'Rio'. Fleetwood Mac didn't do horror movies or beach holidays, but they did do Stevie Nicks as a time-travelling gypsy.

'Gypsy' was a nostalgic song. Its lyric about going 'back to the velvet underground' referred to a boutique at 471 Broadway, San Francisco, where Janis Joplin bought her clothes, and a penniless Stevie Nicks went window shopping.

'Back to the floor . . . to a room with some lace and paper flowers' was about the spartan apartment, where she and Lindsey Buckingham slept, under a lace coverlet and beside a vase of flowers.

There was sadness, too. 'Gypsy' was also about Nicks' oldest friend, voice therapist Robin Snyder Anderson, who was dying of leukaemia. The line 'lightning strikes, maybe once, maybe twice' referred to the pair's friendship.

By now, though, Nicks was struggling with her own problems. In April 1982, she checked into a rehab treatment centre in Newport Beach. But she'd forgotten about the 'Gypsy' video shoot and left two weeks later. After the first day's filming, Nicks acquired a phial of cocaine, which she wrapped in tissue paper and hid behind her dressing-room mirror. When a cleaner threw the tissue and phial away, Nicks demanded someone – anyone – climb into the dumpster to find it. Nobody volunteered.

In the meantime, Russell Mulcahy's team had built a boudoir-meets-dance studio set and filled it with dolls, trinkets, feather boas, vintage lamps and crystal balls. A poodle-permed Stevie, wearing legwarmers and ballet pumps, was later filmed pirouetting, doing the splits and singing into the boudoir mirror.

The story began with Fleetwood Mac in a Depression-era soup kitchen and Nicks walking past her impoverished bandmates while wearing a shawl and bucket hat. The action then moved to a speakeasy, with palm fronds, champagne flutes and Christine McVie brandishing a cigarette holder.

Now cast as a Hollywood femme fatale, Nicks performed an excruciating slow dance with leading man Buckingham. 'I didn't want to be anywhere near Lindsey,' she admitted, 'and I certainly didn't want to be in his arms – and he wasn't a very good dancer.'

'I was coupling up the members of Fleetwood Mac and people were pulling me aside, saying, "No, no. Those two were fucking and then they split up,"' recalled Mulcahy. 'I got very confused.'

Nicks was then shown fleeing the club and running into a fake downpour. Off camera, she almost collided with a low-flying rainmaker. The final scene had her sashaying through a fairy-tale forest, flanked by dancing children; like *A Midsummer Night's Dream* meets a budget supermarket Christmas ad.

Mulcahy included brief shots of the others at the end, with Christine and Lindsey miming through rictus grins, while Mick Fleetwood played the bongos and looked to the heavens as if praying for divine intervention.

Was the video worth $750,000? Of course not. But it helped 'Gypsy' become a US top-twenty hit when the group needed it most. However, those unfamiliar with their story might have presumed its glamorous time-traveller was a solo star and the others her backing band. Before long, the rest of Fleetwood Mac were wondering the same.

Prince

When the Purple Imp Met the White-Winged Dove

Stevie Nicks and Prince's unconsummated love affair began in January 1983. Stevie had just married her best friend's widower, Kim Anderson, and the couple were driving to a ranch in Santa Barbara on honeymoon when Prince's new single 'Little Red Corvette' came on the radio.

Stevie started crooning her new song, 'Stand Back', over its melody. The two songs were like twins. The newlyweds found an electrical store, bought Prince's new album, *1999*, and a cassette player into which Stevie sang a demo of her new song.

Back in LA and working on her second solo LP, *The Wild Heart*, Stevie asked her producer Jimmy Iovine to get Prince's number. She wanted to tell him how much she loved 'Little Red Corvette' and wanted him to hear 'Stand Back'. Stevie was surprised when Prince himself answered the phone and agreed to come to the studio.

Prince arrived at Sunset Sound, flanked by an enormous white-haired bodyguard, and began playing basketball on the court outside. 'He was spinning the ball on his finger and throwing it backwards into the net, like one of the Harlem Globetrotters,' recalled Stevie.

Prince liked 'Stand Back', and agreed to play on the song. He recorded his symphonic-sounding synthesiser part in twenty minutes, asked not to be credited, but settled on 50 per cent of the publishing. A shrewd move, when 'Stand Back' and *The Wild Heart* both became US top-five hits.

In July, Stevie played at the Met Center in Prince's hometown of Minneapolis. He showed up after the gig and swept her away in his bright purple Camaro. The pair stayed up all night at his house in Paisley Park, trying to write a song together until Nicks fell asleep on the kitchen floor. 'We never went to bed together,' she insisted.

The next afternoon Prince drove Stevie to the local airstrip, where a private plane was waiting to take her to the next date. 'We got into the purple Camaro again, he bombs it down the freeway, right onto the tarmac alongside the jet,' she recalled.

The couple embraced while her bandmates gawped at them through the plane windows. Once inside, Nicks faced down the smirks and raised eyebrows and insisted, '*Nothing* happened.'

The pair's mutual admiration continued, though. Prince later told Stevie her solo hit 'Edge of Seventeen' had inspired his song 'When Doves Cry'. He also sent Stevie the backing track for 'Purple Rain', hoping she'd write some lyrics. 'But it was ten minutes long with this big guitar solo, and I was a bit overwhelmed,' she said.

Prince once asked Stevie why she didn't write more sexual songs. 'And I said "because that's not the way I am in real life",' she replied. 'I am not a person who walks naked through the house.'

'I think Prince would have liked a romance with me,' Nicks told *Mojo* magazine in 2013. It never happened, despite Stevie being single again by the time 'Stand Back' became a hit. Not that Stevie let Prince's death in April 2016 stop her communicating with her old musical partner. 'When I'm nervous I'll talk to Prince,' she claimed, 'and before I go on stage, I always say, "Walk with me Prince." I feel like Prince is with me.'

The Everly Brothers

Bye Bye Love

In 1983, Christine McVie guested on Phil Everly's latest solo album, singing harmonies on a cover of McGuiness Flint's 'When I'm Dead and Gone'. It was an easy fit: the Everly Brothers' cut-glass vocals echoed through many Fleetwood Mac hits, including Christine's 'Over My Head' and 'Say You Love Me'. But Phil and his older brother, Don, also had walk-on parts in the group's story.

It began when Christine was a seventeen-year-old art student. 'My friend Theresa and I were always singing and playing guitars and pretending to be the Everly Brothers,' she recalled. 'I was Phil, and she was Don.'

In April 1960, the Everlys played Christine's local venue, the Birmingham Odeon. Christine and Theresa couldn't afford tickets, but on the day of the show sat outside with their sketch pads, pretending to draw the backstage door. When an unsuspecting staff member left it ajar, the girls slipped inside and hid in a backstage cupboard, where they stayed until showtime.

'Finally, we decided we couldn't take it anymore, got out and just mingled – and nobody took any notice,' said Christine. After the gig, she plucked up the courage to approach Phil Everly and showed him some of her illustrations. It was her first encounter with a real-life pop star.

Decades later, Everly asked Christine to sing on his self-titled solo album. Christine told him about their first encounter, and he remembered. 'She was a young girl and an artist, and she gave me a drawing,' Everly told the BBC. 'It was a drawing of hands, like a Leonardo da Vinci study. I still have it in my house in Nashville, and if I can find it again, I'll show it to Chrissie.'

Unfortunately, Phil and Don's relationship was even more fractious than Fleetwood Mac's. The brothers' popularity waned in the early '60s, and both developed drug problems and stopped speaking to each other when they weren't performing. In July 1973, during a gig at Knott's Berry Theme park near Los Angeles, Phil smashed his guitar and walked offstage, leaving Don to finish the show alone.

A year later, Don released a solo album, *Sunset Towers*, and hired a then-unknown Lindsey Buckingham to sing and play in his backing band. 'It was an economic decision,' said Buckingham. The *Buckingham Nicks* album had flopped, and Stevie was waiting tables to pay the rent on their apartment.

Out on the road, a bearded Don Everly arrived on stage looking nothing like his teen-idol self and played a bunch of bluesy country-rock songs. The audience's reaction was the same every night. 'People would shout for [the Everly Brothers hits] "Bye Bye Love" and "Wake Up Little Susie",' Buckingham recalled. 'It was amazing but heartbreaking. Don was still a relatively young man, only in his late thirties, and he wanted to do something unlike the Everly Brothers. But I could see him getting visibly crushed. We did three or four cities, and then he cancelled the tour. I don't think he could handle anymore.'

There were parallels between Everly's frustration and Buckingham's when he later received a muted reception for his solo records. 'Don had done this album, and people didn't think it was what he should be doing,' said Lindsey. 'But it was something he *felt* he should be doing.'

Buckingham flew home, dejected and frustrated. Within six months he and Stevie had joined Fleetwood Mac. The Everly Brothers stayed apart for the rest of the decade but took the money, re-formed in the summer of 1983 and remained musically co-dependent for the rest of their working lives. Phil Everly died in 2014, and Don in 2021. Sadly, Phil never did find the teenage Christine's Leonardo da Vinci-style drawing.

Dennis Wilson

God Only Knows

Clunk! The noise was almost audible over the roar of Fleetwood Mac at the Philadelphia Spectrum. The band looked to the wings where their friends and familiars usually occupied a row of chairs. Except one had tipped over leaving Christine's boyfriend, the exiled Beach Boys drummer, Dennis Wilson, flat on his back, semi-conscious, with his feet visible to the arena audience.

The band tried not to laugh. But nobody seemed to care: Wilson's collapse typified the mood on the 1979 *Tusk* tour. Fleetwood Mac's next album, *Mirage*, included 'Only Over You', a ballad composed by Christine for her lover. 'People think I'm crazy,' she sings. 'But they don't know . . .'

Mick Fleetwood introduced the couple in the winter of 1978. 'Dennis was an utter loon, and Chris was like my sister,' he explained. 'I watched in trepidation as Chris almost went mad trying to keep up with Dennis.'

'Dennis whisked me off my feet,' recalled Christine. 'He was very charismatic, great looking, very charming, cute – if you can call a guy with a beard and a voice like Satan "cute".'

Days after their first meeting, he'd moved into her Coldwater Canyon home, bringing even more romantic anguish into the band. The Beach Boys had fired Dennis for his boozy antics and inability to play properly. So, he hung around Fleetwood Mac instead. They tolerated his disruptive presence precisely because he'd been a Beach Boy. The Mac's next release, *Live* included a cover of the Beach Boys' 'Farmer's Daughter', and Christine sang backing vocals on one song ('Love Surrounds Me') on the group's *L.A. (Light Album)*.

But Wilson also spent his days and nights attempting to seduce the group's female friends and guzzling their booze and drugs (he and John McVie once had a drinking competition before a show in San Francisco). Ken Caillat's abiding memory of Dennis at the recording sessions was seeing him 'coming in hammered, walking around with a jug of vodka and orange juice in his hand.'

Christine and Dennis's relationship lasted almost three years and was rarely dull. For her birthday, Dennis threw Christine a surprise party, booked an orchestra and serenaded her with a boozy version of Joe Cocker's 'You Are So Beautiful'. One Valentine's Day, he hired landscapers to plant a heart-shaped garden in the grounds of her mansion.

These grand gestures were undermined by the fact he'd charged them to Christine's credit card. Christine finally cracked when she discovered he'd been using the same card to buy skimpy outfits for a secret teenage girlfriend. The pair had planned to get wed, but Christine threw him out for good in December 1981.

With Christine gone, Dennis began a relationship with Beach Boy Mike Love's illegitimate sixteen-year-old daughter. Dennis had re-joined the group, and the affair added an extra frisson to intra-band relations.

Try as he might, Dennis couldn't stay sober. He spent 28 December 1983, drinking on his friend's yacht at Marina del Rey. Dennis had thrown some of his ex-wife's possessions into the bay after they'd divorced. Now, he wanted them back.

He'd already dived down several times and retrieved certain items. Then he went down again but never resurfaced. The subsequent forensic report suggested Wilson had experienced a shallow-water blackout and drowned.

'My secretary called me at eight in the morning. So I knew something was wrong,' recalled Christine. 'She said, "Dennis drowned today." And my first reaction was, "My God, is he all right?" I still really can't believe it. He just seemed indestructible.'

Seven months later, Lindsey Buckingham released his second solo album, *Go Insane*. Its closing track, 'D.W. Suite', was a nostalgic homage to *Pet Sounds* and dedicated to the late Beach Boy. 'Christine had loved Dennis with all her heart,' said Mick Fleetwood. 'It was a fascinating, if exhausting, episode in her life.'

'The Green Manalishi (With the Two Prong Crown)'

Money, Money, Money

Fleetwood Mac didn't appear at either of the Live Aid charity concerts in London or Philadelphia. It's not known whether organiser Bob Geldof even asked them. In July 1985, the group were in limbo, and Stevie Nicks was finishing a solo record.

While the world tuned in to watch Queen, U2, Madonna, Bob Dylan and a re-formed Led Zeppelin, Peter Green was performing with his new group, Kolors, at Dingwalls, a club in Camden, north London. Among the songs played at this 'Alternative Live Aid' benefit was 'The Green Manalishi (With the Two Prong Crown)'. By now, though, Green's public profile was so low that his appearance went almost unreported.

Instead, Judas Priest flew the flag at Live Aid by performing 'The Green Manalishi . . .' at Philadelphia's JFK Stadium. The Midlands heavy rockers had recorded their cover of Fleetwood Mac's hit in 1979, long before breaking the US. Now Judas Priest were in the ascendant and even their older songs had been embraced by a generation of MTV-watching heavy metal fans. Many of the Philadelphia audience had probably never even heard the original.

Fleetwood Mac had a hit with 'The Green Manalishi . . .' in May 1970. Its wrecking-ball riff was a startling contrast to their earlier chart-topper, 'Albatross'. But its composer, Peter Green, was in a different mindset now.

Green wrote the song after experiencing a drug-induced nightmare. He'd taken the hallucinogenic mescaline and imagined a green dog barking at him. Green believed that he and the canine were both dead and later talked about 'fighting my way back into my body'. The following day, he sat down in Richmond Park and began composing the lyrics about black nights and full moons, despite it being a balmy spring day.

Fleetwood Mac played the song live before recording it at Warner/Reprise's studio in Hollywood in April. Green played the others his demo and demanded that they copy his drum and bass parts. 'It put my nose right out of joint,' recalled John McVie.

The song sounded like monsters fighting and evoked Green's psychedelic dream state. Peter later refused to perform it on *Top of the Pops* when the producers declined to let him recreate its ghostly wails and cries.

But what was a Manalishi? Green or otherwise? On Judas Priest's watch, it became a common-or-garden heavy metal demon. But its composer believed the green dog in his dream was a metaphor for 'greenbacks' or money. He'd also hallucinated about seeing a shop assistant waving a thick roll of pound notes at him, 'And saying, "You're not what you used to be, you used to be an everyday person, now you think you're better than them."'

This all dovetailed with Green's growing unease with fame, stardom and how much 'manalishi' Fleetwood Mac were making. He'd recently been moved to tears by TV footage of famine in the Nigerian state of Biafra and urged his bandmates to send money. 'I just wanted to make a contribution,' insisted Green. 'The band thought I wanted to give all our money away, but not all of it.'

Green wrote cheques for large sums to various charities, including Save the Children. However, the rest of the group and their management were reluctant to do such a thing. Perversely, 'The Green Manalishi . . .' would make them even more money after it reached the UK top ten that summer.

Dreams

By 1985, the message was lost on many, but the song was oddly appropriate for Live Aid. There was Judas Priest, absurdly clad for the ninety-five-degree heat in studded black leather and chainmail, cranking out a cautionary tale of financial avarice at a fundraiser for drought-stricken Africa. Surely Peter Green would have approved?

'Jewel Eyed Judy'

The Band Mother's Tale

Fleetwood Mac's album *Tango in the Night* is dedicated to Judy Wong, their secretary, confidante and self-professed spiritual adviser. This was their equivalent of giving a gold watch to a long-serving employee. In 1986, Judy was let go after eighteen years spent managing Fleetwood Mac's LA office. 'Because of our solo careers, we all have our own managers, secretaries and lawyers now,' explained Christine at the time.

Judy was the first of several women to play a crucial, if often overlooked, role in the group's success story. Born of Chinese descent in California in 1943, Judy moved to Hampstead, north London, after graduating from college in the mid-'60s. Her arrival coincided with Britain's beat-pop boom, and she quickly became a regular at Klooks Kleek, an R&B club above the Railway Hotel in West Hampstead. It was here she first met Mick Fleetwood, drumming in her then-boyfriend, keyboard player Peter Bardens' band, the Peter B's. 'Mick was so tall, and he looked comical,' she recalled.

Over time Judy befriended many musicians, including the Peter B's' new guitarist, Peter Green, Eric Clapton, the Kinks and Eric Burdon. She became a familiar presence on London's nascent blues rock scene, working for the Gunnell brothers' booking agency in Soho, and attending the recording sessions for John Mayall's Bluesbreakers' groundbreaking *Beano* album.

293

By 1968, Judy had returned to San Francisco, where she ran the Passionflower boutique in the hippie-chic Haight-Ashbury district. She sold stage clothes to Janis Joplin and employed Mick Fleetwood's wife, Jenny, as a shop assistant when she came to town for a summer vacation.

In February 1969, Judy appeared in a *Rolling Stone* cover story, 'The Groupies and Other Girls'. She was upfront about her appreciation of musicians; detailing how she and her girlfriends decided which member of the Moody Blues they each wanted to meet. But at twenty-six years old, she was already concerned about some of her younger peers. 'I've seen it happen where a chick will go up to a guy and say, "I'm 18, I'm clean, let's fuck,"' Judy marvelled. 'Imagine that. It's got nothing to do with a personal relationship.'

By the end of the '60s, Judy was back with Fleetwood Mac. *Kiln House*, released in 1970, included Danny Kirwan's song, 'Jewel Eyed Judy', supposedly written in her honour but coinciding with her marriage to Jethro Tull's bassist Glenn Cornick. The marriage lasted two years, although the pair remained friends.

Really, Judy was wedded to Fleetwood Mac, a union that became official when 'Wongie' began managing the office of their new company, Seedy Management, in Hollywood. She worked tirelessly on their behalf: offering a shoulder to cry on and a sounding board for ideas, but tempering her pragmatism and organisational nous with a passion for astrology and star charts.

'Judy was tiny, strikingly beautiful, with black hair to her waist, and spoke faster than anyone I had ever seen,' remembered one of the group's entourage.

When Jeremy Spencer bailed, Judy recommended her old high-school friend, Bob Welch, as his replacement. She was present when Stevie Nicks first met the group in 1975, and Ken Caillat credits her for suggesting the final running order of *Rumours*.

However, Judy's job ended when Fleetwood Mac's fortunes changed, and Seedy Management dissolved. The '90s and '00s were a difficult time. In March 2005, Judy had been hospitalised after complaining of chest pains for several weeks. But she ignored doctors' orders and checked herself out after a few days. She later suffered a fatal heart attack.

That her body lay undiscovered in her LA apartment for a week prompted Ken Caillat to accuse Fleetwood Mac of neglecting one of their own. 'Judy did everything for the band,' he said, 'and for her not to be given whatever she needed . . . She died toothless.'

Fleetwood Mac paid for Judy's funeral, and Mick Fleetwood spoke at her memorial. Sadly, her story illustrated a familiar pitfall of the music business. When big bands break up and the party stops, the faithful are sometimes left behind. Few were more faithful than 'Jewel Eyed Judy'.

Tango in the Night

Songs from the RV

In January 1987, Lindsey Buckingham owned a *bona fide* rock star's house in the Santa Monica Mountains. It had a swimming pool, a manicured lawn, a home studio known as 'The Slope', and a rented Winnebago parked on the driveway.

The motor home had a specific purpose. Whenever Mick Fleetwood's or Stevie Nicks' behaviour became too much, Buckingham banished them to the RV. 'I couldn't stand having you punks in my house,' Buckingham told them years later. 'You'd turn up at the studio with people you'd met the night before and were too fucking crazy.'

Despite this turmoil, Buckingham managed to oversee *Tango in the Night*, Fleetwood Mac's second biggest-selling album and the last of the classic line-up's imperial run.

Until then, Fleetwood Mac had been in limbo since 1982's *Mirage*. Naturally, drama was never far behind. Mick Fleetwood filed for bankruptcy after over-investing in property; Stevie enjoyed two more hit solo albums (*The Wild Heart*, and *Rock a Little*) but had become a full-blown cocaine addict, and Buckingham was hurting after his second solo LP, *Go Insane*, failed to crack the US top forty. Meanwhile, Christine McVie had a US hit, 'Got a Hold on Me', without really trying, while her ex-husband went sailing around the Caribbean.

Then Christine was asked to record a song for *A Fine Mess*, a romantic comedy directed by Blake Edwards and starring Ted Danson. Nicks was away on tour, but McVie persuaded the rest of the band to contribute to her version of Elvis's 'Can't Help Falling in Love'.

A Fine Mess's title was prophetic: the film and the soundtrack were a resounding flop after Edwards disowned the project and urged the public not to waste their money seeing it. Nevertheless, the movie succeeded in getting four-fifths of Fleetwood Mac back together, which was always Mick Fleetwood's intention.

Only some people were sold on the idea of a reunion, though. 'A new Fleetwood Mac record was not on my radar,' insisted Buckingham, who was busy making another solo LP. While Fleetwood plotted, Buckingham and his co-producer, Richard Dashut, recorded solo songs at Rumbo Recorders, a little facility owned by yacht-rock power couple Captain & Tennille, in Canoga Park.

Fleetwood deployed charm, low cunning and emotional blackmail to change Buckingham's mind. Meetings were held with 'name' producers, including Nile Rodgers, but nobody from the outside could referee the band. Mick told Lindsey they could only make another Mac record with him and even rented a studio at Rumbo's so Buckingham could flit between the band and his solo project.

Having gone bankrupt to the tune of $3,697,163, Fleetwood *really* needed a new Fleetwood Mac album. Buckingham also knew he'd have a bigger payday with the band. 'Staying honest and creatively alive is tricky in a commercial business,' he admitted.

In the end, Buckingham put his album on ice, and he, Dashut and their engineer, Greg Dorman, moved down the corridor to work with Fleetwood Mac. The band was in disarray. Christine had some songs, but John was drinking too much and often couldn't play. Meanwhile, Fleetwood was staying up for days with his party-animal friends, Robin Williams and Gary Busey, and Stevie had gone straight from her latest solo tour to the Betty Ford Center for a twenty-eight-day treatment. 'I knew I was going to die, and I didn't want to die,' she said.

Buckingham insisted that they complete the record at his home studio. He had the power after surrendering his solo songs to the project. Among them were 'Tango in the Night', 'Caroline' and the future hit 'Big Love'. Back at the Slope, Buckingham looked for the sweet spot between art and commerce and tried to make music that 'flexed my creative muscles' but would still get played on MTV.

It was hard work, and *Tango in the Night* took eighteen months. Tour manager John Courage logged how many days the band spent on each song, claiming one took two months and wasn't even included on the record. Buckingham might spend hours recording up to twenty guitar tracks using different models and tunings. Sometimes he'd fashion the results into a finished piece, sometimes he'd abandon them altogether.

Technology had also progressed since *Mirage*. Everybody was in awe of the Fairlight CMI, a digital synthesiser that sampled and manipulated sound. Despite Buckingham's studio team poring over the Fairlight's manual, it was sparingly used. Still, the decade's nouveau technology left its fingerprints all over 'Big Love's breathy electro-pop and 'Family Man's oscillated sped-up vocals.

As well as a co-producer credit, Buckingham's name was on seven of the finished album's twelve songs. Some entries were highly personal: 'Caroline' and the title track were borne out of his recently ended relationship with studio manager-turned-model Carol Ann Harris. 'Tango in the Night' finished with a cathartic heavy-metal solo, and 'Caroline' with Buckingham chanting like a Gregorian monk.

He also buddied up with Christine McVie. It would be thirty years before Fleetwood Mac's platonic couple made an album together (*Lindsey Buckingham Christine McVie*), but they laid the groundwork here. Buckingham's searing backup vocals elevated McVie's 'Mystified' and 'Isn't it Midnight'. Meanwhile, the pair closed the album with the charmingly sweet 'You and I, Part II', whose chorus sounded like a radio jingle-in-waiting.

Christine wrote the big hits, though. Despite attributing 'Everywhere's musical box intro to Buckingham and giving her husband, musician Eddy Quintela, a credit on 'Little Lies', both were hall-marked with her textbook melodies.

'"Little Lies" was very much my song,' she said later, 'and it's not about me, and it's not about Eddy. It's just a song I wrote, lying out by my pool with a pad and paper.'

There was plenty of time to lie by the pool. Like a bookish school-boy hiding his work from his classmates, Lindsey wasn't big on sharing his vision. Christine kept coming to the Slope but often left without playing a note and was none the wiser about what Buckingham was doing.

Having completed her stint in rehab, a fragile Stevie Nicks finally appeared at the house in January 1987. She clambered out of a limousine with an entourage of familiars trailing behind. 'Stevie was the worst she's ever been,' divulged Buckingham. 'I didn't recognise her. She wasn't the person I'd known.'

Like Buckingham's post-break-up numbers, Nicks' songs were also personal, but much sleight of hand was required to bring them to life. 'I had to pull performances out of words and lines,' he said, 'and make parts that sounded like her that weren't her.'

'Welcome to the Room . . . Sara' was a husk of a song about Nicks' time at the Betty Ford Center. 'When I See You Again' had a pretty melody, but Nicks sounded like she was singing, half asleep, on the RV floor. 'Seven Wonders', co-written with Nicks' solo collaborator Sandy Stewart, was the pick of the bunch, thanks to its big hook and her bandmates' heavy lifting.

Years later, Nicks admitted that in her befuddled state, she'd misheard Stewart's lyric and sung 'all the way down to Emmeline' instead of 'all the way down you held the line'. She only discovered the error later, and her wrong lyrics were printed on its sleeve. Nobody minded, and Stevie's followers presumed 'Emmeline' was another mystical character, like 'Sara' or 'Rhiannon'.

Nicks spent three weeks in the studio, and only three of her songs made the final cut. Demos for others surfaced on 2017's expanded *Tango in the Night*, including a half-cooked, Stones-y rocker titled 'Julia', which she repurposed for her solo LP, *The Other Side of the Mirror*.

Stevie complained of being under-represented at the time, so the ever-pragmatic Christine suggested she add backing vocals to their songs. Doing so helped make *Tango in the Night* sound more like *Rumours*. Listen to Nicks whispering away on 'Little Lies'; the song wouldn't be as good without her.

Fleetwood Mac were done by March, and the rental company towed the Winnebago off Lindsey's driveway. 'People think of *Rumours* as being the turmoil time, and it was,' said Buckingham. 'But on *Tango* . . . everyone's level of crazy hit the wall. It was the worst recording experience of my life.'

Tango in the Night was released a month later and dedicated to Judy Wong, whom the band had just made redundant. Artist Brett-Livingstone Strong's tropical sleeve painting was a homage to post-impressionist Henri Rousseau. In the back cover photo, Fleetwood cradled Christine and Stevie, whose make-up suggested Pierrot the Clown's; John McVie peered at the back of his ex-wife's head, and Buckingham stared down the lens while standing on one leg – like a rock-star Long John Silver.

Mick Fleetwood often compared life in Fleetwood Mac to the army. This meant following orders and presenting a united front in the press. It worked. *Tango in the Night* went top ten in several countries and reached number one in the UK. Warner Bros squeezed six singles from the LP, with 'Big Love', 'Seven Wonders', 'Little Lies' and 'Everywhere' all US top-twenty hits.

Today, it's not Nicks, but Mick Fleetwood, whose absence is the most felt, though. 'That album is too electronic-y,' he suggested later. But, like every rock 'n' roll group from the '60s, Fleetwood Mac were terrified of being left behind in the '80s.

It was all too much for Buckingham, though. After agreeing to a ten-week tour, he changed his mind once the dates were booked. Buckingham told his bandmates the news during a summit at Christine McVie's house. Nicks flew into a rage, and Buckingham responded. 'Lindsey grabbed Stevie, slapped her, and bent her backwards over the hood of his car,' claimed Fleetwood in his 1990 memoir.

Buckingham insisted that this never happened. Days later, though, the band had replaced him. 'The show must go on,' declared Fleetwood. 'But there was a comedic sense to it. There we were, promoting an album that was mainly Lindsey's work, and it was like Brian Wilson and the Beach Boys – "I've made the album, now I'm staying home."'

Tango in the Night would sell 10 million in the US and more than 2 million in the UK. But it's never enjoyed the kudos heaped on *Rumours* or even *Tusk*. It's one of those big '80s albums, like *Brothers in Arms* or *No Jacket Required*, guaranteed to upset music snobs.

Strip away the date-stamped technology, though, and it's full of smartly crafted pop songs in the *Rumours* tradition. Several advertising agencies later thought the same. This century, 'Seven Wonders' was licensed to promote the online travel agency Booking.com, and 'Everywhere' did the same for the Three mobile-phone network and Chevrolet's electric car.

Even Buckingham and Nicks' bust-up couldn't keep them apart for ever. But the pain of making the record lingered. During a group interview in 2012, a journalist asked Buckingham about *Tango in the Night*. Instead of answering him, Lindsey turned to Mick and Stevie instead. 'I just couldn't stand to see what you were doing to yourselves,' he told them. 'Did you ever realise that? You were so out of control, it made me incredibly sad, and I couldn't take it anymore.' As soon as he said it, the pair started crying.

'Big Love'

Fleetwood Mac Love Kate Bush

In the summer of 1978, Fleetwood Mac invited the young British songwriter Kate Bush to support them on their next US tour. Bush, flush from her hit single, 'Wuthering Heights', was a reluctant live performer and declined.

'Maybe someday our paths will cross,' said Buckingham wistfully.

'Kate's an interesting, on-the-edge writer,' said an admiring Stevie, 'and she looks like a ninja in her videos.'

Buckingham and Nicks later fell hard for Bush's 1985 hit, 'Running Up That Hill', a song about love and sex, propelled by the futuristic-sounding Fairlight digital synthesiser and the LinnDrum machine. 'Running Up That Hill' inspired Buckingham to compose 'Big Love', a song intended for his third solo album but hijacked for 1987's *Tango in the Night*.

On 'Running Up That Hill', Bush wanted to swap places with her partner to understand each other better. On 'Big Love', Buckingham sang about being in his 'house on the hill' (Bel Air, Santa Monica, to be precise) and being wary of love after another doomed romance.

Like Bush's song, 'Big Love' opened with a long, sustained note (sounding like a backwards cymbal splash) followed by a hypnotic mechanised drum beat. What drove the piece, though, was

Buckingham underpinning the riff with a repetitive bass note and making his guitar sound like multiple duelling banjos.

'Big Love' gave Fleetwood Mac a chic electro-pop makeover, and went top ten in the UK and the US. But any po-facedness was turned upside down by what Buckingham called 'the love grunts'; those 'Ooohs' and 'Aahs' suggesting a couple grunting in ecstasy.

Listeners presumed the 'Oohs' were Lindsey, and the 'Aahs' were Stevie. Buckingham took mischievous delight in this: 'Everybody keeps asking me if it's Stevie Nicks. It's so funny.' Both were actually Buckingham, who created the 'Aahs' by tweaking his voice with a variable-speed oscillator. Nicks was absent from the song, although her backing vocals were later added to a twelve-inch mix.

Really, 'Big Love' was always the Lindsey Buckingham show. In the promo video, he gazed into the camera, looking broody with kohl-rimmed eyes, while Stevie swished her skirts back and forth but didn't do much else.

When Buckingham bailed after *Tango in the Night*, 'Big Love' wasn't included in the live set. It was *too* Lindsey Buckingham for his replacements to play on. When he returned for 1997's reunion tour, it became a showcase for his solo voice and guitar picking. Buckingham performed the 'Oohs' and 'Aahs' alone, but one couldn't help wishing Stevie Nicks would join him. Or, better still, Kate Bush.

'Little Lies'

Fleetwood Mac's Second Saddest Song

Many of the greatest moments on 1987's *Tango in the Night* are Christine McVie's. But for this one, Christine spent days hanging around Buckingham's home studio while he did his Wizard-of-Oz routine behind the curtain.

It was worth the wait. Buckingham's weepy fanfare on 'Little Lies' sounds like pan pipes at dawn (Irish folk-poppers the Corrs later recorded a cover with the real thing). But the rest demonstrates Christine's flair for sounding both upbeat and melancholy. Christine is basically telling a lover to keep bullshitting her, as she's not ready to face the truth. But unlike Fleetwood Mac's saddest song, 'Man of the World', this throws the listener off guard with a bright, shiny chorus.

Sonically, 'Little Lies' is as '1987' as Arnold Schwarzenegger hunting an invisible *Predator* or Glenn Close's boiling bunny in *Fatal Attraction*. But Fleetwood and Mac's crisp drum rolls and basslines cut through the twittering synths and sequencers.

Director Dominic Sena had just made a video for Janet Jackson when he took on Fleetwood Mac. Sena filmed the band down on the farm, using a pencil-sketch animation technique like the one on A-ha's 'Take on Me' promo. It all looked a bit forced, though. The contrast between the rustic locale and Nicks' and Buckingham's frosted tips and Beverly Hills tailoring added to the disconnect.

Though Stevie was game enough to risk her Victorian-style ivory dress cantering around a muddy field on horseback. In one scene, Buckingham walked out of a barn and completely faded away. It was the perfect metaphor. He'd leave Fleetwood Mac soon after.

'Everywhere'

The Dancing Pony Song

In spring 2013, the mobile-phone network provider Three broadcast a new TV advert showing a Shetland pony moonwalking to Fleetwood Mac's 'Everywhere'. The ad went viral and introduced a new generation to *Tango in the Night*'s top-ten hit. A blessing after NY art-rockers Vampire Weekend's earlier discombobulated-sounding cover version.

These were strange times for its composer Christine McVie, though. She'd long since spurned the music business and was living in rural isolation, reading books, walking her dogs and watching the telly. Then up popped a dancing pony and one of her old tunes in the ad break.

Three's marketing department presumably heard in 'Everywhere' what illustrator Lindsey Loch had when she drew the single sleeve in 1988. Loch's drawing showed a little girl floating in space, surrounded by twinkling stars and smiley-faced planets. Not such a great leap to a cutesy moonwalking pony.

Musically, 'Everywhere' takes the quickest route to get where it's going, but McVie sounds brilliantly disengaged like she's not quite there. There's a coolness to this song. The intro sounds like a whirring musical box (you can almost see the spinning ballerina) and an enduring sadness lasts until its doleful outro.

Christine was newly wed to songwriter Eddy Quintela at the time of recording but had to negotiate a malfunctioning working relationship. Buckingham was overseeing the LP from his home studio. Stevie, fresh from rehab, floated ghost-like around the place, and Fleetwood stayed up for days before sleeping it off in the Winnebago parked outside. John McVie was only present when absolutely necessary.

The impression of Christine as the voice of reason, the 'sane one' even, lingers on this, her greatest contribution to the album. It was tough, though. Buckingham was producing, and Christine didn't know what he would do with her songs – which drove her mad. 'Like watching somebody else paint a picture,' according to one source.

Maybe that's why she sounds a bit cautious on lines such as 'You know that I'm proud and I can't get the words out.' Maybe she was distracted by Buckingham's control freakery and sick of seeing Mick Fleetwood out of his mind. Really, 'Everywhere' sounds like a love song sung by someone who doesn't want to admit they're in love. It's haughty but charming; peak Christine McVie – with or without the dancing pony.

Billy Burnette

The Understudy's Tale, Part I

In 1987 Billy Burnette had a great rockabilly voice and a great rock-abilly quiff and was being groomed for stardom. He'd been making music for over a decade but had just signed to Curb Records, later home to country stars Merle Haggard and Lyle Lovett. Curb had a game plan all mapped out, then Burnette threw it away to join Fleetwood Mac.

He was an obvious choice. Burnette had played with Mick Fleetwood's side hustle, the Zoo, performed on Christine McVie's solo album and backed up Lindsey Buckingham on an episode of *Saturday Night Live*.

Burnette came with a fine pedigree too. Born in Memphis, Tennessee, in May 1953, his father, Dorsey, and uncle, Johnny, were members of the pioneering rockabilly group, the Rock and Roll Trio. Fleetwood Mac covered the Trio's 'Honey Hush', the Yardbirds and Aerosmith re-recorded their hit, 'Train Kept a-Rollin', and Led Zeppelin's Jimmy Page was their biggest fan. Billy even made his recording debut at age seven, singing 'Hey Daddy (I'm Gonna Tell Santa on You)', with country-pop star Ricky Nelson.

Burnette took the call from Mick Fleetwood after Buckingham walked out on the eve of the *Tango in the Night* tour. Burnette knew the catalogue, but his first job was to cut two new tracks, 'No Questions Asked' and 'As Long as You Follow', for an upcoming greatest hits set. Neither was going to challenge 'Dreams' or 'Go Your Own Way' and foreshadowed the creatively lean years ahead. 'But how could I say no to Fleetwood Mac,' he reasoned, 'and we all had a lot of fun.'

Lawyers were appointed to get him out of his Curb Records deal, and Stevie Nicks and Christine McVie insisted that he was made a full band member. On stage, rhythm guitarist/vocalist Burnette and fellow understudy, lead guitarist Rick Vito, were required to 'do' Lindsey Buckingham enough to make it sound like the records but not so much as to become a parody.

Burnette sang 'Go Your Own Way', but Lindsey's vocals were a little high and he had the band drop the key down. Audiences didn't notice and he sometimes wondered how many watching presumed he was Buckingham anyway.

Off stage, Burnette and Fleetwood were the band's mischief-makers, staying up all night boozing with *Ghostbusters* movie star Bill Murray and nodding off on the couch during a German TV interview. The band's management nagged Fleetwood to fire Burnette and get Buckingham back, but he stayed around until the '90s.

Burnette knew the next album, 1990's *Behind the Mask*, would be a struggle. Christine's interest was waning and Stevie had become addicted to painkillers. 'Also grunge had just started to come in, and it was a different time,' he recalled. 'The business was changing. I knew it, but I don't think the band knew it.'

Burnette co-wrote several songs on *Behind the Mask* and was frustrated when it failed to sell (5 million was deemed a flop). Sure enough, most of the new songs were dumped after the first night of the tour in favour of more hits. Yet the group still lived like kings and queens: flying between dates on Michael Jackson's private jet and bagging $1 million to play London's Wembley Stadium, where Burnette's mother broke royal protocol by inviting Prince Andrew to the after-show.

Stevie Nicks disappeared at the end of the tour, and, eventually, Burnette realised she'd left the band. He also discovered Fleetwood

Mac would never treat him the same as Buckingham, regardless of his full-member status. Billy was the go-between when President Bill Clinton's people asked Fleetwood Mac to play 1993's inauguration ball. But he was rowed out of the deal when a returning Stevie insisted that they get Lindsey instead.

Fleetwood Mac made another album, *Time*, with new lead vocalists, Bekka Bramlett and ex-Traffic man Dave Mason, but faced widespread indifference, not least from Mick Fleetwood, who called it 'a big mistake'.

Burnette had heard whispers from the Stevie Nicks camp that plans were afoot to get Lindsey back for a full bells-and-whistles reunion tour. 'I tried to tell Bekka and Dave, and they didn't believe me,' he recalled. 'But I knew something was up.'

When the time came, Burnette stepped aside gracefully. He'd made plenty of money, but would for ever be known as 'ex-Fleetwood Mac guitarist Billy Burnette.' In the years since, Burnette has made solo albums, written songs covered by Ray Charles and Tom Jones and toured in Bob Dylan's backing band.

When Burnette heard Lindsey Buckingham had quit in 2018, he phoned Mick Fleetwood to offer his services again. Fleetwood told him the job had already gone to Neil Finn. 'I'd never heard of Neil Finn,' he said. 'I saw a couple of shows and thought, "Oh this doesn't sound very good."'

Burnette and Fleetwood didn't speak for a year and a half after the call, before kissing and making up. 'I'll always be part of the family,' said Burnette. 'I guess that will never change.'

Rick Vito

The Understudy's Tale, Part II

Rick Vito was in the house band at the Peter Green tribute concert in 2020. 'I'm not an Alpha big dog,' said the guitarist, who shared the London Palladium stage with such big dogs as Pink Floyd's David Gilmour, Aerosmith's Steven Tyler and ZZ Top's Billy Gibbons.

Vito performed a spinetingling version of 1968's 'Love That Burns' early on in the show. He strung out and sustained the guitar notes, à la Peter Green, and even sang some lyrics from the edge of the stage, away from the microphone. It was one of the night's best performances, but many of the 2,000-strong audience probably didn't know who he was.

Vito only recorded a handful of Fleetwood Mac songs and performed on two tours in the late '80s and early '90s. But he was the dictionary definition of a Fleetwood Mac stunt guitarist: a consummate musician who could play both Green's heart-wrenching blues and Lindsey Buckingham's spiky art rock.

Richard Vito was born in October 1949 in Darby, Pennsylvania. His first big break was joining roots rockers Delaney & Bonnie and Friends in 1970. After that, he was in and out of studios and on the road with Bonnie Raitt and Bob Seger before Mick Fleetwood asked him to join the band in the summer of 1987.

Vito was friends with Fleetwood Mac's new rhythm guitarist and vocalist, Billy Burnette, and met Fleetwood at an earlier session.

Dreams

'We talked about the Peter Green era,' Vito recalled, 'and I mentioned seeing Fleetwood Mac in Philadelphia with Peter and Danny Kirwan.' A couple of months later, Fleetwood attended a club date Vito was playing. It was an audition, though Vito didn't realise it at the time.

Like Burnette, he was also made a full member of Fleetwood Mac. While this was a good deal financially, it could be creatively stifling. Vito squeezed some of his blues and soul influences into the music. But it was the mid-'80s, and there wasn't so much call for slide guitar in mainstream radio rock. Visually, the band were also at their glitziest. Vito and Burnette's hairstyles expanded to keep up with Stevie Nicks – though there could only be one winner.

Fleetwood Mac were also touring *Tango in the Night* without the musician who'd masterminded it all. 'There was no pressure to become a Lindsey clone,' Vito insisted. 'I don't sing like him, and I don't play like him.' But he and Burnette had to mimic him enough for the songs to sound authentic.

Vito had four writing credits on the group's next album, 1990's *Behind the Mask*. While Burnette worked with Christine, Vito brought his demos to Stevie Nicks, who'd fill in the gaps with lyrics or a bridge, but she wasn't at her best. The LP's weak sales figures started arriving during the subsequent tour.

Christine and Stevie said they were leaving, and Vito felt like he was aboard a sinking ship. His happiest moments were playing 'Oh Well' and other Peter Green-era numbers, which wasn't necessarily what an arena audience in the middle of Indiana wanted to hear in 1990.

Vito also didn't share some of his bandmates' recreational habits. So, getting trapped in a room with Fleetwood and Burnette as they snuffled up half of Peru didn't help. Vito quit for what he called 'personal reasons' at the end of the tour.

He kept busy making solo records, touring and playing sessions for Maria Muldaur, Peter Frampton and Hank Williams Jr. In 1996, his soaring slide solo on Bob Seger's 'Like a Rock' was heard daily on a US TV ad for Chevrolet trucks.

312

But Mick Fleetwood still kept him close. 'It's like you can never really leave,' said Vito, who formed the Mick Fleetwood Blues Band Featuring Rick Vito in 2004.

Like Burnette, he wasn't asked to re-join Fleetwood Mac when the infamous 'smirking incident' led to Buckingham's departure. Instead, he watched the drama from a healthy distance. 'I was curious,' he said. 'Let's leave it at that.'

Bonnie Raitt once said that Rick Vito's slide guitar sound was 'as sharp as a tail fin'. It was the perfect description. Listening to him playing 'Love That Burns' at the London Palladium, he was the right guitarist for Fleetwood Mac, but at completely the wrong time.

'The Mini Mac'

Remembering Behind the Mask *and* Time

The video for Fleetwood Mac's single 'As Long as You Follow' is a 1988 period piece. John McVie aside, they look like the wedding band in an episode of the swanky US soap, Dynasty: all satin shoulder pads, pendulous earrings, bolero ties and Class-A smiles.

Christine sang the verses, and Stevie just had to mime the chorus while sitting on the arm of a sofa. During one take, the camera panned towards her just as the director yelled 'Cut!' The singer had taken too much of something, toppled off the couch and was comatose on the floor. A couple of crew members gently returned Stevie to her perch and normal service resumed.

Stevie's collapse was emblematic of this chapter in Fleetwood Mac's story. 'A strange lost period of the band,' suggested Mick Fleetwood, 'for which I take full responsibility because I refused to give up.'

In summer 1987, lead guitarist Rick Vito and rhythm guitarist/vocalist Billy Burnette replaced Lindsey Buckingham for the *Tango in the Night* tour. Instead of auditioning, the pair attended a band meal at an upscale French restaurant in LA, where Stevie gave them a gladiatorial thumbs-up.

A month after Buckingham walked out, the redux Fleetwood Mac made their debut at Kansas City's Kemper Arena on 30 September 1987. Several Buckingham songs, including the recent hit

314

'Big Love', were discarded in favour of more of Stevie and Christine's songs. The shows sold out and a 'Lindsey Who?' banner was spotted in the crowd at one date.

Playing the hits live was a breeze compared to making new music, though. The new Fleetwood Mac recorded 'As Long as You Follow' and Nicks' 'No Questions Asked' to bolster an upcoming *Greatest Hits* collection. The LP went platinum but 'As Long as You Follow' dropped out of the charts as quickly as Stevie off the arm of that sofa.

The group Fleetwood nicknamed 'The Mini Mac' went on to make two LPs, 1990's *Behind the Mask* and 1995's *Time*. 'I don't think anyone likes those albums,' said Christine McVie years later. 'They're scrubbed under the carpet, they're terrible.'

Behind the Mask was the better of the two, because both Christine and Stevie were still present. Vito and Stevie Nicks' 'Love is Dangerous' had some gas in the tank, but 'Skies the Limit' and 'Affairs of the Heart' were overwhelmed by the vogueish technology. Greg Ladanyi had been hired to co-produce, partly because of his sterling work on Don Henley's *Building the Perfect Beast*. But Henley had the songs, Fleetwood Mac didn't. Lindsey Buckingham stopped by to play acoustic guitar on the title track. But without his manic energy, the rest was vanilla soft-rock with a crashing '80s hangover.

At Mick Fleetwood's request, the band were replaced by six models on the LP cover, one of whom could have been mistaken for Stevie Nicks through a record shop window in a snowstorm. Released in April 1990, there was enough residual goodwill to push *Behind the Mask* to number one in Britain, but not into the US top ten.

Christine's chipper-sounding single, 'Save Me', sounded like a cry for help but scraped into the US top forty. 'Warners thought it logical to continue putting out Stevie's and Chris's songs as singles,' explained Rick Vito. 'But they weren't bringing their A-game.'

Vito and Stevie Nicks both left at the end of the next tour. Meanwhile, Christine refused to play live but was contractually bound to make another album. Fleetwood Mac's revolving door started spinning. In came ex-Traffic guitarist/vocalist Dave Mason and singer Bekka Bramlett.

Mason hoped Fleetwood Mac would revive his flagging career and twenty-four-year-old Bekka hoped it would raise her profile.

The now multi-generational Fleetwood Mac went out on the road in 1994, with Christine's place taken by session musician Steve Thoma (fresh from performing on Bruce Willis's *The Return of Bruno* album). But instead of private jets and Madison Square Garden, they travelled by bus and supported Crosby, Stills & Nash at Orlando's Disney-themed Pleasure Island.

The Mini Mac also clashed with each other on tour and while recording a new album, *Time*, in Los Angeles. Bekka Bramlett was young and outspoken and Dave Mason thought he knew better. Christine liked Bekka but not Mason, and recorded her songs separately from the others.

Fleetwood still hoped she'd change her mind about touring. But the lyrics to Christine's song 'Hollywood (Some Other Kind of Town)' suggested a woman packing her Louis Vuitton for the first flight back to Heathrow. Even the return of Richard Dashut (and Lindsey singing backing vocals on Bekka's 'Nothing Without You') couldn't salvage the project. Fleetwood poured out his woes on the album's closing spoken-word track, 'These Strange Times', a song so out of character most of the group refused to play on it.

In between recording sessions, the band embarked on a cash-grab tour, sharing the bill with other heritage acts. Where they'd once played to rapt fans in arenas and stadiums, Fleetwood Mac were now in competition with the rollercoaster and water slide at Cincinnati's King's Island Amusement Park. 'Did I feel depressed seeing Fleetwood Mac opening for Pat Benatar and REO Speedwagon?' pondered Buckingham. 'Yes, I thought it was very sad.'

Time was released in October 1995. Fleetwood claimed the egg on its cover symbolised Bekka's arrival and the birth of a new Fleetwood Mac. But it didn't chart in the US, stalled outside the UK top fifty and became the band's worst-selling album. 'Warner Bros didn't bother with it,' griped Dave Mason. 'So it died a death.'

The Mini Mac played its final date at the Las Vegas Hilton on New Year's Eve 1995. 'It was a good band, with the wrong damn name,' said Fleetwood. 'We'd made an album that was a total failure and I couldn't see myself starting over, so we just stopped.' Mick Fleetwood had finally, unexpectedly, given up.

The Reynolds Girls

The (Not So) Anti-Fleetwood Mac

Smash Hits readers laughed, and disgusted rock fans reached for the dial to change radio stations. It was the pre-digital age (April 1989 to be precise) and the Reynolds Girls were in the UK top ten with 'I'd Rather Jack'. 'Golden oldies, Rolling Stones, we don't want them back,' they sang. 'I'd rather jack, than Fleetwood Mac.'

'I'd Rather Jack' was the latest creation from Stock Aitken Waterman (SAW), the production trio who'd turned tea boy Rick Astley and *Neighbours* actor Kylie Minogue into pop stars. SAW's dance-pop productions were massive hits but scorned by critical tastemakers and stuffy radio presenters beholden to pop's old guard.

Pete Waterman – the song's lyricist and producer – first encountered Fleetwood Mac while working as a club DJ in the late '60s. He didn't dislike them at all and rated Peter Green as a guitarist. But Waterman wasn't above creating mischief and once upset Pink Floyd's Afghan-coated disciples by playing the novelty hit 'Leap Up and Down (Wave Your Knickers in the Air)'? three times before one of their club gigs.

Two decades later, Waterman was presenting a show on Liverpool's Radio City, and often saw eighteen-year-old hairdresser Linda Reynolds and her sixteen-year-old sister, Aisling, waiting outside. The siblings were wannabe pop singers and would give

318

him copies of their latest demos, which he'd discreetly throw in a bin on his way to the car.

Then Waterman played one of the tapes, discovered the girls could sing and signed them to his PWL production company and label. He wrote 'I'd Rather Jack' to make a point. 'The Jack' was a body-popping dance move popular on the Chicago house scene a few years before. But Waterman deemed it recent enough to signify youth. Meanwhile, his Fleetwood Mac-baiting lyrics also laid into Dire Straits and Pink Floyd.

'It was a song attacking the blanding out of youth culture,' he explained. 'It's just a bit of fun, but it's time the old codgers moved over. The music industry shouldn't revolve around the personal taste of a few select forty-year-olds.'

'I'd Rather Jack' was released just a few weeks after Mick Fleetwood's disastrous co-presenting gig with model Samantha Fox at the BRIT Awards. That night, PWL's hit acts were overlooked again in favour of Phil Collins and Cliff Richard.

Critics and DJs were forced to take notice as the Reynolds Girls raced up the charts in the UK, Ireland, Finland and the Netherlands. Linda and Aisling appeared twice on the BBC's *Top of the Pops*. Wearing Converse trainers and stonewashed denim, they looked like ordinary teenage girls found in towns up and down the country. Maybe that was the problem: they were too ordinary.

Either way, after appearing *Top of the Pops*, the single dropped like a stone, and PWL dropped the Reynolds Girls. 'The public didn't believe them,' said Waterman, who claimed the song would have been a number-one hit if he'd given it to his other sibling duo, Mel and Kim.

Meanwhile, the Reynolds Girls' father, Walter, re-mortgaged his house to fund a follow-up single, 'Get Real'. When it stiffed, his daughters disappeared from show business. Attempts to contact them for a 2012 PWL reunion show and accompanying TV documentary both failed. Even the *Liverpool Echo* joined the search: 'Do you know where the Reynolds Girls are now? Are you Linda or Aisling?' they asked. Nobody replied.

Fleetwood Mac never publicly commented on 'I'd Rather Jack', and the Reynolds Girls found them less offensive than their producer. 'I think they're quite good at what they do,' admitted Linda, a little sheepishly, in a TV interview. Then she paused before confirming what everybody had long suspected. 'They just suited the idea of the song . . . mainly because their name rhymes with "jack".'

Bill Clinton

'Go to it, Mr President'

In 1992, Fleetwood Mac were hardly the hippest band in the world. In fact, they were considered so 'un-cool', that Democratic presidential candidate Bill Clinton's advisers suggested he stop using 'Don't Stop' as his campaign song.

Clinton refused. He loved 'Don't Stop'. Perhaps it reminded him of becoming Arkansas Attorney General when *Rumours* came out in 1977. By then, the saxophone-playing Clinton had given up any hope of becoming a professional musician and was focusing on politics.

Years later, when Clinton was considering running for the White House, he flew to Los Angeles to make a speech about education. His nineteen-year-old chauffeur asked him if fancied being president. 'At the time, nobody but my mother thought I had a chance,' Clinton recalled.

His driver told him he should go for the job, and that 'Don't Stop' should be his campaign song.

'This was the stone age when we all had tape decks,' said Clinton. 'He flipped it open, put in a Fleetwood Mac tape and played "Don't Stop". My first reaction was, "You weren't alive when that song was made."'

Clinton followed his chauffeur's advice and adopted 'Don't Stop' as his campaign song. Billy Burnette recalled Fleetwood Mac playing a corporate gig attended by Republican President George Bush Snr and being asked not to perform the song because of its connection to the Democratic Party. When they refused, Bush left the event early.

When Clinton became the 42nd president of the US, his people asked Burnette if Fleetwood Mac would play at his inauguration gala. Mick Fleetwood and John McVie were still in situ, but Stevie Nicks and Lindsey Buckingham had quit to focus on solo careers, and Christine McVie no longer wanted to tour.

Burnette made the calls and set the wheels in motion. Stevie and Christine agreed to reunite with the others. Then Stevie told Burnette that his services were no longer required; Lindsey Buckingham was coming back.

Buckingham told a press conference that he couldn't consider performing more than one song, though, and his body language suggested that he found the reunion excruciating. But he also found it hard to say no, to the president or Stevie Nicks. 'I called Lindsey and said, "If you cheat me out of this moment, I'll never speak to you again,"' claimed Nicks.

The inauguration gala was held on 19 January 1993, at the Capital Centre, Landover, Maryland, and broadcast nationwide. Aretha Franklin, Little Richard, Chuck Berry and Michael Jackson all performed, with actors and comedians, including the later-disgraced comedian Bill Cosby sidling on stage to congratulate the incoming president.

The grand finale featured Fleetwood Mac performing 'Don't Stop', complete with a wailing guitar solo and just one dirty look from Nicks to Buckingham. For what? The TV cameras didn't reveal.

Halfway through the performance, Clinton, his wife Hillary and their daughter Chelsea wandered on stage. All three looked mortally embarrassed. Nicks took pity on Clinton and handed him a tambourine. He recoiled at first. 'But I just said, "Go to it, Mr President!" And he did – he rocked out.' Unbeknown to Clinton, the bells had been muted with gaffer tape.

Clinton tried to make a noise before giving up and handing the tambourine to a roadie. By then, Michael Jackson had sauntered on stage and stolen his limelight. Jackson's arrival was the cue for the show's other performers to join in. Several generations of entertainers, including a bemused-looking Jack Lemmon, surrounded the five Macs, everybody singing along or at least pretending to.

Clinton's arrival ended a thirteen-year run of Republican presidents, and he continued to use 'Don't Stop' during his tenure in the White House. But while the seed had been sown, it took more than four years for the classic Fleetwood Mac line-up to get back on the road.

The group's relationship with Clinton resumed in 2001 when Hillary invited them to make a surprise appearance at his presidential going-away party, to be held in a marquee on the White House grounds. Minutes before showtime, Mick Fleetwood realised he needed to use the bathroom, but the nearest one could only be reached via the audience. As he was wearing his tights, waistcoat and knickerbockers, this would have blown the surprise.

Mick's manager approached one of the armed guards nearby and asked if he had a solution. The guard paused for a moment before replying, 'Mr Fleetwood is free to piss on the White House lawn, sir.'

Emotions were running high that night. Clinton was shocked to see Fleetwood Mac and, according to Stevie, started sobbing during 'Landslide'. However, Clinton's fling with former White House intern Monica Lewinsky had led to his impeachment and subsequent fall from grace. 'I did not have sexual relations with that woman,' he famously told the press. Though he clearly had.

Fleetwood Mac bowed out with the inevitable 'Don't Stop'.

After the show, Christine wondered whether they should have picked another song. Given Clinton's denial of his affair, wouldn't 'Little Lies' have been a better choice? she asked mischievously.

Dave Mason

The Understudy's Tale, Part III

Dave Mason probably shouldn't have joined Fleetwood Mac. But it's easy to understand why he did. When Mick Fleetwood offered him a berth in 1993, both parties needed a helping hand. 'Dave's career is like Fleetwood Mac's,' said the drummer. 'He's been here, there and everywhere, but he's always found a way of prevailing.'

On paper, it made sense. Born in Worcester, in May 1946, Mason was the same generation as Fleetwood and Mac; another ration-book kid raised on Elvis and Buddy Holly. Their musical paths were also intertwined. Mason helped form Traffic with Christine McVie's teenage friend Steve Winwood, and wrote their 1967 hit, 'Hole in my Shoe', which partly inspired 'Albatross'.

But Mason kept leaving Traffic, re-joining and then leaving again. A gifted vocalist, guitarist and writer, he had his eye on a solo career and moved in distinguished circles. He sang backing vocals on Hendrix's 'Crosstown Traffic' and played second guitar on 'All Along the Watchtower', and whacked a bass drum on the Rolling Stones' 'Street Fighting Man'.

Sadly, drugs, booze, bad business decisions and changing musical trends took their toll in the years ahead. Mason's career nosedived after 1978's US top-twenty hit, 'We Just Disagree', and he lost his record deal.

Fleetwood Mac were also in the doldrums after 1990's underperforming *Behind the Mask*. Over lunch at his Malibu house, Fleetwood told Mason that he was tired of auditioning hotshot guitarists to replace Rick Vito. 'They're all notes and no content,' he sighed. 'I'm almost tempted to ask you.'

'And I said, "Why not? Let's try it, and see what happens,"' replied Mason, who joined Fleetwood Mac in time for a short US tour opening for Crosby, Stills & Nash.

Unfortunately, both Christine McVie and Fleetwood Mac's other new vocalist, Bekka Bramlett, disliked Mason. 'I couldn't stand him,' said Bekka. 'It was acrimonious with Dave Mason and me,' concurred Christine.

There were still a lot of drugs and alcohol floating around Fleetwood Mac, which may have played a part. But, ultimately, Mason was a solo artist parachuted into a group whose core members were still pining for Buckingham and Nicks. He only managed to get two songs on their next album, *Time*, which was loaded with Christine's numbers in a bid to sound like the classic Fleetwood Mac.

Audiences didn't want to hear any new material on their subsequent 1995 dates, though. So, Mason became the third guitarist, after Vito and his current bandmate Billy Burnette, paid to 'do' Lindsey Buckingham. The pain showed on his face, as he stood there – all tight ponytail and pirate beard – grimacing through 'The Chain' and 'Go Your Own Way'.

Mason was happier performing Traffic's 'Feelin Alright' and 'Dear Mr Fantasy', but was aggrieved to discover the reunited Traffic were touring the US at the same time and hadn't asked him to join them.

Mason has never publicly criticised Bekka Bramlett or Christine McVie and believed Christine's absence from both tours cost them dearly. 'All you had was Mick and John McVie, so it was classified as a Fleetwood Mac covers band,' he said. 'It was never going to work. Warner Bros was also trying to force the issue of getting Stevie Nicks and . . . Whatshisname back in there.'

By January 1996, it was all over. A year later, Stevie and *Whatshisname* were back in Fleetwood Mac, and Mason was rehearsing with Ringo Starr & His All-Starr Band. Though he never made it to the subsequent tour. 'C'est la vie,' he said at the time. 'There you go.'

Bekka Bramlett

The Understudy's Tale, Part IV

Fleetwood Mac's ex-lead singer, Bekka Bramlett, still remembers the day that she phoned her father from a hotel in Switzerland to complain about one of her bandmates. It was December 1995 and the group were about to play the picture-postcard town of Interlaken, but without Stevie Nicks, Christine McVie or Lindsey Buckingham.

Instead, twenty-something Bekka was sharing vocal duties with Dave Mason, whom she did not get along with. Mason's latest crime was smoking cigars on their tour bus. Bekka poured out her grievances to her dad, Delaney Bramlett, who told her to take a moment and calm down. Delaney and his wife Bonnie had been a country-blues duo in the '70s and worked with Eric Clapton, George Harrison . . . and Dave Mason. He's not so bad, Delaney told her. But his daughter wouldn't be swayed.

This was not a happy time for Mick Fleetwood, who spent most of that tour mediating between his warring vocalists. 'Bekka had known Mason since she was a kid,' he said. 'I imagined there would be chemistry between them. Apparently not.'

Rebekka Ruth Bramlett was born in Westwood, California, in April 1968, and came from a musical dynasty. Delaney and Bonnie had been on the road since they were teenagers, performing with the likes of Albert King and Leon Russell. Bekka was always destined to follow them into the business.

Dreams

Mick Fleetwood hired Bekka to sing with his side-project group the Zoo, before inviting her to replace Stevie Nicks in Fleetwood Mac. Fleetwood hoped Stevie's hiatus would be temporary while she took care of her drug problem. However temporary, Bramlett took the job, and made her live debut on 1994's Another Link in the Chain tour.

She sang a mean, stripped-down version of Stevie's 'Gold Dust Woman' but refused to sing her signature songs 'Dreams' or 'Rhiannon' and dyed her blonde hair brown so no one could mistake her for you know who. Meanwhile, Christine McVie, who was still officially a member but wouldn't tour, gave Bekka her blessing to perform her hits, 'You Make Loving Fun' and 'Don't Stop'.

However, Bekka was a blues-soul singer with a New Orleans barrelhouse of a voice, which wasn't right for some of the Mac songbook. Out on the road, she and Billy Burnette maintained the group's reputation for romantic intrigue by having an affair. 'I just kind of threw myself at him,' she later told *Rolling Stone*. The couple wrote a song, 'Dreamin' the Dream', after their first kiss in a Four Seasons hotel lift.

The song appeared on Fleetwood Mac's next album, 1995's *Time*, but nobody was listening. Instead, the group were back on tour, playing the hits; both theirs and other people's, including Hendrix's 'All Along the Watchtower' and John Lennon's 'Imagine'.

Fleetwood Mac's stock had dropped. But while Bekka didn't mind them sharing the bill with other vintage acts, she was annoyed by Fleetwood and John McVie picking holes in every performance like a rock 'n' roll Statler and Waldorf. One night, after a few drinks, Bekka told them she wished she was in co-headliners REO Speedwagon because at least they high-fived each other after a good gig.

Believing she still had a future with the band, Bekka bought a million-dollar house before playing what turned out to be her final date on New Year's Eve 1995. A few weeks later, Fleetwood sent her a fax: 'And on my fax, Mick said, "You wish you were in REO Speedwagon, so I'm going to go ahead and fire you now."'

Stevie re-joined Fleetwood Mac soon after. Her only comment when asked about her predecessor was that 'she over-sings'. Bekka quietly returned to session work with Billy Joel, Buddy Guy and numerous country artists.

She lost the expensive house but insists she isn't bitter. Bekka grew up hearing songs from *Rumours* on the radio. When she hears them now, they remind her of happy childhood summers rather than being trapped on a cigar-smoke-filled tour bus in Switzerland. After Fleetwood Mac, she never saw Dave Mason again.

'These Strange Times'

Fleetwood Mac's Most Hated Song

Nobody, other than Mick Fleetwood, likes 'These Strange Times'. Fleetwood's only songwriting contribution to 1995's *Time* is a seven-minute, eight-second spoken-word piece at odds with the rest of the album's unassuming blues-rock. Christine and John McVie loathed it so much they refused to play on it. But the group's new vocalist, Bekka Bramlett, took pity on the boss and helped him out.

Over a backdrop of mournful cello, doomy percussion and Bekka's gospel wails, Fleetwood narrates a tribute to Peter Green and a frank admission of his own struggles. 'I, too, my friend, find the devil trying to make me do things I don't want to do,' he intones. 'God is nowhere, and this is hell.'

At the time, Fleetwood's life was 'awash with free-flowing substances', and his band was in disarray. Never one to stay down for long, his words took on a more positive spin as the song progressed. The line 'God is now here, and that was hell,' suggested some light at the end of a long, dark tunnel.

In 2020, Fleetwood released a new version of the song, recorded with Rick Vito. The piece acquired a new meaning during the global pandemic. 'My hope is that by sharing these thought-provoking moments in my world I can open the eyes of others to things in their world,' he wrote on his website, 'and to

330

the existence we all share, which is more and more endangered with each passing day.'

The sentiment was admirable, but the original still has a compelling, car-crash quality. It's the sound of a rock star unravelling in public.

Part Six

'This is *not* about art'

An uneasy détente brings the classic Fleetwood Mac line-up back on the road but not quite into the studio.

The Dance

The Highs and Lows of Fleetwood Mac's 1997 Reunion Show

One afternoon in 1996, Lindsey Buckingham walked into what he called 'an intervention'. He'd arrived at Christine McVie's house with his new wife, Kristen, to find the rest of Fleetwood Mac waiting. 'They all stood around me in a circle and said, "You gotta come back. You gotta come back." And I said, "Okay."'

The following May, the *Rumours*-era line-up reunited for a live album and concert film recorded at Warner Bros studios, Burbank, California. It was a slick, hits-heavy show performed by musicians in their fifties and keen to reassert their relevance. *The Dance* live album debuted at number one in the US and sold 1 million in just two months.

'My lawyers and manager both signified that this could be a good move for me in the long term,' said Buckingham. 'Sure, go ahead, talk about the money. But this isn't the same as the Eagles.'

Fleetwood Mac's soft-rock nemesis had recently put aside two decades of internecine resentment to clean up with the two-year Hell Freezes Over tour. Fleetwood Mac only had to suppress the urge to strangle each other for thirteen weeks.

The Dance album and film was big on nostalgia, creative brilliance and emotional resonance. As Stevie Nicks said at the time, 'America wants a happy ending.'

'The Chain'

A spine-tingling call to arms. Fleetwood's hat even falls off due to the ferocity of his drumming. After one minute and thirty-seven seconds, Stevie exchanges her first reproachful look with Lindsey. One down, many more to go . . .

'Dreams'

'Thunder only happens when it's raining,' croons a honey-voiced Stevie. A highlight of the show with its Beach Boys-alike harmonies ('Ow-ow-ow . . . you know . . .') and Buckingham and Nicks swapping dewy-eyed smiles. ('Sure, we're playing it out,' admitted Buckingham. 'But when I quit the band, Stevie and I still had unresolved issues. It's kinda nice to be getting along again.')

'Everywhere'

'Welcome to our little soirée,' says Christine McVie, sounding like the headmistress at a fee-paying girls' school addressing parents before the annual fundraiser. Christine ventures out from behind her Yamaha and shakes some maracas, while an under-used Stevie wafts her tambourine overhead as though trying to swat an invisible fly.

'Gold Dust Woman'

Full of spooky peyote-trip-in-the-desert vibes. Stevie dons a glittering gold shawl for some earnest fist-clenching and more reproachful looks in Buckingham's direction. Includes her first 360-degree twirl of the night. (Afterwards, the camera cuts to Hole frontwoman and

Kurt Cobain's widow Courtney Love frantically applauding in the audience.)

'I'm So Afraid'

Lindsey's doomy showcase is a bit overwrought, especially so soon after 'Gold Dust Woman'. An under-used Stevie does her crazy lady-shaking-a-tambourine-at-the-bus-stop routine, while the guitar solo lasts until the new millennium. (Receives a standing ovation.)

'Temporary One'

Christine's new song is a summery pop number with lyrics about being in Fleetwood Mac. 'The sea that divides us is a temporary one,' etc. (None of the audience can comfortably slip out and use the facilities because of the cameras.)

'Bleed to Love Her'

Lindsey's new song – all peerless three-way harmonies – is prefaced by a nervy speech about how 'the reconvening of these, uh, five people was kind of an, uh, organic thing . . .' His body language screams: 'Get me outta here!' until everyone starts playing and he visibly relaxes.

'Gypsy'

Sluggish reading of the non-sluggish 1982 hit. Redeemed by another of Stevie's 360-degree twirls. (Later on the Dance tour, the group collectively agree that 'the set is a bit sluggish in parts.')

'Big Love' and 'Go Insane'

Buckingham's solo version of the 1987 hit spliced with the title track of his second solo album – full of frantic picking and manic 'Ooh,

Aahs'. Prefaced by a speech in which he claims to be a 'different man' from the one that presumably pissed them all off in the '80s. (Receives another standing ovation.)

'Landslide'

Stevie's song was written when she and Lindsey were unhappily in love before they joined Fleetwood Mac. It gives the estranged couple an opportunity for lingering looks, hand-holding and hugs. 'Thanks, Lindsey,' she murmurs at the end. 'Thanks, Stevie,' he replies. ('I'm sure there were people out there who genuinely believe that Stevie and Lindsey will be reunited,' said Fleetwood. 'Let me say now, that will never happen.')

'Say You Love Me'

Christine's 1977 hit reimagined as a country waltz featuring 'my ex-husband' on backing vocals. Cue, a sheepish-looking John McVie. Contains some nimble Lindsey Buckingham banjo picking. ('Christine seems to take great pleasure in saying, "My ex-husband's going to sing for you,"' complained John. 'I wish she'd knock that off.')

'You Make Loving Fun'

Christine's pillow-soft West Coast pop, with a boggle-eyed Fleetwood riding the beat. Under-used Stevie resumes her fly-swatting tambourine dance.

'My Little Demon'

'We all have demons,' says Lindsey, beginning another confessional speech. 'I think there have been times when we've let them get the best of us ... I think it's important to learn from your mistakes ...' Camera cuts to Christine and a stony-faced Stevie.

'. . . And to fight for the positive choice.' A new song follows with pre-recorded demonic grunts and growls.

'Silver Springs'

First Mac live outing for the *Rumours* song that got away. Another highlight, full of brooding, accusatory looks between Mr and Mrs Buckingham Nicks: 'You'll *never* get away from the sound of the woman that loves you,' etc. ('I realised a long time ago that there is no Fleetwood Mac without Lindsey,' says Nicks. 'If it can't be with him, then let's not do it.')

'Over and Over'

Christine's breakthrough '*White Album*' hit was partly written about the creatively bumptious and demanding Lindsey. Almost slips by unnoticed, though.

'Rhiannon'

Christine's dainty piano intro cues up Stevie's ode to the titular white witch/Welsh goddess, accompanied by lots of dramatic eye-rolling. Lindsey stays in the shadows until it's time to solo or sing on the chorus. ('It's working at the moment,' says Buckingham, 'But there have already been times when I'm up there hammering away and start thinking, "Jesus, how did I end up back here?"')

'Sweet Girl'

Stevie's new song – a sunshiny country rocker about zooming around the globe and never stopping. 'I chose to dance across the stages of the world,' she trills while sporadically looking at Lindsey. (Again, none of the audience dares slip out to use the facilities.)

'Go Your Own Way'

On the home stretch now ... Fleetwood boggles his eyes during the extended teasing intro, and Stevie flashes a sour look at
Lindsey during the 'shacking up is all you wanna do' line. For the
victory lap, she stands on Christine's side of the stage and lets the
gentlemen partake in the musical equivalent of brandy and cigars:
Lindsey plays his one-man Lynyrd Skynyrd 'Freebird' guitar solo
and even the immovable John McVie moves. (Afterwards, a min-
ion drapes a cape around Fleetwood's shoulders, like he's a boxer
leaving the ring.)

'Tusk'

Fleetwood Mac's mad-genius 1979 hit features the present-day
University of Southern California (USC) Trojan Marching Band,
wearing matching sunglasses. Buckingham does his elephant-with-
a-gammy-leg dance, and Stevie swats a swarm of imaginary flies
with her tambourine.

'Don't Stop'

The USC Marching Band stick around to play on Christine's
cheery 'Dear John ...' letter to ex-husband McVie. 'Oooh, doncha
look back ...' etc. Ends with Fleetwood walloping his gong before
everybody slopes off the stage one by one.

'Songbird'

Christine's spot-lit tearjerker closes the night, just as it did in the
Mac's '70s heyday before Fleetwood leads the others back on for a
final curtain call: 'Thank you for making this such a special night
for us. It's been a l-o-o-o-ng time.'

Fleetwood Mac followed the Dance with a sold-out North American tour in autumn 1997. 'If we go to Europe, great. If we split

up at Christmas, that's fine too,' said Fleetwood. 'Let's be dignified about it.'

America's happy ending never happened. Instead, the tour finished in November in Landover, Maryland. By then, Christine McVie was telling journalists that she was leaving the band to open a restaurant in England.

'John McVie asked me the other day, "What are we going to do when this is all over?"' confessed Fleetwood at the time. 'And I don't have a clue.'

Say You Will

How (Not) to Make a Comeback Album

In January 2002, Stevie Nicks arrived at Lindsey Buckingham's home studio carrying an appliance made of wood, leather, hemp and bird feathers.

'What is that?' asked Lindsey.

Stevie told him it was a spirit catcher from her house in Phoenix. 'Where can we put it?' she asked briskly.

'Well . . . um . . . in this area,' replied a baffled-sounding Lindsey. 'Or, if you want it to wash out over the whole area, maybe put it on the mantel.'

Mick Fleetwood watched, bemused, before unfolding his gangly frame from the couch, kissing Stevie, and gently placing her spirit catcher on the mantelpiece.

'The bad news is I've had no rest at all,' Stevie announced to the room. 'The good news is I've written four songs . . . and they're *totally* Fleetwood Mac.'

Stevie and her spirit catcher appeared in *Destiny Rules*, a documentary about making 2003's comeback album, *Say You Will*. The film was revealing and even voyeuristic. When the crew went home, discreet microphones and cameras around the studio captured many after-hours moments, like a rock-star version of *Big Brother*.

The film also exposed the delicate psychology involved in putting Fleetwood Mac back together: how Stevie and Lindsey

342

bickered like an unhappily married couple, how Mick Fleetwood played both sides and how John McVie preferred sailing his boat to enduring 'a hundred-and-fifty replays of the same track'.

Say You Will had been on the cards for years, but the stars aligned in 2001. Fleetwood and John McVie had been performing on Buckingham's next planned solo album, and Lindsey had just played on one track from Stevie's recent solo LP, *Trouble in Shangri-La*.

Then Warner Bros passed on releasing Buckingham's album, and Nicks' manager, Howard Kaufman, told her about a new thing called Napster and how internet file-sharing was killing revenue streams. He suggested that she get back to Fleetwood Mac fast.

Mick Fleetwood always wanted the band to reunite, but they didn't have a record deal or Christine McVie. 'It took us a long time to figure out what we were going to do without Christine,' said Stevie. 'Or even if we could do it without her.'

However, the power had also shifted in her favour. Kaufman knew Fleetwood Mac would only get a deal if Stevie were on board, and insisted she had as many songs on the album as Lindsey. So, Buckingham proposed making *Say You Will* a double CD. 'I'll eat a shit load of money if needs be,' he said.

Fleetwood cautiously agreed to this until his manager, Carl Stubner, explained just how much a double CD would cost them. Buckingham wouldn't budge, though. 'Look at filmmakers,' he said to Fleetwood on camera. 'A good example is [New York satirical filmmaker] Todd Solondz. He's not getting rich off it, but he's contributing to the culture of cinema. Ridley Scott isn't. Whether it sells 300,000 or three million, I'd hate to see [this album] chopped up into something it's not meant to be.'

Fleetwood then appeared, via 'hidden' camera, talking on the phone. 'Lindsey says he doesn't care if it sells 300,000 copies, which I don't believe,' he told Stubner. 'Then he quotes a filmmaker who lives in a two-bedroom *kennel* . . . The only way Lindsey can say that is because he will never live in a two-bedroom house.' With perfect comic timing, the film cut to Buckingham standing on the plot of land where his new 10,000-square-foot mansion was being built.

'Do we really think people our age are lying around on the floor smoking dope, thinking about what the next record they're going to buy is?' asked Stevie to no one in particular. 'Nobody wants to rock the boat and hurt Lindsey's feelings. We all want Lindsey's dream to come true, but this is not about art.'

Warner Bros chairman Tom Whalley and vice chairman Jeff Ayeroff dropped by the studio to listen to Fleetwood Mac's new songs. By the last chorus of Stevie's infuriatingly catchy 'Say You Will' the two executives were singing along.

'Commercial enough?' implored Stevie. 'I prayed to the commercial gods.'

'And the gods delivered,' beamed Ayeroff.

Warners re-signed Fleetwood Mac, after which an almighty row ensued over what songs would make the album's final cut. 'And all the joy of making another album went out the window,' said Buckingham, who ditched the idea of a double CD after discovering how much touring he'd have to do to make it pay. 'And I can't take the chance Stevie might pull out after forty dates. I have a family and a new home to pay for.'

Say You Will was released in April 2003, still with a bumper eighteen tracks split between Buckingham and his ex-partner. A supporting cast of session musicians, co-producers and engineers, including new blood Rob Cavallo and John Shanks, helped push it over the finishing line.

Shanks even asked Buckingham to get his 1976 white Les Paul Custom, as heard on 'Go Your Own Way', out of storage. Shanks wanted the *Rumours* guitar, and Buckingham did as he was asked.

Christine played Hammond on two tracks as a hired hand, and Sheryl Crow sang backing vocals on two more. Stevie floated the idea of Sheryl joining them on tour. But Buckingham was concerned that hiring someone to perform Christine's songs might 'degrade Fleetwood Mac to a lounge level act'.

Crow then prematurely announced she was touring in Fleetwood Mac, upsetting the others. 'After the friction that incident created between her and Stevie, Sheryl decided she should step back from the idea,' said Buckingham.

Christine was upfront when asked about *Say You Will*. 'It was like a glorified Buckingham Nicks album,' she sniffed. 'I think that element of me might have been missing.'

Buckingham's uplifting 'What's the World Coming To' and 'Peacekeeper' worked hard to fill the hole. Meanwhile, Nicks' title track (with young female backing singers, including her niece, Jessica, and John McVie's daughter, Molly) was offset by the soul-searching 'Destiny Rules' and 'Illume (9-11)', the song inspired by the Twin Towers attack.

The uneasy détente resulted in the album containing two 'goodbye' songs: Buckingham's 'Say Goodbye' and Stevie's 'Goodbye Baby'. The first became a tear-jerking highlight of future live shows. Both composers also wrote about their respective love lives. Buckingham's song 'Come' was about an unnamed ex-girlfriend; Stevie's 'Thrown Down' was about Lindsey.

In the film, Lindsey advised Stevie to keep the tenses consistent in 'Thrown Down'.

'Who are you talking about [in the song]?' he asked.

'I'm talking about you,' she replied.

Buckingham ignored this information. 'It's a rule of thumb in writing that you don't shift your tense or person,' he explained.

'Well, I don't think you could say that to Bob Dylan because he would say to you, "I write what I want to,"' she fired back.

'Okay, okay,' said Lindsey. 'But it's not as abstract as Bob Dylan would write in those situations.'

'It's the way I write,' Stevie replied.

Fleetwood Mac's comeback tour began in May 2003. *Destiny Rules* showed Fleetwood and Buckingham pacing up and down before the first date in Columbus, Ohio. 'How do you feel?' Lindsey asked Mick, who was wearing a beret and a cape, like a cross between a French Resistance fighter and Harry Potter.

'Like a god,' Fleetwood grinned.

345

Say

Dreams

Say You Will reached number three in the US, and the tour grossed $28 million in sixteen months. The final scene in the documentary showed Stevie and Lindsey holding hands as they walked to the stage. It was all part of the act.

'I didn't like Say You Will,' Nicks later admitted. 'I didn't like making it, and I didn't like the songs, so that tour was very hard for me.'

The spirit catcher had failed, and Fleetwood Mac never made another album.

'Come'

Fleetwood Mac's Bad Sex Guide, Part II

Once Fleetwood Mac left their priapic blues and racy stage props behind, they rarely sang overtly about sex. Financial greed, UFOs, flying shamans, gypsies, 9/11, witches, dragonflies, each other? Yes. But love and heartache took priority over sex, with Stevie Nicks especially coy on the subject.

Lindsey Buckingham was more forthcoming. 'Come' was supposedly written about an ex-lover, and contained 5:59 minutes of lyrical handwringing, squalling guitar solos and Buckingham sounding like he was singing through a keyhole at the woman who'd spurned him. 'Think of me, sweet darling,' he hissed, 'Every time you don't come.' It was the one song on Fleetwood Mac's comeback LP that truly belonged on a solo album.

Mick Fleetwood later named 'Come' as one of his favourite songs on *Say You Will*. But Stevie Nicks was noticeably absent from the stage whenever Fleetwood Mac performed it on tour.

It was rumoured that 'Come' was written for a girlfriend who'd left Buckingham for another woman. Lindsey has never discussed its subject matter. But this hasn't stopped some from putting two and two together, and coming up with his ex-girlfriend, the actor Anne Heche, who later embarked on a relationship with TV host Ellen DeGeneres.

Lindsey and Anne met in 1992 when they were sat next to each other on a flight to Los Angeles. Heche wrote about the meeting in her memoir, *Call Me Crazy*.

'Are you a musician?' she asked Buckingham, who was twenty years her senior.

'Ah . . . yes, yes I am,' he replied.

'What do you play?'

'Guitar.'

'You ever play with anyone I might have heard of?'

'You ever hear of Fleetwood Mac?'

'Fleetwood Mac . . . I don't think so, no, why should I have?' claimed Heche, which either suggested she'd somehow managed to avoid popular music since childhood or was deliberately playing dumb.

'Lindsey and I travelled for a while, while he was on tour, and I tried to be the good girlfriend groupie,' wrote Heche, who died in 2022. 'We had fun for about a year, but I needed my own career and wasn't willing to sacrifice it for a rock star.'

Buckingham later revealed that 'Down on Rodeo', from his solo LP, *Under the Skin*, was partly about Anne Heche. 'More broadly it was about people who spend all their time window shopping through their life,' he said. 'Looking through the window at stuff and not going in and engaging, or keeping a distance. Even relationships that you've had for a long time, a lot of people don't get beyond a certain point.'

'Can you hear me, Annie?' he sings, imploringly on the fade.

'Illume (9-11)'

A Song About the End of the World

In the early morning of Tuesday, 11 September 2001, Stevie Nicks checked into the Waldorf Astoria Hotel in New York. She was in town to play two shows on her Trouble in Shangri-La solo tour. But when she woke up a few hours later, the World Trade Center was on fire.

'My assistant woke me right after the second plane hit the second tower,' she recalled. 'I walked over to the window and looked down. Everything was grey. There were no cars, there were no yellow cabs, there were no people. It looked like the end of the world.'

Stevie and her entourage witnessed the aftermath of one of the worst terrorist atrocities in living memory while spending forty-eight hours inside the Waldorf. Nicks watched the TV news, called her mother and ex-boyfriend Don Henley ('Asking them, "Should I go home?"'), lit candles and stuffed towels against the windows to keep out the stench of burning iron.

The two NY shows were cancelled, but a date in Atlantic City on 15 September went ahead. Nicks performed in front of a stars-and-stripes flag and stayed out on the road until the tour was done. 'But it was hard not to walk on stage and burst into tears every night,' she said.

Nicks started composing 'Illume (9-11)' soon after the attack, with notes from her journal: 'I've never been a political person, but

I felt like I was in the middle of history.' That said, the lyrics contained a reference only Stevie Nicks could have conjured up. 'The smell of Nag Champa' referred to the brand of incense candle she'd lit in her hotel suite that day.

'I saw history go down/I cannot pretend/That the heartache falls away,' she intoned, over pattering drums and Lindsey Buckingham whispering in the distance. Neither the song nor the album challenged 'Dreams' or *Rumours* for popularity or sales figures. Despite its terrible provenance, this was a welcome foray into the broader world after decades of songs about their love lives. 'I didn't set out to write a September 11 song,' insisted Nicks. 'It just happened.'

Bob Weston

The Curse of the Fleetwood Mac Guitarist, Part IV

Fleetwood Mac were touring the US when they appeared on NBC's music programme *Midnight Special* in autumn 1973. The group's new guitarist, Bob Weston, was a fine musician but his white suit, floral shirt and sharp sideburns also brought a little rock-star glamour to the male frontline. However, Mick Fleetwood kept his head turned away from Weston throughout the performance. With good reason, as Bob was having an affair with Mick's wife, Jenny.

Born in Devon in November 1947, Bob Weston was another post-war baby besotted with Chuck Berry and Muddy Waters. He moved to London in the early '60s and joined Brit blues pioneer Long John Baldry's band. In the summer of 1973, Fleetwood Mac saw Weston playing with Baldry and offered him a job. Bob later ran into his predecessor, Danny Kirwan, at the Speakeasy in London's West End. 'Good luck,' said Kirwan, when he learned about Weston's new job. 'You're gonna need it.'

Weston moved into the group's communal house, where he recorded two Mac albums, *Penguin* and *Mystery to Me*, in quick succession. His slide guitar playing fitted Christine McVie and Bob Welch's songs, he sang and co-wrote a duet with Christine called 'Did You Ever Love Me', and arranged and played all the guitars on Christine's song 'Why'.

Away from the music, Weston also befriended a lonely Jenny Boyd. 'There was a spiritual empathy,' he said. 'If you believe in such things, from an astrological point of view, but we were born within an hour of each other.'

'I was alone in the country, tied down with children, and I thought, "Wow, someone to talk to,"' explained Jenny. 'We had the same birthday and understood each other.'

Jenny and Bob began a clandestine affair, and Fleetwood tried to ignore it for the good of the band. Fleetwood Mac's US autumn 1973 tour lasted two weeks before tour manager John Courage summoned Weston from his bed the morning after a show and fired him.

'I hadn't even had a cup of tea,' recalled Weston. 'Next thing, there was a knock at the door, and the entire road crew stood there. They were all looking daggers at me. I was unceremoniously handed a plane ticket, bundled off to the airport and flown home.'

Back in England, Bob and Jenny moved in together for a week before she realised that she still loved Mick and ended the relationship. 'It was the most expensive affair I've ever had,' said Weston, years later. 'It cost me my career. But I became the dumping ground for everybody else's angst – "It's not us, it's him." I took the can to a greater degree than I should.' The group's impending line-up changes and Mick and Jenny's subsequent divorces (plural) suggest some truth in this.

After Fleetwood Mac, Weston played sessions for ex-Small Faces frontman Steve Marriott and folk singer Sandy Denny, performed on Murray Head's 1975 hit, 'Say It Ain't So, Joe', recorded TV soundtrack music and made solo records for a French label. He even had a cameo, playing guitar and suppressing a laugh in the video for Lindsey Buckingham's solo hit, 'Trouble'. Time proved a great healer, too, and his 1980 solo album, *Studio Picks*, featured Mick Fleetwood playing on one track.

Weston later read the drummer's first autobiography and was moved by Mick's recollection of events. 'I decided to ring and compliment him,' said Weston. He made it as a far as Fleetwood's secretary, who told him the boss wasn't available. Three days later, the secretary called back. 'What did you want him for?' she asked. 'Oh . . . nothing,' Weston replied, wearily.

The new century brought new challenges. Weston played regularly in a covers band at a pub in Hampstead, north London, but landing another record deal proved elusive. By 2011, he was living alone at a flat in Brent Cross, and friends raised the alarm when they didn't hear from him after Christmas. On 3 January 2012, the police broke into the apartment and found the TV on and a body on the couch. Weston had previously been diagnosed with cirrhosis of the liver and died from a gastro-intestinal haemorrhage. He was just sixty-four years old.

A journalist once asked Mick Fleetwood if any past member had come close to derailing his precious band. Mick seemed stuck for an answer. What about Bob Weston? suggested the interviewer cautiously. 'Oh no,' Fleetwood replied as if the thought had never crossed his mind. 'Bob was cool.'

Extended Play

Au Revoir, *Fleetwood Mac*

One of the occupational hazards of having as many different line-ups as Fleetwood Mac is that song titles get recycled without anyone realising. 'Without You' appeared on 2013's *Extended Play*, despite the band recording a song with the same name in 1970.

Stevie Nicks could be forgiven, though. She'd composed her harmony ballad before joining Fleetwood Mac and probably never heard Danny Kirwan's 'Without You'. Or maybe the universe was sending them a message: you're repeating yourselves, it's time to stop.

By April 2013, it had been a decade since the last Fleetwood Mac album, *Say You Will*, and there was a world tour imminent. Hence, the four-song, digital-only *Extended Play* EP.

Stevie's 'Without You' had been earmarked for the second Buckingham Nicks album, and missing, presumed lost, until she found the demo some forty years later. She and Lindsey revisited their younger selves and layered some imperfect harmonies over a tale of imperfect love.

This was Nicks' only contribution, though, and there was an unfinished feel to most of *Extended Play*, as if Buckingham and his co-producer Mitchell Froom were battling with limited time, resources and interest from some of the group.

As 'Without You' had already re-opened old wounds, Buckingham wrote the brisk, poppy 'Sad Angel' for Stevie Nicks. 'We fall

354

to earth together/The crowd calling out for more,' he sang before a climactic 'Go Your Own Way'-style guitar solo. 'Of all the things we cut, "Sad Angel" was, for lack of a better term, the most Fleetwood Mac-y,' he said.

It was also the most complete sounding. Buckingham's 'Miss Fantasy' was a lovely chorus in search of a song, while 'It Takes Time' was a superior exercise in self-flagellation. 'Maybe I couldn't admit I was wrong . . . maybe I've just been lying to myself,' whispered Buckingham over dainty piano chords and sampled strings.

The group performed 'Sad Angel' and 'Without You' every night of their world tour. And every night Stevie prefaced 'Without You' with a lengthy, convoluted explanation of its origins ('Lindsey says I wrote it in 1974, I say 1971 . . .') and claimed it was 'the most beautiful thing I have ever written about he and I', before gesturing towards Buckingham stood in the wings with his acoustic guitar.

Christine McVie re-joined the band a year later, but the five of them never made it back to the studio. Instead, *Extended Play* became Fleetwood Mac's swansong: less of a bang, then, more of a loud whimper. Though it was comforting to find them still writing songs to each other after all this time. As Lindsey Buckingham might say, '*Very* Fleetwood Mac-y.'

Rock Royalty

Mick Fleetwood's Blue Blood Revealed

In September 2013, the Scottish *Daily Record* reported that Mick Fleetwood was related to the British royal family. Conveniently, this news arrived in the middle of Fleetwood Mac's UK tour.

'All we know is that it's on my mother's side,' claimed Fleetwood. 'It had always been a bit of a family joke, but it seems her family were connected to William the Conqueror – probably through a gardener or something.'

Fleetwood's sixth great-grandfather, Edward Lascelles, a customs officer in eighteenth-century Barbados, was discovered to be Princess Diana's ninth great-grandfather; meaning Fleetwood Mac's drummer and Diana's eldest son, Prince William, the heir to throne, were sixth cousins, three times removed.

It wasn't Fleetwood's first brush with royalty. The Queen's son, Prince Andrew, had previously attended a Fleetwood Mac show at Wembley. Now, though, blue blood was officially running through the drummer's veins.

'This connection has now been made official,' said Fleetwood. 'Imagine my shock when I saw a big picture of Prince William next to a picture of me in the newspaper. My mind was blown. It's a good dinner table conversation now. If anyone in the band starts disagreeing with me, I'll tell them I can have their head taken off.'

Harry Styles

Fleetwood Mac's (Not So) Secret Love Child

Mick Fleetwood met One Direction singer Harry Styles in 2014. The drummer had taken his twin daughters, Ruby and Tessa, to see the boy band play in Pasadena. After the show, the girls were thrilled to meet their heroes. But so was Harry Styles, who adored Fleetwood Mac and used to sing along to 'Dreams' growing up as a kid in the West Midlands and Cheshire.

A year later, the band arranged for Harry to present a birthday cake to Stevie Nicks backstage after a Fleetwood Mac date in London. The Styles/Fleetwood/Nicks love-in had officially begun, and they couldn't keep away from each other.

One Direction were the platinum-selling offspring of the TV music show *The X Factor*. But by 2017, twenty-three-year-old Harry had left to pursue a solo career. Fleetwood Mac were integral to the birth of solo Styles. He performed 'The Chain' on his debut tour, and Stevie joined him at LA's historic venue, the Troubadour, to duet on 'Landslide'. In January 2018, Styles joined Fleetwood Mac to sing 'The Chain' during a charity fundraiser at New York's Radio City Music Hall.

But Styles and Ms Nicks had their own thing going on. Harry declared her, 'Everything you've ever wanted in a lady, a lover, in a friend.' Stevie described him in *Vogue*, 'as the type of person you'd want to live next door to. He'd look out the window and see you

357

were having a hard time planting flowers and rush out asking, "Can I help you with those roses?" He's the son I never had.'

Their mutual appreciation peaked in 2019 when Harry inducted Stevie into the Rock and Roll Hall of Fame. During his introduction speech, Styles explained that his parents used 'Stevie Nicks' as both an adjective and a verb: 'To quote my father, "That was *so* Stevie". And to quote my mother, "I Stevie Nicks-ed that shit so hard."' He then dropped to his knees and presented her with a statuette.

It didn't end there. Two years later, Harry chose pensioner Mick Fleetwood as the new face of his skin and nail-care brand, Pleasing. The company's 2021 campaign, Shroom Bloom, put a psychedelic twist on its face serums, hand balms and nail polishes. 'To evoke the feeling of lying in a park in early spring,' according to their sales pitch, 'a singular blade of grass moving in the breeze . . . a ladybird landing on a petal.'

In the subsequent ad campaign, the septuagenarian Fleetwood was photographed reclining on a patch of grass, his fingernails painted with *Vine Ripe* red and *Sprouting* green polish, and dressed by Harry's personal stylist in a violet top hat and zebra-print romper suit. The ensemble screamed, Gandalf moonlighting at Willy Wonka's Chocolate Factory. Fleetwood kept the nail polish on for two weeks and declared the whole experience 'magical'.

It seems Stevie Nicks wasn't the only one who wanted to be a surrogate parent. 'Mick has always wanted a son,' she divulged, 'and I think he's adopted Harry.'

'Greeny'

The Ghostly Guitar

In 2014, Metallica's lead guitarist Kirk Hammett was in a hotel suite in London, feeling bored and restless. 'So I called my friend up, a guitar collector, and said, "Got anything interesting?"' he said.

The collector, Richard Henry, told him that he'd acquired Peter Green's 1959 Gibson Les Paul Standard, aka 'Greeny'. Hammett had previously heard that Henry wanted $2 million for the guitar: 'But he told me this was poppycock, it was nowhere near that much, not even one million.' Hammett fought the urge, before giving in and asking Henry to bring the instrument to his hotel.

Hammett lifted 'Greeny' from its case, watched the light glint off its now-faded sunburst finish, and plugged it into a vintage Vox amp. Within seconds of his fingers touching the strings, he turned to Henry and said, 'I am not giving this back.'

Hammett phoned a mutual friend, who called Led Zeppelin's Jimmy Page. 'And Jimmy passed on the message – "You need to buy that guitar now."' Within two hours, Hammett had wired the money, believed to be just shy of half a million dollars, into Henry's account.

What makes 'Greeny' so irresistible is its tone. In technical terms, it has a reversed-neck pickup, meaning that when the guitar's toggle is in the middle position it creates a unique out-of-phase sound.

Or, in layman's terms, it has that otherworldly sound heard on those early Fleetwood Mac hits.

'It's a Les Paul that sounds like a Fender Strat,' explained Hammett. 'When I first put it in the middle position, I thought, "Are we dealing with the occult here?" You can hear these ghost notes, like other notes than the ones you're playing.'

Green bought the guitar in 1967 and used it on John Mayall's Bluesbreakers' *A Hard Road* album. Its ghostly echo was all over the LP's standout track, 'The Supernatural', and it became Green's go-to instrument on Fleetwood Mac's run of peerless singles, including 'Black Magic Woman' and 'The Green Manalishi (With the Two Prong Crown)'. Though not 'Albatross'.

Then Green started giving his possessions away. In 1970, he befriended Gary Moore, the future Thin Lizzy guitarist, then playing in Northern Irish rockers Skid Row. Moore made the mistake (or not) of complimenting Green on his woollen overcoat, only for Peter to insist he accept it as a gift.

Then Green told Moore he was leaving Fleetwood Mac and asked if he wanted to borrow his Les Paul. 'I was living in a bedsit in Belsize Park and didn't have a lock on my door, so I had to take the guitar everywhere,' recalled Moore. 'I was terrified something was going to happen to it.'

After a few days, Green offered to sell him the instrument. Moore said he couldn't afford it, so Green suggested that he sell his Gibson SG Standard and give him the proceeds. Moore sold the SG, but Green refused to accept all the money. In the end, Moore acquired 'Greeny' for around £100, several pounds less than Green originally paid.

He wasn't the first young guitarist to experience Green's generosity. Moore's future Thin Lizzy bandmate Snowy White had previously turned down Peter's offer to buy the guitar. 'I told Peter, "Look, don't sell it. If you don't feel like playing it, just keep it in the attic,"' recalled White. 'But the next thing I heard, he'd sold it Gary.'

Despite Moore treating the guitar like a Ming vase, he couldn't protect it forever. 'Greeny's neck was shattered after a lorry ploughed into the back of Gary's car on Chiswick flyover. The guitar was restored with the aid of a steel rod, and Moore later took it for a spin on Thin Lizzy's *Black Rose* album and his signature song, 'Parisienne Walkways'.

In 1995, Gary Moore released *Blues for Greeny*, a tribute album to his Fleetwood Mac mentor. He brought the Les Paul with him when he met Green for the first time in over two decades. 'How much did you pay for that then?' asked an incredulous Peter. 'Moore replied, "You should know!"' But Green looked at him blankly and claimed not to recognise his old guitar.

'Greeny' stayed with Moore until 2006, when he ran into financial difficulties and sold it to a dealer. The guitar disappeared from the market for several years before ending up with Richard Henry.

In 2020, Kirk Hammett performed at the Peter Green Tribute Concert in London and recorded a new version of 'Man of the World' for an official Green CD and tribute book. Like Gary Moore, Hammett took 'Greeny' to show its former owner and fell for Peter's dark humour.

'Peter was sat on a couch, and for the first ten minutes we were just checking each other out,' he recalled. Hammett finally showed him his old guitar, but Peter shook his head. 'He said, "Nah, that's not mine." But his buddy sitting in the corner silently mouthed to me, "He *knows* it's his."'

Since then, 'Greeny' has toured the world with Metallica, and Hammett played it at the 2023 Jeff Beck and Friends Tribute concert, alongside Green's old sparring partners, Eric Clapton and Rod Stewart.

'Greeny' and its owner now have an unbreakable bond. 'From the day I bought it, I have played it every single day,' claimed Hammett, 'and I sleep with that guitar never less than a hundred feet away from me.'

John Courage

The Fixer's Tale

Tour manager John Courage was on the road with Christine McVie's solo group in 1984, when he met his on-screen alter-ego. During a day off somewhere in Texas, the band and their entourage went to the cinema to watch the new spoof rock documentary, *This Is Spinal Tap*.

The first appearance of the fictional group's manager, 'Ian Faith' (played by satirist and future *Spitting Image* writer Tony Hendra), was followed by much stifled laughter and nudging of elbows among Christine's party. That's because 'Faith', with his crisp British accent, floppy blond hair and whiff of menace was uncannily like John Courage.

In one scene, he interrupts a bickering Spinal Tap. 'Whenever a single bump or ruffle comes into this little fantasy, adolescent world that you guys have built around yourselves, you start screaming like a bunch of poncey hairdressers!' he roars.

Courage understood how 'Ian Faith' felt and would have expressed himself in the same uncompromising terms. Courage, aka 'The Colonel', aka 'JC', had been getting Fleetwood Mac around the world since 1973. He too smoothed the bumps and ruffles, as their tour manager, surrogate parent, confidante, drug buddy, massager of egos and teller of home truths.

Stevie Nicks (who nicknamed Courage 'Sister Golden Hair' after a song by the folk-rock group America) had this to say: 'Everybody

362

has their road manager. JC was ours, and the road managers are the ones who know everything.'

Courage died in 2016 and, despite knowing everything, took most of his secrets to the grave. 'JC' was born in Belfast in 1950, the son of an army captain and part of the Courage beer brewing family. He was raised in Aylesbury and moved to London where he worked as a theatre curtain-puller before becoming a stagehand at the Roundhouse, the scene of many psychedelic 'happenings' in the '60s.

Courage was so short of money that for a while he slept in the Roundhouse rafters, like an angry blond bat, before becoming a road manager for the homegrown blues bands Chicken Shack and Savoy Brown, and visiting US jazz rockers Chicago Transit Authority.

Fleetwood Mac met Courage on a 1972 US tour with Savoy Brown, where he told them that their American road manager was lazy and useless. After Courage undertook an amphetamine-fuelled night drive from Chicago to Boston, John McVie told him to look them up when he was back in England.

Within a month, Courage had moved into Fleetwood Mac's communal house, Benifold, and become their go-to guy. This was the post-Peter Green, pre-Buckingham Nicks era when the group spent most of their time shedding members. One of Courage's first assignments was firing guitarist Bob Weston. The deed was done in Lincoln, Nebraska, and he had him in a cab to the airport before the others had woken up.

Soon after, Courage was looking after $2,000 of the band's tour money when he was busted for possession of pot and an unpaid car rental. He used the cash to hire a lawyer, which forced him into working for Clifford Davis's 'fake' version of Fleetwood Mac to clear the debt.

Courage frequently clashed with Davis. In one tale worthy of *This Is Spinal Tap*, he walked out on the eve of a tour until Davis agreed to pay the cost of shipping Fleetwood's orchestral gong to the States. When Bob Welch announced that he was leaving the band, Courage was so outraged on their behalf that he tossed Welch's guitar and amp out of a window.

After Fleetwood Mac became multi-platinum stars, their tours became longer and their demands more extreme. 'Do you know what I do?' 'Ian Faith' tells Spinal Tap in another famous scene. 'I find lost luggage, I locate mandolin strings in the middle of Austin . . .'

Courage's jobs included sourcing vintage wines and English ales in foreign climes, convincing commercial airlines to check twenty items of passenger luggage, and even marching onto the tarmac to supervise the load in.

When Australian customs officers impounded two crates of bottled Gatorade believing they were spiked with LSD, Courage had crates of the canned soft drink couriered from the US the next day. Gatorade was Mick Fleetwood's preferred vodka mixer, and he didn't want to let him down.

Courage ruffled feathers too. Regardless of what garish hippie fashions he was wearing, his English accent and moustache always gave him a rather military bearing. Ken Caillat called him 'an arrogant son of bitch' and compared him to an SS officer, but also respected how much he loved the band.

The trouble is, Courage put Fleetwood Mac before everything else, regardless of the cost, upset or legality. He'd bribe, threaten, connive and charm to get things done. 'If you want a job in this business, then shut your mouth and get on with it,' he once said.

Courage's pre-gig ritual involved giving his charges a ten-minute countdown before curtain-up ('Three minutes, everyone . . .' 'Two minutes, everyone . . .') and filling bottle tops with cocaine to fortify some of them before, during and after. His was the last voice heard over the PA before the show began. 'Ladies and gentlemen,' he announces at the start of 1980's *Live* album. 'Will you please give a warm welcome . . . to Fleetwood Mac.'

Courage married his wife, Dina, in 1983, worked with a solo Bob Welch, became Christine McVie's personal manager, and was back with Fleetwood Mac on their 1997 reunion tour. He still had the moustache, the sharp tongue and the military comportment, but it was a different era now.

One evening, a drunken middle-aged man in a Michigan hotel bar mocked Mick Fleetwood's ponytail. 'Getcha hair cut!' he slurred. After he said it a third time, Courage strode over, planted his hands palms down on the table, leaned into his face and briskly threatened to 'fuck him up the arse' if he didn't 'shut his fucking mouth'. The victim's face crumpled, the bar's patrons fell into an awkward silence and Mick Fleetwood stood up and left. Courage threatening a hotel guest in front of a journalist from *The Times* really didn't play well with anybody.

Away from the harshness of touring life, Courage was a cherished friend and family member. But he'd become institutionalised by decades on the road. When he was diagnosed with cancer, he 'shut up and got on with it' and kept its severity a secret from many. By then, he was back in Aylesbury and spent his final weeks in a hospice, where his room was decorated with Fleetwood Mac pictures to remind him of the good old bad old days.

John Courage died in October 2016. One of his last wishes was that his funeral be held as near to Bonfire Night as possible. After all, it was a life that had been full of loud explosions.

Penguins

Fleetwood Mac's Favourite Bird

Long before his death in 2019, Lyle Tuttle was feted as 'the father of modern tattooing'. He opened his first studio in San Francisco in the '50s, tattooed Janis Joplin and Joan Baez, and once appeared on the cover of *Rolling Stone*, inking a spider onto a woman's behind.

Throughout the '70s , Tuttle's studio on LA's Sunset Boulevard was a magnet for rock stars staying at the Hyatt House hotel opposite. Among them was John McVie, who emerged from Tuttle's one day with a penguin tattooed on his right forearm. 'I find the birds visually interesting and fascinating,' he said later.

McVie's obsession began when he and Christine lived in Chalk Farm, north London, during the late '60s . On days off, the couple visited the nearby London Zoo, where amateur photographer John took pictures of the animals. McVie even joined the Zoological Society of London, whose annual fee granted him unlimited visits to the zoo. Over time, he gravitated towards the penguin pond and learned how to identify the Adélie from the gentoo, the rockhopper from the Humboldt.

When asked to pose for a photograph on the back of 1971's *Future Games*, McVie insisted they use a shot of a penguin instead. Two years later, the band named their latest album *Penguin* and put a cartoon bird on its cover. By then, McVie had visited Tuttle's after a few hours of drinking at the Hyatt House. 'As an afternoon of complete delirium wore on, the idea of a tattoo became a *great* idea,' he later recalled.

The penguin was now Fleetwood Mac's mascot. They called their touring company Penguin Promotions, their publishing companies Rockhopper and Gentoo Music and McVie named his boat, Adélie. In 1977, he and Christine donated a female Humboldt penguin to Cleveland Zoo. Three years later, John came back and donated a male. McVie's tattoo has faded, but his favourite avian is now Fleetwood Mac's world-famous mascot, lurking in the undergrowth on the cover of *Tango in the Night*, and resplendent in top hat and tails on the cover of 2018's best-selling *50 Years – Don't Stop* collection.

Part Seven

'They chose to keep her'

Fleetwood Mac get torn asunder in the twenty-first century, but discover that the music itself can survive anything.

Desert Island Discs

Christine McVie Gets Marooned

On 22 December 2017, BBC Radio 4 broadcast an episode of its world-famous show, *Desert Island Discs*, with guest Christine McVie. Christine had rejoined Fleetwood Mac after more than a decade away and just released a new album with Lindsey Buckingham.

Christine had to imagine she was abandoned on a desert island and was asked to choose a book, a luxury item and the Beach Boys, 'Angel Come Home' to make the isolation more bearable. She told the host, Kirsty Young, that she'd take historical author Alison Weir's epic *Henry VIII: King and Court* ('the largest, biggest, fattest book on Henry VIII I could find'), a baby grand piano ('the one I played "Songbird" on') and the following music:

Antonio Vivaldi, 'Concerto No. 4 in F Minor'

Taken from the Venetian composer's most famous work, *The Four Seasons*, this was Vivaldi's greatest hit, his 'Don't Stop' or 'Everywhere'. It reminded Christine of her father, concert violinist and music teacher, Cyril Perfect: 'An eccentric, who lived beyond his means and was one for going to the bar and having a couple of Scotches with the chaps.'

Fats Domino, 'Ain't That a Shame'

Christine credited the New Orleans pianist's 1955 hit as 'the moment the classical scales fell from the eyes'. Her brother John had acquired the sheet music that his sister found stashed inside the piano stool, like illicit contraband. Domino's pumping, left-handed bass here inspired hers on 'Don't Stop', 'Say You Love Me' etc.

The Beatles, 'Roll Over Beethoven'

The Fab Four's take on Chuck Berry's hit appeared on their second album, *With the Beatles*, Christine's Christmas present from her parents in 1963. 'I played it until there was nothing left of it,' she recalled. 'Singing along to the tracks with a hairbrush and shaking my head.'

Later, John Lennon said 'Albatross' had inspired 'Sun King', and was heard in the 2021 documentary, *The Beatles: Get Back*, describing Fleetwood Mac as 'sweet, man, and their lead singer's great'. Paul McCartney added that he thought they sounded like Canned Heat. 'Yeah, but better than Canned Heat,' insisted Lennon.

Fleetwood Mac, 'Man of the World'

Christine was playing in Chicken Shack when she first met Fleetwood Mac. While she later 'fell head over heels' for John McVie, she was initially drawn to Peter Green and named this 1970 single, recorded almost two years before she joined, as one of her favourite pieces. 'A reflective song, which still gives me a tear in my eye,' she explained. 'They gave him a tab of acid at a party in Germany – and he never came back.'

The Everly Brothers, 'Cathy's Clown'

The American duo's 1960 hit demonstrated the kind of pristine harmonies Fleetwood Mac later deployed on Christine's 'Say You Love Me'. Serendipitously, Lindsey had once played in Don

Everly's solo band and Christine had hidden backstage at the Birmingham Odeon to get brother Phil Everly's autograph. Decades later, she sang on one of his solo albums.

The Beach Boys, 'Angel Come Home'

Co-written by his brother Carl, Dennis Wilson sang this entry from the Beach Boys' *L.A.* (*Light Album*), a record patched together in trying circumstances. 'I just adored him,' said Christine of Dennis. 'We had a rollercoaster affair for a couple of years. He was bad . . . but it was the drugs.'

Ralph Vaughan Williams, 'The Lark Ascending'

The English composer's 1914 one-movement piece for piano and violin moved Christine to tears the first time she heard it. The song reminded her of her father, but Vaughan Williams' work also inspired Peter Green, who brought its subtle poetry to his playing on 'Albatross', 'Oh Well' and 'Man of the World'.

Etta James, 'I'd Rather Go Blind'

Chicken Shack's cover of the Californian blues singer's 1967 hit put them in the chart and earned Christine the accolade of *Melody Maker*'s Best Female Vocalist, 1969. Also trailered her English home-counties take on the blues, as heard on the mid-period Mac albums, *Mystery to Me* and *Heroes are Hard to Find*.

Lindsey Buckingham
Christine McVie

The Greatest Album Fleetwood Mac Never Made

Lindsey Buckingham was taking a quiet moment in the bathroom at Los Angeles' Village Recorder when he had a revelation. It was 2016, and the studio had barely changed since Fleetwood Mac recorded *Tusk* here in the '70s. 'You take a piss, and even the tiles are the same,' he marvelled.

Buckingham had returned to Village Recorder's Studio D, the room Fleetwood Mac built, to make the *Lindsey Buckingham Christine McVie* album. Christine had re-joined the band, but conflicting schedules and issues kept them all out of the studio. Instead, she and Buckingham started working together, with John McVie and Mick Fleetwood as their rhythm section.

Just as 2003's *Say You Will* was a Fleetwood Mac album without Christine, this was Fleetwood Mac minus Stevie Nicks. It was also their finest work since 1987's *Tango in the Night*. 'But absent of the politics and the complexity of the emotional language,' as Buckingham tactfully put it.

Not that this was the plan to begin with. 'Chris, John, Lindsey and I had the greatest time,' said Mick Fleetwood in 2015, a year before the album's release. 'We went back to the Village and cut a whole lot of songs. Lindsey and I hope that Stevie will find time. I really hope there will be another lovely album from this band.'

When Nicks wouldn't commit, the 'lovely' album came out under the Buckingham McVie name. Lindsey and Christine had been batting song ideas back and forth for two years or more. Both trusted the other but also acknowledged their respective strengths and occasional weaknesses.

'Christine's stuff is more literal and easier to read,' suggested Buckingham. 'Mine is maybe a little more obscure and open to whatever Rorschach test you're going to put on there. It's a different kind of deep.'

'Lindsey takes a song and builds on it,' said Christine. 'He's very good at that.'

In other words, Christine smoothed off some of Lindsey's sharper edges. The die was cast on the sunny opener, 'Sleeping Around the Corner'. Some of this material was initially for a Buckingham solo project. But while 'Love is Here to Stay' and 'Lay Down For Free' would have fitted on his *Seeds We Sow* or *Gift of Screws* albums, but would they have had quite such joyous choruses without Christine?

Similarly, Buckingham bent Christine's straight-ahead pop songs slightly out of shape: giving her sugary calypso 'Feel About You' an awkward rhythm, and sticking a blast of martial drumming in the middle of 'Too Far Gone'.

They both knew when to step back, though. 'Red Sun' and 'Game of Pretend' were charmingly simple and uncluttered, while Buckingham's 'In My World' was the LP's standout. A wonderfully melancholy song, which, with its 'Big Love'-style 'Oohs' and 'Aahs' and swinging rhythm section, could have come off of *Tango in the Night*. Only the lyrics belied its age. 'It's a song about idealism and growing older,' explained Buckingham, 'which had an extra resonance when Donald Trump came to power.'

There were mixed emotions too when they all reconvened in Studio D. Despite having the same glass, woodwork and bathroom tiles, the old place wasn't quite how Fleetwood Mac left it. Former owner, Geordie Hormel, had died, and while *Tusk* was created on a steady diet of Dom Pérignon and Class As, everybody was now in their sixties and seventies and marginally better behaved.

'I've grown up a lot since the last time I worked with Christine,' said Buckingham. 'I am a completely different person. So there was a bittersweetness to it, as the room represented different incarnations of one's selves.'

There was a bittersweetness to the music too. Buckingham wrote 'On with the Show' before Christine re-joined Fleetwood Mac: 'Then she heard that song and fell in love with it, so it took on an enhanced meaning.'

Christine's was the last voice heard on the record. 'Travelling girl is moving north, west, east and south,' she sang on the closing track, 'Carnival Begin', a song about returning to the band.

Released in June 2017, the album bucked the trend of Buckingham and McVie's solo works by becoming a US top-twenty and UK top-five hit. Neither party saw their collaboration as a career move. 'It's a nice splinter off the main artery of Fleetwood Mac,' joked Christine.

Nevertheless, the pair took the show on the road in the summer of 2017, playing to a smidgeon of Fleetwood Mac's audience in modest-sized theatres across the US. They were doing it by choice, though, not necessity. They played the new songs and the hits, but also deeper cuts, including 'Wish You Were Here' and 'Hold Me'. Best of all, they looked like they were having fun.

The grand English dame and the jittery Californian made an odd couple. But it was an easy relationship unspoiled by any lingering romantic resentment. Nobody said it explicitly, but Buckingham appeared visibly relaxed in a way he rarely was around Stevie Nicks.

The fun ended in 2018, though, when Buckingham left Fleetwood Mac just before a world tour. Having made their best record in thirty years, Lindsey and Christine never had the opportunity to work together again. 'The politics and the complexity of the emotional language' had returned with a vengeance.

'The Last Mac'

How the 'Smirking' Incident Ended Fleetwood Mac

Stevie Nicks loves to talk. 'Am I boring you, dear?' she once asked a writer while giving a lengthy answer entirely unrelated to the question asked. On 26 January 2018, though, Stevie Nicks talked, and her band ended up in disarray – again.

The group were at New York's Radio City Music Hall to receive the Person of the Year award from the MusiCares charity foundation. 'I just finished a tour where I talked for forty-six minutes and sang for two hours,' Stevie warned the audience before beginning her acceptance speech.

She delivered her monologue while the rest of Fleetwood Mac stood behind her. The speech was witty, self-aware, emotional and wide-ranging, and lasted for six minutes and ten seconds. After four minutes, Mick Fleetwood whispered to Christine McVie, who jokingly looked at her watch, before the pair joined hands and waltzed back and forth for a few seconds.

Lindsey Buckingham then offered his hand to a grinning John McVie, who refused to take it, before performing a rather awkward wiggle of his hips. It all seemed very light-hearted. When Stevie was done talking, her bandmates and the audience, including Bill and Hillary Clinton, gave her a round of applause.

Then, in October 2018, Fleetwood Mac's An Evening with Fleetwood Mac world tour went ahead without Lindsey Buckingham.

A few days after their appearance at MusiCares, Buckingham had received a call from the group's manager, Irving Azoff, who outlined a list of grievances Stevie had with him. One was that he'd smirked during her MusiCares acceptance speech; another was that he'd complained about having 'Rhiannon' as their intro music at the event.

'It wasn't about it being "Rhiannon",' Buckingham insisted. 'It just undermined the impact of our entrance, and the irony is that we have this standing joke that when Stevie talks, she goes on a long time. I may or may not have smirked. But I looked over and Christine and Mick were doing the waltz behind her.'

At the end of the call, Buckingham presumed Stevie had quit the band. He emailed Mick Fleetwood saying he hoped they'd carry on. When Fleetwood didn't reply, Buckingham contacted Azoff again, who intimated that Nicks had told the group she wouldn't work with him anymore.

'They chose to keep her,' said Buckingham. 'The other members were stuck in the middle and had to make a choice that was not tenable whichever way they went.'

Naturally, 'the smirking incident' captured the public's imagination, but was just one of many factors in Buckingham's departure. Mick Fleetwood blamed the falling-out on Lindsey's refusal to sign off on a world tour that had been in the works for over a year. Ever the diplomat, Fleetwood refused to say he was fired, though, because 'that's an ugly word'.

In 2021, Buckingham admitted that he'd wanted Fleetwood Mac to delay their tour by three months to accommodate some solo shows: 'That's not something Stevie particularly wanted to do. So at that point, other things began to come into the mix.'

Buckingham insisted he wanted to keep the lines of communication open. He offered to fly to Maui to speak to Fleetwood and Nicks in person. But it didn't happen. 'My God, after forty-three years and all the stuff we managed to rise above,' he said. 'It was a shame to let this happen at this point in our careers. It didn't speak well for the legacy and I was disappointed in Stevie being the one who orchestrated it.'

'We were not happy,' Fleetwood later admitted. 'It is no secret that Lindsey and Stevie are in a continuum Liz Taylor/Richard Burton type of life, and it went in and out of valleys and mountain-tops and God knows what through the years – and that support really could not be given to ask the situation to continue. It was too challenging.'

Just as they'd done in 1987, Fleetwood Mac replaced Buckingham with two new musicians, Mike Campbell and Neil Finn. Both were sold the idea that this new Fleetwood Mac could make new music.

In the meantime, An Evening with Fleetwood Mac opened in Tulsa, Oklahoma, on 3 October, and Buckingham filed a lawsuit for several claims, including breach of fiduciary duty and intentional interference with prospective economic advantage. The matter was quietly settled in December. 'We've all signed off on something, I'm happy enough,' was all Buckingham would divulge.

The drama didn't end there. In February 2019, Buckingham suffered a heart attack during a minor surgical procedure. He woke up to discover he'd undergone an emergency triple bypass and his vocal cords had been damaged by a breathing tube. 'While it is unclear if this damage is permanent, we are hopeful it is not,' wrote his wife, Kristen Messner, on social media. 'This past year has been a very stressful and difficult year for our family.'

Buckingham made a full recovery and said that Stevie Nicks had contacted him after the surgery, but she'd not responded to his subsequent messages. In the meantime, 'Crowded Mac/Fleetwood House' played to sold-out audiences across the US, Europe and Australasia.

'There's a faction of people who are coming only for the brand, *per se*,' admitted Buckingham. 'They aren't going to differentiate in terms of members as long as Stevie is up there.'

The new additions were consummate pros and fitted right in. Campbell, with his shades, braids and hat, looked like a rock star, and Finn had the assuredness of a seasoned pop star. Without needing to accommodate Buckingham, this Fleetwood Mac dug deep into the catalogue. They'd earned the right to indulge themselves and revived 'Black Magic Woman' (with Stevie unwisely singing lead vocals), 'Man of the World' and 'Oh Well', and, briefly, Danny Kirwan's 'Tell Me All the Things You Do' and Bob Welch's 'Hypnotized'.

The trouble was these songs were unknown to most of the beer-and-popcorn-guzzling audience who'd come to hear 'Don't Stop' and 'Go Your Own Way'. Even Christine McVie's 'Isn't It Midnight' from the monster hit *Tango in the Night* drew blank looks, while 'All Over Again' from *Time*, the 1995 Mac album that nobody remembers, was a bizarre choice of encore, and swiftly dumped.

The setlist also included Split Enz's 'I Got You', Crowded House's 'Don't Dream It's Over' and Tom Petty's 'Free Fallin'. Audiences knew these songs, as they'd been on MTV back when they were young and unencumbered by kids and responsibility. 'I Got You' was from 1980, and even sounded like something jittery and intense from an early Lindsey Buckingham solo album. But none of this stuff was Fleetwood Mac.

'I didn't see the show,' said Buckingham. 'But I heard it described as a little generic, and verging on being a covers band. Having looked at the setlist I thought some of the material ran a little broad. There was a lot of Peter Green stuff, which is fine, but you've got "Free Fallin'" and "Don't Dream It's Over", which might be considered a little off-the-radar.'

An Evening with Fleetwood Mac ended in Las Vegas in November 2019 and earned the band $49 million over eighty-seven shows. Soon after, Mick Fleetwood claimed that he and Buckingham had reconciled and he was open to the idea of a reunited Fleetwood Mac, *yet again*.

Then Stevie broke her silence in a letter to *Rolling Stone*. 'Following an exceedingly difficult time with Lindsey at MusiCares in New York, I decided for myself that I was no longer willing to work with him,' she explained. Nicks claimed that there was a 'very precise litany of events why I will not work with him' but didn't reveal what they were.

However, she refuted Buckingham's claim that he'd been dismissed: 'I did not have him fired. I did not ask for him to be fired. I did not demand he be fired. Frankly, I fired myself. I proactively removed myself from a situation I considered to be toxic. I was done. If the band went on without me, so be it.'

'It would be so appropriate for the five of us to go out again,' said Buckingham, sounding regretful, in 2021. 'Then if you wanted to call it a farewell tour have it be *the* farewell tour and it would have meant something. But, hey, that's rock 'n' roll.'

Mike Campbell

The Final Guitarist's Tale

Stevie Nicks' old friend and singing partner Tom Petty died on 2 October 2017. Tom Petty and the Heartbreakers guitarist Mike Campbell had been Petty's foil forever, co-writing the hits, 'Refugee' and 'Runnin' Down a Dream', and helping produce platinum albums including *Full Moon Fever*.

Shortly after Petty's death, Campbell was in his backyard when his mobile rang. It was Mick Fleetwood asking if he wanted to join Fleetwood Mac. Campbell had co-written a song on 1990's *Behind the Mask* but was only on nodding terms with the drummer. Now, though, Fleetwood Mac had a world tour pending and needed a replacement for Lindsey Buckingham. Fleetwood also insisted he wanted Campbell to join as a full band member. 'That carried a lot of weight for me,' he said. 'Because I wasn't interested in being a sideman.'

Campbell asked for twenty-four hours to think about the offer, before accepting. On 3 October 2018, almost a year to the day since Petty's passing, he walked on stage with Fleetwood Mac in Tulsa, Oklahoma.

Campbell and Stevie Nicks went way back, though. Nicks developed an all-consuming crush on Tom Petty's music after hearing the Heartbreakers' 1976 debut LP. But Florida-born Petty was an un-starry, unreconstructed Southern rocker and instinctively dubious about starry Stevie Nicks.

'I didn't know whether to like Stevie or not,' Petty admitted. 'Because we saw this big corporate rock band, Fleetwood Mac, and kept thinking, "What does she want from us?" But she was this stone-gone huge fan.'

'I loved the Heartbreakers and would have joined them,' claimed Stevie. However, Petty was never sure how serious she was, and his band were a boys' club. 'Tom would say, "There are no girls in the Heartbreakers, I'm sorry,"' recalled Campbell. '"But you can sing back-up here and there."'

Nicks sang backing vocals on two songs from their fourth album, *Hard Promises*. But her dream was to make, what she called, 'a girl Tom Petty record'. Stevie played the long game and landed most of the Heartbreakers and their producer, Jimmy Iovine, for her 1981 debut, *Bella Donna*.

The album included the hits 'Edge of Seventeen' (its title inspired by Petty's wife, Jane, who told Stevie she'd met her future husband when she was on the 'edge of seventeen') and 'Stop Draggin' My Heart Around', a duet composed by Campbell, which cast Petty and Nicks as a gnarly voiced Romeo and Juliet. The song raised Petty's profile and launched Nicks as a solo star.

Their platonic affair peaked in the mid-'80s when Stevie trailed the Heartbreakers around Australia, just so she could sing a couple of numbers on stage. The authorities eventually ordered her to leave the country as she didn't have a work permit, and her producer Jimmy Iovine told her to get back to LA and start promoting her new solo album. 'God bless her,' said Campbell, 'Stevie always connected with us musically and spiritually.'

However, Campbell didn't find it easy being in Fleetwood Mac. He could stretch out on the Peter Green songs and Danny Kirwan's 'Tell Me All the Things You Do', but he had to play by the rules on 'Rhiannon'. 'It was tricky,' Campbell admitted. 'I was not used to copying other people's songs *per se*. So I had to dig in.'

The An Evening with Fleetwood Mac tour sold out around the world. But with Crowded House's ex-vocalist Neil Finn also in the band, the set included songs by both Campbell and Finn's former bands.

'Stevie sang the shit out of [Tom Petty's] "Free Fallin",' said Campbell. But he found it tough to see the collage of Petty through-the-ages images on the screen behind him. 'I cannot look at it, or I get too emotional,' he said at the time.

However heartfelt, the tribute also showed how much sway Stevie Nicks had over Fleetwood Mac. Petty was her guy, and she'd continue to pay homage to him and sing 'Free Fallin' on her solo tours. Maybe it was hard for her to let go. In the late '70s, when Fleetwood Mac was riven with musical and emotional tension, the Heartbreakers offered an escape. Stevie was the kid who ran away to join their circus.

Mike Campbell never played another note with Fleetwood Mac after the final date in Las Vegas in November 2019. Talk of more shows and a new record were derailed by the pandemic and, later, Christine McVie's passing. 'If Fleetwood Mac asked me, I'd do it again,' said Campbell in 2022. 'But I don't really see that ship leaving port again.'

Neil Finn

The Final Lead Singer's Tale

Neil Finn was on his way to a soundcheck when Mick Fleetwood's name flashed up on his mobile phone. It was May 2018, and Finn was about to perform with a choir and an orchestra at the Sydney Opera House, but he answered anyway. After twenty minutes of pre-amble, Fleetwood asked if he fancied trying out for Fleetwood Mac. 'I was,' said Finn, 'rather surprised.'

New Zealand-born Finn had his first hit, 'I Got You', with new wave-ish pop-rockers Split Enz, in 1980. But it was his next group, the harmony-heavy Crowded House, that put him on Fleetwood's radar. 'Especially one song, "Don't Dream It's Over",' said Mick.

A few months after the call and against all expectations, Neil Finn found himself singing 'Don't Dream It's Over' on stage with Fleetwood Mac. He'd go on to perform it every night on tour as the group's new lead vocalist.

By 1996, Crowded House had sold more than 15 million records and scored further hits with 'It's Only Natural' and 'Weather With You', before going on what Finn called 'an indefinite hiatus'. By then, he'd released hit solo albums and collaborated with members of Radiohead, the Smiths and Pearl Jam.

Finn and Fleetwood first met backstage at the Royal Albert Hall in 1999. Finn was performing at a tribute concert for Linda McCartney, and Fleetwood was hanging out. Finn later realised that Fleetwood had sowed 'one of his little seeds', during their conversation. 'They get planted when he meets people,' Finn explained. 'It's not a conscious thing, but it's a strategic thing.'

The pair met again at the 2015 New Zealand Music Awards, after which Fleetwood played on Finn and his son Liam's album, *Lightsleeper*. Apparently, Fleetwood flew to New Zealand and spent days chasing the Finns around the island while they played small pubs and civic halls off the beaten track. But the seed was growing.

After hiring Mike Campbell, Fleetwood Mac still needed a lead vocalist. Several auditioned. 'Some of them were great, but they just weren't right,' said Fleetwood, before throwing Finn's name into the mix.

'We sat around a table and started listening to everybody we could think of, aged between twenty-seven and sixty-five,' said Stevie. 'Neil just made it.'

When the others agreed, Fleetwood made the call. Finn was too shocked to say anything other than to tell him he'd ring back tomorrow: 'Then my kid said to me, "Why wouldn't you want to stand in a room and sing songs with Fleetwood Mac?"'

Finn flew to Hawaii ('Mick spent an hour telling me it wasn't an audition but it was, and I was auditioning them too') and was hired as a full-time member of Fleetwood Mac. With Campbell already in situ, it took some of the heat off him. But Finn seemed more comfortable with the early songs and tried not to think too deeply about Buckingham's words to 'Second Hand News' and 'Go Your Own Way'. After all, Stevie, the subject of their composer's displeasure, was standing a few feet away.

'I could never be capable of singing like Lindsey,' he insisted. 'But I put a similar intensity into some of his songs.' Nevertheless, he noted that when Campbell stretched out for too long on some solos, Stevie complained. 'She would get exhausted playing tambourine,' he recalled. 'And say, "Fucking hell, Lindsey only did twelve bars!"'

Nicks also insisted they perform 'Don't Dream It's Over' and told audiences she'd sung along whenever it came on MTV in the

'80s. 'A song like this comes around once in a lifetime,' she gushed. 'If you have one of those songs, you have to sing it all the time.'

For all Mick Fleetwood's talk of a new band and new music, Finn knew there was 'a big journey' to be made before actually doing it. After the tour, he heard that Fleetwood had been speaking to Buckingham again, and told the press he hoped they'd reconcile.

Aged sixty at the time of the tour, Finn thought he was inured to everything that the music business could throw at him. But learning how Fleetwood Mac dealt with their upheavals taught him a lesson. In 2020, a newly inspired Neil Finn re-formed Crowded House. 'It's amazing,' he later said, 'how crazy things become normal.'

Peter Green Tribute Concert

Where's Wally?

On 25 February 2020, five months before Peter Green's death, Mick Fleetwood and Friends staged a concert in his honour at the London Palladium. Band members and audience alike hoped Green would attend. This meant some of the audience spent the minutes before showtime squinting up at the boxes flanking the Grand Circle.

Anyone with a bald head in their sixties or over was considered fair game. Considering the demographic tonight, this was the equivalent of playing 'Where's Wally?' One husband and wife couple, flourishing a pair of bird-watching binoculars, quickly spotted a gentleman answering Green's description settling into a box.

'Is it Greeny?' asked the wife, excitedly.

'I don't know! I can't see him any better than you can!' snapped her partner.

It turned out it wasn't. But anticipation ran high, accelerated by nobody knowing exactly who was going to perform beyond a couple of famous names. Mick Fleetwood, in trademark waistcoat and neckerchief, played MC, though it was strange seeing him transplanted from the multi-tiered arena to a modest-sized theatre. Fleetwood was also visibly nervous and apologised for needing an autocue during his introductory speech. As the evening wore on, though, he relaxed and delightedly announced several 'dear, dear friends' to the stage.

Fleetwood's house band included the Who's Zak Starkey on additional drums, and guitarists Andy Fairweather Low, Jonny Lang and former 'Mini Mac' band member Rick Vito. The show's premise was that a cast of Green's contemporaries and acolytes would perform his Fleetwood Mac-era songs. All credit to Rick Vito, though, a musician who'd spent his time in the band understudying Lindsey Buckingham, but delivered one of the best performances of the night on 'Love That Burns'.

There was something refreshingly un-starry about it all, though. ZZ Top's inscrutable guitarist Billy Gibbons, complete with backwoodsman beard and blinged-up shower cap, husked his way through 'Doctor Brown', before being joined by Aerosmith's Steven Tyler, who injected some stadium-rock glamour by waving his scarf-festooned mic stand around during 'Rattlesnake Shake'.

In marked contrast, Christine McVie and Brit blues standard-bearer John Mayall both showed up to sing and play keyboards, before sloping off stage again, as if they'd gone to put the kettle on. At some point, ex-Rolling Stone Bill Wyman sauntered on to play bass and disappeared again, before anyone noticed.

The first change of gear came when Fleetwood and his house band perched on stools and were joined by ex-Oasis songwriter Noel Gallagher carrying an acoustic guitar. 'I know what you're thinking,' said Gallagher in a deadpan Mancunian accent. 'Has he got the fucking blues? Well, we'll soon find out.' There then followed a lovely 'The World Keeps Turning' and 'Like Crying', neither of which would have sounded out of place on one of Gallagher's High Flying Birds albums.

As the evening wore on, the more obvious was Peter Green's influence on these musicians. Pete Townshend was the first to address it; drolly hacking out the guitar figure to the Who's 'Won't Get Fooled Again' to demonstrate its similarity to 'Station Man'. Townshend spent the song windmilling his arm and rocking back and forth. 'Station Man' was from *Kiln House*, Fleetwood Mac's first album *without* Peter Green. But nobody seemed to mind.

389

Neither Townshend nor Gallagher could compete with history, though. Jeremy Spencer's performance of 'The Sky is Crying' was so sublime in its Zen-like calm, that Fleetwood almost started weeping. This was the first time the pair had shared a stage in more than fifty years.

Not everything was quite as assured. Neil Finn's 'Man of the World' couldn't match the bruised feel of the original, and 'Oh Well (Part I)', with a returning Gibbons and Tyler, took time to find its mark.

Then, like a relay runner passing the baton, Gibbons ducked out and Pink Floyd's David Gilmour ambled on to play the song's instrumental second half. Gilmour then settled down behind his lap steel for 'Albatross', reinforcing the link between vintage Green and '70s Floyd – from 'Albatross' to 'Shine on You Crazy Diamond'.

Metallica's Kirk Hammett, the current owner of Green's 1959 Les Paul, as played on many of tonight's songs, joined Billy Gibbons and the house band for a very heavy metal-sounding 'The Green Manalishi (With the Two Prong Crown)' and an almost all-star grand finale of 'Shake Your Moneymaker'. Highlighting the casual nature of the show, David Gilmour and Noel Gallagher failed to make a reappearance.

'We love ya, Peter! Wherever you are!' roared Steven Tyler, before tottering off stage. Wherever Green was, he wasn't here, though. He didn't fancy it. 'If music be the food of love, then play on,' declared a grinning Mick Fleetwood, before waving goodbye. Within three weeks, all gigs were off as the UK went into lockdown. It's a shame Green missed it.

Barbie

Stevie Nicks' Fairy-Tale Princess

In October 2023, global toymakers Mattel Creations launched the Stevie Nicks signature Barbie doll. Their timing was perfect. Stevie was in the middle of a US tour and the recent fantasy comedy *Barbie*, with Margot Robbie in the lead role, had made over $1.4 billion at the box office.

'I have a surprise,' Stevie told the sold-out audience at New York's Madison Square Garden. Most hoped it would be a rogue member of Fleetwood Mac past or present. Instead, she unveiled the doll modelled on her twenty-seven-year-old self. 'The age I was when we made *Rumours*,' Nicks explained.

Stevie had sent Mattel her original *Rumours* cover outfit, from which they fashioned a replica chiffon skirt, platform boots, feathered blonde hair and a tiny tambourine. Stevie was consulted at every stage, suggesting changes to the features ('Make the nose bigger, change the mouth' etc), until giving her final approval.

Stevie's Barbie followed replicas of Tina Turner and David Bowie and was launched with a message of female empowerment. 'Encouraging girls to awaken their inner rock star,' ran the blurb. The doll went on sale for $56 a few hours after the New York show, and quickly sold out. Stevie saw its appearance as evidence of her good taste in clothes and footwear. After all, she was still wearing a variation of the same outfit. 'I was totally right when I was 27 and said, "This is what I want,"' she told the *New York Times*. 'It's who I was, and who I still am.'

Stevie went on to photograph her mini-me at venues and hotels across the US, creating a sort of fantasy tour diary. Those hoping 'Barbie' might kiss and make up with her original 'Ken', aka Lindsey Buckingham, were in for a long wait, though. There would be no fairy-tale happy ending here.

Christine McVie

'I'm Good at Pathos . . .'

'I didn't write the hits. Christine wrote the hits.'

Stevie Nicks

'The finest blueswoman and piano player in all of England.'

Mick Fleetwood

'I feel very lucky to have known her.'

Lindsey Buckingham

'She's a lovely, lovely lady, even though she told me to fuck off.'

John McVie

Christine McVie's Greatest Fleetwood Mac Moments

'Show Me a Smile'
'Spare Me a Little of Your Love'
'Why'
'Over My Head'
'Say You Love Me'
'You Make Loving Fun'

Dreams

'Don't Stop'
'Songbird'
'Think About Me'
'Brown Eyes'
'Honey Hi'
'Hold Me'
'Everywhere'
'Little Lies'

Soon after the royalties from the multi-million-selling *Rumours* began to arrive, Christine McVie phoned up her business manager. 'I told him I wanted to buy a Rolls-Royce and drive it out of the showroom today,' she recalled.

That afternoon, Christine wrote the cheque, turned the ignition key and watched the spirit of ecstasy bonnet ornament nosing towards the showroom's open doors. 'And for the first half hour, I was terrified I'd crash the thing.'

Christine loved being able to buy a Rolls-Royce, but the fantasy was better than the reality, and she soon traded it in for something smaller. The story illustrated her approach to stardom: unafraid to over-indulge and display some extraordinary airs and graces, but, deep down, grounded and pragmatic.

Christine McVie passed away after suffering a stroke on 30 November 2022. Phrases such as 'Fleetwood Mac's secret weapon' circulated in the obituaries. Really, there wasn't anything secret about her contribution, but it took her death for it to be fully acknowledged. Christine composed the big hits, 'Don't Stop', 'You Make Loving Fun', 'Everywhere' and 'Little Lies', but didn't cheerlead from the front, like Lindsey Buckingham and Stevie Nicks. When she left the band in the 2000s, though, they sorely missed her.

Fleetwood Mac's all-singing, keyboard-playing songwriter was born Anne Christine Perfect in Cumbria on 12 July 1943. She never liked her surname: 'Because teachers would always say, "I hope you live up to it."'

Raised in Smethwick, on the border between Birmingham and the Black Country, Christine was the second child of music tutor and violinist Cyril and medium and faith healer Beatrice.

'My mum belonged to the psychic society of Birmingham,' she explained. 'I didn't want to hear about that side of her life growing up. It scared me. I just wanted her to be an ordinary mum, but she had a group of friends she would have seances with.'

One night, Beatrice placed her healing hand on a wart under her daughter's nose: 'She told me it would be gone by the morning, and it was.'

Christine's talent for art saw her fast-tracked into Moseley Junior Art School and on to Birmingham Art College, where she studied sculpture. By now, Christine could play the cello and piano and had been introduced to the Fats Domino songbook by her brother, John. Domino's seesawing left hand on 'Ain't That a Shame' and 'Blueberry Hill' – 'the boogie bass' as Christine called it – would reappear in some of her hits.

Christine and her school friend, Theresa, played acoustic guitars, mimicked the Everly Brothers and caught the train to London to visit talent agencies. Christine composed her first song, the worldly wise sounding 'I'll Never Stop Loving You', aged sixteen.

She was remarkably candid about her early life and loves in a 1977 *Rolling Stone* interview. Christine told the magazine that she was 'a tubby teenager' who went on a crash diet to attract a boy at the college folk club. 'I just fell in love with Spence,' she said. 'I swore I would get thin and go out with him – and I did.'

Apparently, Christine stopped eating chocolate and she and 'Spence' sang together in a local jazz band before he formed the Spencer Davis Group with fourteen-year-old prodigy Steve Winwood. Christine attended every gig and was smitten by the music: 'The blues was raw and dark and dirty and sexy. It was a releasing of passion undisturbed for so long.'

Christine soon found her way into another local group, Sounds of Blue, playing bass alongside future Traffic flautist Chris Wood. 'I was a novelty, though, like the girl bass player in the Applejacks or the drummer in the Honeycombs,' she said. 'We weren't over-ground, we were underground. We were followed by university students and people who would come to pubs, get their pints and watch us sweat in an upstairs room.'

In 1966, Christine graduated with her national diploma in sculpture, but no idea what to do next. Her parents suggested teaching, 'but I couldn't handle a room full of kids,' she said.

Instead, she became a window dresser at Dickins & Jones department store on London's Regent Street: 'It was boring and the uniform was awful.' Salvation arrived via ex-Sounds of Blue bassist Andy Silvester and guitarist Stan Webb, who asked her to play piano in their blues group, Chicken Shack.

'She didn't want to do it,' recalled Webb in 2017. 'I don't think she fancied the idea of going on the road. I heard some other piano players, but we decided to give her one more try. I think just to shut us up, she said, "Yeah, okay, I'll try it for a while."'

Silvester lent Christine his Freddie King records and told her to listen to the piano player, Sonny Thompson. 'So I just copied his licks,' she said. 'But I never play on black notes, the white notes are the good ones. If a root note starts with a black note I'm in trouble.'

Christine joined Chicken Shack in time for a six-week residency at Hamburg's Star Club. 'We worked seven nights a week, five hours a night,' she said. Chicken Shack treated her like 'one of the lads', and club owners often presumed she was somebody's girlfriend.

'Nobody chatted me up. I wasn't even like a bird to them,' Christine told *Disc* magazine in 1970. 'The groupies used to glare daggers at me, and it put them off their stroke when I was around.'

Passions ran high in her private life, though. Christine spent two years with a Swedish boyfriend and told *Rolling Stone* she 'ran around screaming' when he broke off their engagement. Christine thought she first saw Fleetwood Mac play London's Saville Theatre in November 1967. After the show, bassist John McVie asked her out for a drink, 'even though I fancied Peter Green'. John thinks he first met her after Fleetwood Mac's debut gig at the Windsor

National Jazz and Blues Festival when he was still in John Mayall's Bluesbreakers.

Either way, Christine was drawn to McVie's dark good looks, dry humour and 'Fu Manchu moustache'. McVie persuaded his new girlfriend to play piano on Fleetwood Mac's second album, *Mr. Wonderful*. The couple married quickly in the summer of 1968, as her mother Beatrice was dying of cancer and wanted to see her daughter wed. Really, Christine was marrying into Fleetwood Mac.

'I thought it was extremely romantic,' she said, years later. 'Obviously, a bit of the glamour rubbed off. It was almost like someone marrying a Beatle. You married one of the links in the chain, and you were part of them.'

Meanwhile, Christine's career was taking off. She composed Chicken Shack's first single, 'It's Okay With Me Baby', sang their hit, a cover of Etta James's 'I'd Rather Go Blind', and played on their 1968 debut, *40 Blue Fingers, Freshly Packed and Ready to Serve*.

But she also signed to Fleetwood Mac's label, Blue Horizon, and released a solo LP, *Christine Perfect*. 'For which I wrote a couple of tracks but I had no confidence in myself as a songwriter,' she claimed.

Christine winning *Melody Maker*'s Best Female Vocalist two years running challenged this lack of confidence. 'But there was only me and Julie Driscoll and Janis Joplin,' she insisted. Then she experienced stage fright during her first solo tour and burst into tears at a club date in Nottingham. The remaining dates were cancelled: 'The solo thing wasn't for me, I couldn't sustain it. I need a group.'

Soon after, Christine abandoned Chicken Shack and her solo career because she wasn't seeing enough of her husband. 'It always destroys me when John's away,' she explained at the time. 'It's like having my right arm missing.'

This vulnerable Christine McVie seemed at odds with what Ken Caillat later called 'the tough, talented Christine, who drank like one of the guys and swore like one too.' Caillat claimed Christine could outswear even Grace Slick (presumably, the gold standard in sweary female rock singers), and that her laugh reminded him of comedian Barry Humphries' female alter-ego, Dame Edna Everage's.

In 1970, Fleetwood Mac began living communally in a converted oast house in rural Kent. Christine spent the first three months playing den mother: cooking stews and rolling joints while 'the boys' wrote songs.

It was Mick Fleetwood who suggested she join the band. They'd booked a US tour and decided they needed a piano player. 'I knew all the songs, anyway. So I just came chiming in and did a couple of harmonies,' she explained. 'Ten days later I was on stage in New Orleans.'

'They treated me very well,' she continued. 'I never had a problem with being the only girl in the band. They treated me as one of the guys, but with respect, like a sister. But they never excluded me from the boy jokes. I had to get used to that, so now I have a mouth like a sewer.'

Christine's early compositions lightened the mix alongside guitarist Danny Kirwan's songs. But it was guitar player Bob Welch who encouraged her to write. Between them, the pair composed most of those shadowy, mid-period Mac albums. Christine's 'Show Me a Smile', 'Why' and 'Heroes are Hard to Find' gave this phase of the group an illusion of continuity.

'I got fed up with 12 bars,' Christine explained. 'I did more chord selections and different tempos, which made it more commercial. But my left hand always stayed with the boogie.'

By 1973, though, her marriage was on the skids, and Christine had a fling with the group's sound engineer Martin Birch: 'And the strain of being in the same band as John had started to take its toll. He's not the most pleasant of people when he's drunk.'

The relationship was in jeopardy by the time Buckingham and Nicks joined in 1975. Their arrival upended Fleetwood Mac on every level. The three singers' voices blended beautifully. 'But I now had to sing with a slight American accent,' explained Christine. 'I had to adapt my vocal accent, but you could always tell I was English. I think that was an important part of our sound.'

Christine's 'Over My Head', from *Fleetwood Mac* (aka the '*White Album*'), became the group's first US top-twenty hit. It was partly written about Buckingham, whose perfectionism intimidated her. But Christine proved a good foil for Lindsey. Songs such as 'World Turning' demonstrated how well they worked together, partly because neither had any emotional dogs in the fight.

Christine and Stevie bonded quickly too. 'We made a pact, probably in our first rehearsal, that we would never accept being treated as second-class citizens,' explained Stevie. 'That we would be so fantastic and so strong and so smart that none of the uber-rock star group of men would look through us. And they never did.'

'Before Stevie, I was the only girl and I was also with John twenty-four hours a day – for years – and that's exactly why everything went wrong,' said Christine in 1976. 'So I had to decide – either I'll be lonely or I will adapt enough to be like a big sister, to be with the guys and still retain that respect. I love to be with men, generally more than women, but since Stevie's been with us, it's great.'

However Stevie, five years Christine's junior and with a fraction of her experience, swiftly became Fleetwood Mac's on-stage front-woman. 'For a while, I got jealous,' Christine admitted. 'It didn't last long because I saw my role as part of the rhythm section. I could no more do twirls in chiffon than Stevie could play blues on the piano.'

Christine's appearance in the 'Tusk' video, strolling around Dodger Stadium wearing oval sunglasses and cradling a white wine spritzer, compounded the impression of Christine as the group's matriarch.

'Five pm was wine thirty,' recalled Bekka Bramlett. 'Christine was leaving and gave me her blessing to sing her songs, and said, "Give it some soul, girl."'

'I write about romantic despair but with a positive spin,' said Christine. 'But I'm sure people sometimes read things into them. Sometimes they just evoke an emotion somebody can relate to. But if they were all about me personally, I'd have killed myself by now.'

Really, Christine wrote about adult lives and emotions. These were the boy-meets-girl songs of her youth, given a grown-up spin; songs about love, sex and heartache, inspired by her ex-husband ('Don't Stop') and her boyfriend ('You Make Loving Fun') on *Rumours*.

She also mastered the art of appearing to float above her bandmates' drama while having plenty of her own. 'The others would call me the level-headed one, but I was crazy like them,' she admitted. 'The boys were worse than us, but sometimes good stuff comes out of doing bad stuff. Sometimes a cup of tea doesn't quite cut it when you're writing a song.'

There were times, too, when she sailed close to the wind: 'I stayed up for three days with the white powder, washed down by Dom Pérignon. I almost had a heart attack.' In 1980, Christine's car was pulled over by officers from the New York Police Department, who claimed they'd seen her snorting cocaine. When they couldn't find any, they took her to the precinct, where she was strip-searched. Christine was on her way to a *Rolling Stone* cover shoot and was mortified as she was wearing, to quote one band familiar, 'her large, greying, bottom-of-the-drawer knickers'. 'I was saving my new pink silk ones for the shoot,' she explained later.

Unlike Stevie, Christine pulled back from the brink before her drug use became unmanageable. But both women were too committed to Fleetwood Mac to have children. 'There were never any for me,' said Christine. 'There was always a career in the way. It was a case of one or the other. And I never found the right man – not through want of trying.'

After John, she embarked on a relationship with Fleetwood Mac's lighting director, Curry Grant. This was followed by a tumultuous couple of years with Dennis Wilson, for whom she wrote 'Only Over You'. 'I loved him for a while,' she said. 'I mothered him, to be honest. I tend to go for these half-little boy characters.'

With Fleetwood Mac in limbo after 1982's *Mirage*, Christine made a solo album, the Mac-lite *Christine McVie*, and enjoyed a modest hit, 'Love Will Show Us How'. Unlike Buckingham and Nicks, her solo work always seemed like a casual fling until she reunited with Fleetwood Mac.

In October 1986, Christine married Portuguese musician Eddy Quintela and shared the credits with him on several Fleetwood Mac songs, including 'Little Lies'. 'That's not an area I want to talk about,' she said after their divorce. 'Let's just say I wrote most of the songs.'

Christine's pragmatic streak came to the fore again when Buckingham told them he wouldn't tour 1987's *Tango in the Night*. Stevie chased him up and down the corridors of Christine's mansion and out the front door, hurling insults. 'Please don't kill each other on my driveway!' Christine boomed, presumably while waving a glass of white wine spritzer.

'You became used to these dramas and blow-ups, it just seemed like part of everyday band life,' she said. Christine stayed with the group for the underwhelming *Behind the Mask* and *Time* albums, before leaving in the early '90s. Her father was ill, and she wanted to be in England. 'I'd had enough of living out of a suitcase,' she said. 'I'd been on the road for thirty years and missed my roots.'

But she was still 'a link in the chain'. A one-off performance of 'Don't Stop' at President Bill Clinton's inauguration gala was followed in 1997 by a full reunion tour. But Christine had enough months before its end. 'Don't tell anyone,' she said, during a late-night interview in Auburn Hills, Michigan, 'but when this tour's over, I am leaving the band to open a restaurant.'

It was an open secret, and Christine only made it as far as attending cookery school. But she sold her house in LA and her song publishing and bought a nineteen-acre estate in the Kent village of Wickhambreaux. She wanted to get away from the music business and the decadence: 'For years I'd just go to the pub and have fish and chips, not to fancy restaurants in a limousine.'

Christine's marriage to Quintela ended in 2003, and her third solo LP, *In the Meantime* (co-produced by her nephew, Dan Perfect) crept out the following year. 'I was coming out of a relationship and just got it all off my chest,' she said later. 'It's about the darkest thing I've ever written, I was completely paranoid and uncomfortable doing it.'

At the time, Christine told journalists she spent her days walking her Lhasa Apso dogs, 'Dougal' and 'George', reading books and watching *CSI: Miami* and *Have I Got News For You*: 'I used to be a late-night person. But these days, I'm more of an early bird and go to bed about nine in the evening.'

In 2012, the current Fleetwood Mac members were being interviewed for a *Mojo* music magazine story about *Rumours*. Christine had dropped off the media radar. Finding her involved contacting a retired record company manager who put us in touch with her lawyer/manager. Christine replied to some emailed questions with polite but un-illuminating answers. After some gentle persuasion, she agreed to a brief phone interview.

'I understand why you want to talk to me,' Christine said warily. 'As it's *Rumours* I guess I am important. It was a pleasure to listen to the album again. It's nice to take a trip down Memory Lane occasionally . . . It's like if you live next door to Buckingham Palace, you don't go and look at it every day.'

Christine had also been to see Fleetwood Mac in concert at Earls Court. 'I had a good time,' she insisted. 'They are limited in what they can do of mine, though. I think they tried to do "You Make Loving Fun", but I don't think the sound of their vocals was right.'

You could hear the low murmur of a TV set in the background. What are you doing after this interview? 'I'm watching the tennis,' she replied, sounding like she couldn't wait to get back to it.

It turned out Christine had been suffering from agoraphobia. The flight home from Los Angeles in 1998 was one of the last she took for sixteen years. Part of the reason for *In the Meantime*'s low-key release was her refusal to travel for promotion. 'I flew to New York once, but I had to get drunk to do it,' she later confessed.

The full story emerged over time, 'For the first five years in England, I was restoring the house, which took a long time, the gardening and the decorating. I enjoyed all that,' she explained. 'Then I went into a spiral of isolation and decline and drank too much.'

'This is what happens to really famous women,' cautioned Stevie Nicks. 'Read back through the history of famous women. If they're not married and don't have tons of grandchildren, they become reclusive.'

Christine eventually curbed her drinking and sought professional help. In 2013, a psychiatrist asked her if she could go anywhere in the world, where would she choose? She told him the Hawaiian island of Maui where Mick Fleetwood lived. The therapist told her to book a plane ticket for six months' time.

Over the coming weeks, McVie slowly regained enough confidence to leave the house, and sit in her car and then drive into the village. When Fleetwood came to London, she flew back to Maui with him: 'And I barely noticed the plane taking off.'

In Maui, Christine sat in with Fleetwood's blues band before re-joining Fleetwood Mac in 2014. Initially, Buckingham was cautious about her return. 'I was protective of the fact that we'd moved forward as a four-piece,' he said.

'Lindsey said I couldn't leave again,' said Christine, who claimed her guest appearance in London with the four-piece Mac in 2013 was 'Lindsey's way of auditioning me.'

For the following year's world tour, Christine was back behind her keyboard, customised with a wing mirror so she could see the rhythm section behind her. Instead of a new Fleetwood Mac album, though, there was 2017's *Lindsey Buckingham Christine McVie* instead. 'I'm very good at coming up with lyrics, songs and hooks, and Lindsey is very good at making it 3D,' she said. Neither party knew it, but this would be her swansong.

Christine later revealed she had scoliosis and could only stand up to play keyboards, and her performances on the Buckingham-less Fleetwood Mac's 2018–19 tour were less assured. Her death was attributed to an ischemic stroke and came as a shock to most.

John, her ex-husband and the world's most reluctant interviewee, took to social media to comment. 'This is a day where my dear sweet friend Christine McVie has taken to flight,' he wrote.

Initially bound to them by marriage, Christine McVie became vital to Fleetwood Mac's chemistry and success. She wore her talent lightly, though. Christine's final public appearance was at the Peter

Green tribute concert in 2020. She was her usual understated self, wandering on stage without fuss or fanfare.

Christine waved her hand in the direction of the eight-strong, all-male house band and grinned. 'Look at all these *guys*,' she sighed.

'Surrounded you are, Chris!' shouted Fleetwood from behind his drum kit. It was always the case, but Christine McVie had the measure of them all.

Acknowledgements

'Big Love' to my agent Matthew Hamilton at the Hamilton Agency and to all at Nine Eight Books, including publishing director Pete Selby, editor James Lilford and designer Jake Cook.

Also, to the members of Fleetwood Mac for numerous interviews between 1997 and 2020. This book draws on my conversations with Lindsey Buckingham, Mick Fleetwood, Peter Green, Christine McVie, John McVie, Stevie Nicks and Jeremy Spencer, conducted for the music magazines *Mojo*, *Q* and *Classic Rock*. Also, thanks to all the studio engineers, producers and road managers who talked to me about all eras of the band. For more information, please visit markrblake.com

Bibliography

Boyd, Jenny, *Jennifer Juniper: A Journey Beyond the Muse* (Urbane Publications, 2020)

Boynton, Graham, *Wild: The Life of Peter Beard, Photographer, Adventurer, Lover* (St Martin's Press, 2022)

Brunning, Bob, *Behind the Masks* (New English Library, 1990)

Caillat, Ken, *Making* Rumours*: The Inside Story of the Classic Fleetwood Mac Album* (John Wiley & Sons, 2012)

Caillat, Ken, and Hernan Rojas, *Get Tusked: The Inside Story of Fleetwood Mac's Most Anticipated Album* (Backbeat Books, 2019)

Celmins, Martin, *Peter Green: Founder of Fleetwood Mac* (Omnibus Press, 2022)

Clapton, Eric, *Eric Clapton: The Autobiography* (Crown Publishing, 2007)

Clayton, David, and Todd K. Smith, *Heavy Load: Free* (Moonshine Publishing, 2000)

Davis, Stephen, *Gold Dust Woman: The Biography of Stevie Nicks* (St Martin's Griffin, 2017)

Fleetwood, Mick, and Anthony Bozza, *Fleetwood: Play On* (Hodder & Stoughton, 2014)

Fleetwood, Mick, with Stephen Davis, *Fleetwood: My Life and Adventures With Fleetwood Mac* (Sidgwick & Jackson, 1990)

Harris, Carol Ann, *Storms: My Life with Lindsey Buckingham and Fleetwood Mac* (Chicago Review Press, 2007)

Heche, Anne, *Call Me Crazy: A Memoir* (Simon & Schuster, 2001) anzeigen

Dreams

Dreams

Howe, Zoë, *Stevie Nicks: Visions, Dreams & Rumours* (Omnibus, 2014)

Norman, Philip, *We Danced on Our Desks: Brilliance and Backstabbing at the Sixties' Most Influential Magazine* (Mensch Publishing, 2023)

Reed, Ryan, *Fleetwood Mac FAQ: All That's Left to Know About the Iconic Rock Survivors* (Backbeat, 2018)

Stewart, Rod, *Rod: The Autobiography* (Arrow, 2013)

Tannenbaum, Rob, and Craig Marks, *I Want My MTV: The Uncensored Story of the Music Video Revolution* (Penguin, 2011)

Waterman, Pete, *I Wish I Was Me: The Autobiography* (Virgin, 2001)

Wilson, Ann, and Nancy Wilson, with Charles R. Cross, *Kicking and Dreaming: A Story of Heart, Soul and Rock 'n' Roll* (It Books, 2013)

408